Looking the Tiger in the Eye

LOOKING THE TIGER IN THE EYE

Confronting the Nuclear Threat

CARL B. FELDBAUM

RONALD J. BEE

ILLUSTRATED WITH PHOTOGRAPHS

——HARPER & ROW, PUBLISHERS——

Cambridge, Philadelphia, San Francisco,
St. Louis, London, Singapore, Sydney
NEW YORK

Thanks are due to the following for permission
to reprint the copyrighted materials listed below:

William S. Burroughs, for excerpts from "Comments
on Los Alamos Boys Ranch School," copyright © 1985
by William S. Burroughs. Reprinted by permission
of the Andrew Wylie Agency.

City News Publishing Co., for an excerpt
from Dwight D. Eisenhower's "Liberty Is at Stake"
speech, from *Vital Speeches,* Vol. XXVII, No. 8
(February 1, 1961), pp. 228-231. Reprinted
with the permission of City News Publishing Co.

David Grossman Literary Agency, Ltd., for excerpts
from Albert Einstein's letter to Franklin Roosevelt,
as it appears in *Einstein: the first hundred years,*
edited by Maurice Goldsmith, Alan Mackay, and James
Woudhuysen. Copyright © 1980 Maurice Goldsmith and the
Science Policy Foundation. Reprinted by permission of the
David Grossman Literary Agency and Pergamon Press Ltd.

Simon and Schuster, Inc., for an excerpt from William
Faulkner's Nobel Prize acceptance speech, from *A Treasury
of the World's Great Speeches,* selected and edited by
Houston Peterson. Copyright 1954 by Simon and Schuster,
Inc. Reprinted by permission of Simon and Schuster, Inc.

Photo and illustration credits can be found on page 316.

Typography by Andrew Rhodes
1   2   3   4   5   6   7   8   9   10
First Edition

Library of Congress Cataloging-in-Publication Data
Feldbaum, Carl B.
    Looking the tiger in the eye.

    Bibliography: p.
    Includes index.
    Summary: The history of nuclear weapons including decisions
made by political, scientific and military officials is explained to
encourage the public to become part of the nuclear-decision-making
process.
    1. Nuclear weapons—History.   2. Nuclear warfare.
3. World politics—1945–   4. United States—Military policy.
I. Bee, Ronald J.   II. Title.
U264.F45 1988   355'.0217   85-48253
ISBN 0-06-020414-1
ISBN 0-06-020415-X (lib. bdg.)

Acknowledgments

We would like to express our appreciation to the many people who contributed to this book since its inception in 1984. In the course of these past four years, friends, colleagues and acquaintances lent us observations, advice and encouragement during extensive discussions about the nuclear threat and its impact on young people and adults. We also benefited from the fresh perspectives and questions posed by students and teachers at Langley High School (Va.).

Our families were stalwart in the face of our seemingly endless preoccupation with nuclear weapons and war. Their love, devotion and cheerful forbearance were inspirational. Laura, Harley and Mia Feldbaum, Keith and Virginia Bee, you know that this is your book too.

The authors were privileged to have talented and dedicated assistance from other quarters as well. Richard J. Davis, of Weil, Gotshal and Manges, godfathered this project with help from his most able colleagues Harriet Pilpel and Andrea Van Kampen. The team at Palomar Corporation deserves much credit: a special acknowledgment is owed to Anne Johnson Black for her fine editing; to Gail Gorham for her wise counsel and calming influence; to Melissa Gold, Josh Gold, David Lutz and Christopher Buckly for their avid fact checking; to Wendy E. Hucht and Mary Mader McGrath, our often exasperated executive secretaries; and to Will Klingaman, for his assistance during the initiation of this project.

We are also grateful for the tough-minded criticism and editing of George Frampton, Tony Marro, Ronald Ostrow, Bernard Weinraub and Christian Williams. Günter Bischof, Eric Markusen, Jeffrey Dunham and Jonathan Tucker gave us able research assistance and served as sounding boards for many of our ideas. Ron Bee would like to thank the Robert Bosch Foundation for its understanding, and Virginia M. Burke for her patience and support.

At Harper & Row, publisher Elizabeth Gordon and editors Barbara Fenton and Virginia Koeth were steadfast in helping us look the tiger in the eye as far as our audience was concerned. We appreciate their imagination, foresight and dedication.

C.B.F.
R.J.B.

For Aunt Dorothy,
a double Gold Star mother
whose losses, grace and beauty
made me think hard about war.

C.B.F.

In memory of Armin Rappaport,
Professor of History,
who taught his students
the power of principle.

R.J.B.

Contents

I believe that until we have looked

this tiger in the eye, we shall be

in the worst of all possible dangers,

which is that we may back into him.

J. Robert Oppenheimer,

"Atomic Weapons and American Policy,"

Foreign Affairs,

July 1953

INTRODUCTION

In August 1945 the United States dropped two atomic bombs on the Japanese cities of Hiroshima and Nagasaki. Before the attack on Hiroshima only a few people in the world knew that atomic weapons even existed. By the time the second bomb fell, however, it was obvious that an unprecedented force had been unleashed. These two bombs caused so many deaths and such tremendous devastation that the Japanese government surrendered several days after the attack on Nagasaki, thereby ending World War II.

Since that time, no nation has used a nuclear weapon against another country. Yet, over the past forty years, the United States, the Soviet Union, Great Britain, France and China have spent trillions of dollars, rubles, pounds, francs and yuan to develop and produce more than 50,000 nuclear weapons. In addition to the first five members of the "nuclear club," other nations are developing nuclear weapons or may already have a capability to make them. These weapons are so destructive that it is almost inconceivable that anyone would use them; yet nations maintain nuclear arsenals largely because they are afraid their rivals might use, or threaten to use, these weapons against them. We have sought to deter each other from nuclear war by threatening nuclear retaliation.

There now exist enough nuclear weapons to imperil the future of the human race. What led human beings to develop the first bombs, and what drove us, after the devastation of Hiroshima and Nagasaki, to build the vast nuclear arsenals of today? How have the United States and other nations attempted to limit or eliminate these weapons, and why have we not been more successful? What are our choices for the present, and what sort of future can we look forward to?

These are some of the questions that we will explore in the chapters that follow. We do not presume to provide final answers to the problems posed by the existence of nuclear weapons; however, in Chapter XIX, "Nuclear Democracy," we suggest guidelines for achieving reductions in nuclear arsenals and indicate a path to their eventual elimination. The authors' views as to how this might come about are secondary to our primary purpose, which is to provide you with the background and incentive to participate knowledgeably in the current and future debate over nuclear weapons.

Public participation in this debate is essential. Too many discussions about nuclear weapons are dominated by a limited number of people who have mastered the language and technicalities of the issues. Many people, in fact, prefer not to discuss the subject at all, since the prospect of a nuclear war often brings on feelings of anxiety and hopelessness. But these issues are far too important to be left to specialists alone; they involve the future character of American society, the health of the planet and the very existence of the human race. If we choose to remain ignorant of these issues, we allow others to make crucial decisions for us.

Very few people used to participate in debates and decisions about nuclear weapons. When the first atomic bombs were developed, not even the vice-president of the United States knew about them. In recent years, public participation in nuclear weapons issues has increased in the United States as well as in other democratic countries, and the influence of public opinion on nuclear weapons policy has grown significantly. It is now more important than ever that the participants in these debates have the ability and information to exercise sound judgment.

Many people today have expressed their belief that nuclear war is inevitable. They view the chances of a nuclear war as an international game of Russian roulette: sooner or later, they say, the odds will catch up with us and someone will "push the button." Others argue that no one would ever be foolish enough to unleash a nuclear holocaust, knowing that a full-scale war could destroy the aggressor as well as the intended victim.

The authors of this book support neither view. We see very little that is inevitable in human history, including the chances of a future nuclear war. Nor do we think it wise to underestimate the potential for human folly, given past misjudgments that led to war. As we will show, the history of nuclear weapons consists of a series of deliberate decisions made by political, scientific and military officials in the United States and other nations. Some of those decisions were made in secret, away from public view. Others clearly were influenced by the power of public opinion. Many were made on the basis of incomplete or erroneous information and without full understanding of their implications. None of them, however, was "inevitable."

To understand decisions made about nuclear weapons, we must appreciate the circumstances in which they were made. This book therefore includes selections from historical documents and memoirs written by those who participated in the decision-making process. In the chapters that follow, there are recollections of the scientists who built the first atomic bombs, statements by President Truman on his reasons for authorizing the use of these bombs against Japan, excerpts from debates between those who favored and those who opposed the development of the hydrogen bomb, and thoughts expressed by U.S. presidents, Soviet leaders and others on the nuclear arms race that continues today.

We begin by describing the origin of nuclear weapons. We examine the political and scientific events leading up to the development of the first atomic bombs by the United States and the decision to use those bombs against Japan in World War II. We describe the devastation of Hiroshima and Nagasaki that resulted. We trace the circumstances that led the nations of the world to go to war in the first place; in this nuclear age, it is essential to grasp what motivated human beings to fight a war that ended in the use of nuclear weapons.

Next we depict the postwar rivalry between the United States and the Soviet Union. We report the U.S. reaction to the first Soviet atomic test, and describe the subsequent decision to build the H-bomb—over 1,000 times more powerful than the bombs that destroyed Hiroshima and Nagasaki. Also during this period the new "superpowers" developed bombers, missiles, submarines, and other means to "deliver" their fast-growing numbers of nuclear weapons. These were perhaps the coldest years of what became known as the Cold War, when tensions between the United States and the Soviet Union finally led to the Cuban Missile Crisis of 1962.

The third and final part of this book addresses the period from 1962 to the present. After the Cuban Missile Crisis, U.S. and Soviet leaders realized how devastating a nuclear confrontation could be and sought agreements to control nuclear weapons. Despite this period of *détente*, however, nuclear arsenals continued to grow. We examine the arms control process—international attempts to limit or eliminate nuclear weapons. We identify agreements that have been reached and discuss factors that help or hinder these often difficult negotiations.

This book does not delve into the pros and cons of nuclear power reactors designed solely to produce electricity. However, since nuclear materials for peaceful and military uses are virtually the same, we do point out the danger that nations using nuclear power (there are currently twenty-six nations with 397 reactors worldwide) can divert nuclear materials from electricity to weapons production. If allowed to occur, the spread, or proliferation, of nuclear weapons would result in a more dangerous world. We describe the Nuclear Non-Proliferation Treaty (currently signed by 135 nations) and other measures aimed at preventing the spread of nuclear weapons.

Nuclear power and nuclear weapons are related in another way: Although a nuclear reactor cannot explode—even in the worst case—with anywhere near the force of a nuclear weapon, the April 1986 accident at the Soviet reactor at Chernobyl did spread a radioactive cloud across Europe and other parts of the northern hemisphere. The full effects of this radiation will not be known for years. The Chernobyl accident should remind us how devastating a nuclear war would be if even a few (not to speak of hundreds or thousands of) nuclear weapons were ever used.

A few words regarding the organization of this book: Since we choose to tell this story largely from the perspective of the participants, accounts often overlap; also we occasionally use flashbacks to bring in pertinent information and previous events that influenced key judgments and actions. Put simply, we have taken the liberty of not always following a chronological path. We have marked selected passages and quotations with superscripts ([00]) to lead you to the sources and suggested reading that are listed at the end of this book.

It is impossible not to have strong feelings about nuclear weapons unless you choose to ignore their existence. The prospect of a nuclear war deeply concerns the authors of this book just as it must concern others who think about it. Unfortunately, the nuclear threat will not disappear simply because we want it to. The difficult task for all of us is to find the best way to ensure that nuclear weapons will not destroy us, our hopes and those of our children. The authors hope this book will provide some measure of guidance in that quest.

Looking the Tiger in the Eye

1

ZERO HOUR

. . . a great blinding light lit up the sky as if God himself had appeared among us . . . there came the report of the explosion, sudden and sharp as if the skies had cracked. . . .

Dr. James Chadwick,
British atomic scientist,
July 16, 1945

At 1:00 A.M. on July 16, 1945, U.S. Army General Leslie R. Groves awoke after an hour's sleep to make final preparations for Zero Hour. General Groves and his civilian counterpart, the physicist Dr. J. Robert Oppenheimer, had gathered together a group of brilliant U.S. and Allied atomic scientists at Los Alamos, deep in the mountains of northern New Mexico. For three long years, in the midst of the unprecedented violence and bloodshed of World War II, they had been racing Nazi Germany to develop a "super-weapon"—experimenting in secret under the code name "Manhattan Project" to determine whether an atomic bomb could be built and exploded.

By July 1945 the war in Europe was over. Nazi Germany and Fascist Italy had surrendered, but Japan continued to fight on fiercely in the Pacific. At Manhattan Project headquarters in New Mexico, scientific work on the weapon continued in the hope that it could be used to bring World War II to an end.

The Los Alamos scientists had designed and built a device that

1

they believed would produce an atomic explosion, but they were not absolutely certain the weapon would work. Their uncertainty convinced Dr. Oppenheimer to request a full-scale test of the bomb. General Groves hesitated, for he knew that the United States had produced only enough explosive uranium and plutonium to build two or possibly three atomic bombs in the coming months. He ultimately decided in favor of such a test to avoid the possibility of a humiliating failure should the United States decide to drop an atomic weapon on Japan. Groves feared dropping a "dud."[1]

Until this time, no one in the world knew whether man could create an atomic explosion, nor what the results of such an explosion would be if it did occur.

These uncertainties led to extraordinary safety and security precautions for the test, scheduled for 4:00 A.M. on July 16 near a military base at Alamogordo in the desert of southern New Mexico, about 250 miles from Los Alamos. The unassembled parts of the bomb were transferred from Los Alamos to Alamogordo under heavy security on the mornings of July 12 and 13. Manhattan Project scientists, engineers, and truck drivers were not permitted to stop for gasoline or telephone calls between Los Alamos and Alamogordo. They were instructed to stop for food only once during the nine-hour drive, at a café where Groves was thought to have placed a security agent to act as the cook.

On the night of July 12, special teams began to assemble the bomb in an old ranch house at the Alamogordo base. Each part of the bomb had been crafted to precise specifications. For some unknown reason, an important section of the plutonium core stuck and would not drop down into its proper slot. Everyone present simply sat and stared. After three long minutes the section slid into place, and the rest of the device was assembled without further delay.

It took a day and a half to complete the assembly of the complex parts of the bomb. By Saturday, July 14, it was ready to be placed on top of a specially constructed 100-foot-high steel tower, designated "Point Zero." This spot in the New Mexican desert had been chosen because it was isolated, far from any farms or towns. It was located southeast of Albuquerque in a desolate region called Jornada del Muerto, "Journey of the Dead." Centuries before, Spanish colonists had crossed this area on their journeys northward. Studded with lava beds, it had neither wood nor water holes, and in the early days many people died of thirst or were attacked by hostile Indians. It was the center of violent storms and was alive with rattlesnakes, scorpions and tarantulas.[2]

Only a few roads led anywhere near this forbidding site; its inaccessibility minimized the number of unwanted observers. The rest of the country, and of course the rest of the world, had no idea what was about to occur, and the U.S. government wanted to make certain that absolute secrecy was maintained. In case there were questions after the bomb test, the government had prepared a cover story about an accidental explosion of ammunition stored at the Alamogordo base.

As the bomb was lifted by a hoist to the top of the tower, severe thunderstorms swept through the area. Several days earlier, a duplicate bomb containing only ordinary explosives had been placed on the tower as a test model. Lightning had struck and the bomb had exploded. Although Groves's men subsequently took measures to reduce this hazard, the lightning and thunder on July 16 worried everyone present.

When the explosive detonators and the firing mechanism were finally installed, the bomb was ready. It was an awkward-looking contraption. Nicknamed "Fat Man," it was three feet thick, encased in a black, egg-shaped shell. Nearly 12 feet long, Fat Man weighed close to 10,000 pounds.

As Zero Hour approached, the heavy rains and lightning persuaded Groves and Oppenheimer to postpone the test for an hour and a half. Oppenheimer had been unable to sleep and had spent the night pacing around the camp. Several days later Groves recalled that Oppenheimer had been "very nervous, although his mind was working at its usual extraordinary efficiency." Groves tried hard to shield Oppenheimer from his excited assistants, who were disturbed by the imminent event and by the uncertain weather conditions.

By 4:00 A.M. the rain had stopped but the sky remained heavily overcast. Groves and Oppenheimer paced nervously in and out of the control house, situated about six miles from Point Zero. Peering into the darkness, they tried to reassure themselves that the stars looked brighter, that the weather was clearing. At five o'clock the last three men on the bomb tower were ordered to descend and return to the control house. A switch was thrown to connect all the electrical leads between the bomb and the control panel, and searchlights were turned on, illuminating the tower for several miles.

There was nothing left to do but wait for Zero Hour. Some Manhattan Project personnel feared that the bomb would fail to explode, and that their years of effort would be wasted. Others feared that the explosion might set off a chain reaction in the atmosphere. One of the scientists, Enrico Fermi, had half seriously offered to take bets from his colleagues the night before on the chances that the bomb would ignite the atmosphere, and then on whether it would destroy merely the state of New Mexico or the entire world. Others set up a betting pool (one dollar apiece) to predict the force of the bomb if it worked as they hoped. In fact, almost all their predictions on the force of the explosion proved far too low.[3]

At 5:10 A.M. Dr. Oppenheimer's assistant began the countdown at the control center, 10,000 yards from Point Zero. Groves instructed the scientists at the base camp, about 10 miles from the test site, to put on sunglasses and lie down on their stomachs with their heads turned away from the explosion. Everyone correctly assumed that they would be blinded if they tried to view the initial flash without protection. At 20 miles from Point Zero, physicist Edward Teller passed out suntan lotion to protect against the ultraviolet radiation of the bomb.[4]

Groves's assistant, General Thomas F. Farrell, recalled that "as the time interval grew smaller and changed from minutes to seconds, the tension increased by leaps and bounds. Everyone in that room knew the awful potentialities of the thing that they thought was about to happen." Farrell added, "We were reaching into the unknown and we did not know what might come of it. It can safely be said that most of those present were praying and praying harder than they had ever prayed before."

Groves later provided the following account of those last moments before the explosion:

As the remaining time was called from the loudspeaker from the 10,000-yard control station there was complete silence. Dr. Conant said he had never imagined seconds could be so long. Most of the individuals in accordance with orders shielded their eyes in one way or another. There was then this burst of light of a brilliance beyond any comparison.[5]

Eyewitness accounts of the blast reflect the stunning impact it had upon those present, who could look toward the tower only after the initial flash. General Farrell described his view as follows:

The whole country was lighted by a searing light with the intensity many times that of the midday sun. It was golden, purple, violet, gray and blue. It lighted every peak, crevasse and ridge of the nearby mountain range with a clarity and beauty that cannot be described but must be seen to be imagined. . . . Thirty seconds after the explosion came, first, the air blast pressing hard against the people and things, to be followed almost immediately by the strong, sustained, awesome roar which warned of doomsday and made us feel that we puny things were blasphemous to dare tamper with the forces heretofore reserved to The Almighty.[6]

British scientist James Chadwick, whose discovery of the neutron in 1932 had been one of the keys to unleashing the power of atomic energy, was present at Alamogordo; he wrote in his diary that "a great blinding light lit up the sky and earth as if God himself had appeared among us . . . there came the report of the explosion, sudden and sharp as if the skies had cracked . . . a vision from the Book of Revelation."

Dr. Oppenheimer clung to a post to steady himself as the countdown reached zero. He said later that when he saw the explosion, a passage from the Hindu scriptures came to mind:

If the radiance of a thousand suns
were to burst into the sky
that would be like
the splendor of the Mighty One—

As a giant cloud rose into the air, Oppenheimer was reminded of a more ominous line from the same poem: "I am become Death, the shatterer of worlds."[7]

The test was code-named "Trinity," and many of those present felt that they had witnessed an event of almost religious intensity. Their outward reactions, however, reflected a deep sense of relief and tremendous pride. The scientists began to congratulate each other: They now knew that atomic fission explosions were no longer a matter of theory alone. One scientist threw his arms around Oppenheimer and shouted with glee. The pent-up emotions of the past few months were let loose; everyone realized that the force of the blast had far exceeded most of their expectations. Dr. Isidor I. Rabi, an occasional advisor to Oppenheimer at Los Alamos, later recalled that "at first I was thrilled."

The blast was visible for approximately 180 miles in every direction. Even at a distance of ten miles from the test site the intensity of the light was equal to one thousand suns. The roar of the explosion was heard 100 miles away. Within five minutes the atomic cloud towered over 42,000 feet tall. Desert sand was fused into glass by the extreme heat: the temperature at the center of the blast was estimated to be four times greater than the center of the sun. Point Zero was now a crater 1,200 feet across; the steel tower that had held the bomb was vaporized.

After reviewing the test data a week later, Groves and Oppenheimer learned that their bomb had exploded with the power of 17,000 tons of TNT, a form of dynamite that up to that time had been the most destructive explosive known. The atomic bomb's force dwarfed the "blockbuster" bomb, so called because it could destroy a city block. Until that time, blockbusters were considered the most powerful explosive weapons of World War II, each one having the power of 10 tons of TNT. The weapon tested at Alamagordo had the force of 1,700 blockbusters exploded simultaneously. Unlike TNT, however, the atomic blast had also released enough radiation to kill every living thing within a radius of two thirds of a mile.

A small town named Carrizozo was, at 58 miles away, the closest settlement to the test site. Groves and his assistants kept careful watch on the wind direction; a sudden shift to the east would expose its 1,500 inhabitants to the bomb's dangerous radioactive cloud.

No one in Carrizozo knew anything about the test at Alamogordo. To protect the residents, Army trucks and personnel were stationed at the outskirts of town. If the wind shifted, they were to carry out orders to enter all homes, awaken all residents and carry them to safety—without explanation and by force if necessary.

Groves was also concerned that a change in the wind direction could pose a threat to "any town too large to be evacuated." Groves said later, "The city about which we were most concerned was Amarillo [Texas], some 300 miles away, but there were others large enough to cause us worry. The wind direction had to be correct to within a few degrees."[8]

For the time being, the U.S. government kept the test and its results a secret. But since a number of people in the area had seen the unusually brilliant light and had heard the roar of a tremendous explosion, the Manhattan Project press office circulated its story about an accidental explosion of ammunition stored at the Alamogordo base. It added that there had been no loss of life.

General Groves had expected to meet with Oppenheimer and several other scientists after the test to discuss the results, but according to Groves, "no one who had witnessed the test was in a frame of mind to discuss anything. The reaction to success was simply too great. It was not only that we had achieved success with the bomb; but that everyone—scientists, military officers, and engineers—realized that we had been personal participants in, and eyewitnesses to, a major milestone in the world's history and had a sobering appreciation of what the results of our work would be."

Groves telegraphed his secretary in Washington, D.C., with news of the test results. She in turn cabled Secretary of War Henry L. Stimson, who was in Potsdam, Germany, preparing for a conference of American, British and Russian leaders to settle plans for the Allied occupation of Germany and to find the most effective way to defeat Japan. Her two top-secret messages to Stimson read as follows:

16 July 45

Operated on this morning. Diagnosis not yet complete but results seem satisfactory and already exceed expectations. Local press release necessary as interest extends great distance. Dr. Groves pleased. He returns tomorrow. I will keep you posted.

17 July 45

Doctor has just returned most enthusiastic and confident that the Little Boy is as husky as his big brother. The light in his eyes discernible from here to Highhold and I could have heard his screams from here to my farm.

"Little Boy" was a code name for the atomic bomb. "Highhold" was Stimson's home on Long Island and the "farm" was another of his residences at Upperville, Virginia; they indicated the approximate distances from Washington, D.C., that the bomb's flash could be seen and its roar heard.[9]

When the news arrived in Potsdam, Stimson took the message to President Harry S Truman's official residence, a yellow stucco house in the German summer resort town of Babelsberg. For several days after Stimson's visit, observers reported that Truman's confidence and spirits had visibly increased.

On July 19 Truman received a more complete account of the Alamogordo test results from General Groves. "The President was tremendously pepped up by it," wrote Stimson. "He said it gave him an entirely new feeling of confidence. . . ." Truman relayed the news to British Prime Minister Winston Churchill almost immediately. Churchill realized that the Alamogordo blast represented a tremendous step into the future. Compared to this atomic explosion, Churchill exclaimed, "What was gunpowder? Trivial. What was electricity? Meaningless."

Since the United States, Britain and Canada had cooperated on the Manhattan Project, the British at Potsdam knew about the development of the bomb and about U.S. plans to test it. Our Soviet allies, however, had not been part of the Project. Some of President Truman's advisors suggested that sometime during the Potsdam Conference he should inform Soviet Premier Josef Stalin about the successful atomic test so that the Soviets would not be surprised or alarmed if the United States decided to use an atomic weapon against Japan.

On the morning of July 24 Stimson told Truman that the first bomb would be ready for use against Japan sometime after August 3. At 7:30 that evening, at the conclusion of a meeting between the two leaders and their staffs, Truman casually approached Stalin. General Harry Vaughan, one of Truman's advisors, heard the President speak to Stalin's interpreter: "Will you tell the generalissimo [Stalin] that we have perfected a very powerful explosive which we are going to use against the Japanese and we think it will end the war."

By all accounts, Truman did not actually state that the explosive was an atomic weapon.

Stalin's response was equally casual. He told Truman that he was glad to hear the news and that he hoped the Americans would make good use of the weapon against Japan. President Truman and Prime Minister Churchill were unsure whether the Soviet leader understood the significance of Truman's comment.[10] Later evidence indicates that Stalin's understated reaction and his failure to ask questions may have been a ruse. As we will show in Chapter X, Stalin's spies had infiltrated the Manhattan Project, and Soviet scientists were already at work on their own atomic weapon.

II

HIROSHIMA AND NAGASAKI

[The Japanese] may expect a rain of ruin from the air the likes of which has never been seen on this earth.

President Harry S Truman,
August 6, 1945

On July 26, 1945, in a final effort to obtain Japan's surrender before using atomic weapons, the United States and its allies issued a message known as the Potsdam Declaration. It called for the "unconditional surrender of all Japanese armed forces," and warned that the alternative was "prompt and utter destruction." There was no actual mention of an atomic weapon. In return for unconditional surrender the Allies were to ensure humane treatment of the defeated Japanese nation.

Unfortunately, the Japanese government, and especially its military high command, did not consider Japan defeated. On July 28, Japanese Prime Minister Admiral Kantaro Suzuki, rejected the Potsdam Declaration, claiming it was "not worthy of comment." After receiving Japan's response in Potsdam, President Truman ordered that plans proceed for the atomic bombing of Japan.

By August 2, President Truman was on board the heavy cruiser U.S.S. *Augusta*, returning to the United States. Truman's orders were to drop atomic bombs on Japan sometime after August 3, as weather permitted. In preparation for the attack, specially

12

trained American flight crews on the Pacific island of Tinian, within bombing range of Japan, carried out practice runs with a model of an atomic bomb. The Navy cruiser U.S.S. *Indianapolis* was steaming west from San Francisco toward Tinian, carrying a shipment of uranium to arm the weapon. Ironically, the *Indianapolis* was sunk by a Japanese submarine shortly after delivering its cargo.

On the evening of August 5, 1945, the members of the 509th Composite Group, 20th Air Force, gathered in their dingy assembly hall on Tinian. Until that day, only their commanding officer had known that they would be responsible for dropping an atomic bomb on Japan. The men did not even know that such a bomb existed. They had volunteered for this special mission earlier that spring, but they had been told only that they would be doing "something different." During practice flights they were instructed to wear welder's goggles, and warned not to look in the direction of their target after the drop.

Colonel Paul W. Tibbets, Jr., former personal pilot for General Dwight D. Eisenhower, was commanding officer of the 509th. He told his men on the evening of August 5, ". . . we are going on a mission to drop a bomb different from any you have ever seen or heard about. The bomb contains a destructive force of 20,000 tons of TNT." Tibbets paused for questions, but everyone in the room was too stunned to speak.

Tibbets, a top pilot in the Army Air Corps, had been chosen to fly the plane that would carry the bomb. The atomic device, partially assembled, presently hung in the bomb bay of his B-29, the *Enola Gay*, which Tibbets had named after his mother. Earlier on August 5, Brigadier General Farrell, General Groves's assistant, had arrived on Tinian from Los Alamos to explain the bomb mechanism to Captain William S. Parsons, the naval explosives expert who would assemble the weapon in the plane while en route to the target in Japan.[1]

At 1:45 A.M., August 6, three B-29s took off from Tinian to report on weather conditions over Hiroshima and several alternate target sites. Hiroshima had been chosen by a U.S. Target Committee of military and scientific personnel including Groves, Farrell and Oppenheimer. As Groves explained, "I had set as the governing factor that the targets chosen should be places the bombing of which would most adversely affect the will of the Japanese people to continue the war. Beyond that, they should be military in nature, consisting either of important headquarters or troop concentrations, or centers of production of military equipment and supplies."[2]

To demonstrate the immense power of the atomic weapon, and thus convince the Japanese to surrender, the committee decided to choose a target that had not already been damaged; they wanted to leave clear evidence that the city had been destroyed by a single bomb. To fully demonstrate the weapon's effects, Groves urged selection of a city located on a flat plain so that the effects of the atomic bomb could "run out" to their maximum extent.

To the Target Committee, Hiroshima appeared to meet these criteria. It had an army base and had not been attacked from the air. The committee rejected the ancient city of Kyoto as a target because of its cultural importance to the Japanese people. An attack on Kyoto, it was feared, would produce among Japanese bitter hatred of the United States that could far outweigh the shock value and military effect of the atomic bomb.

At 2:45 A.M. on August 6, a second group of three B-29s took off from Tinian. One was the *Enola Gay*.

The planes flew northwest toward Japan in a nearly cloudless night sky. There were no enemy planes in sight. The members of the crew, sobered by the importance of their mission, spoke very little. Captain Robert Lewis, copilot for Tibbets, began a letter to his parents:

At 4:30 we saw signs of a late moon in the east. I think everyone will feel relieved when we have left our bomb with the Japs and get halfway home. Or, better still, all the way home.

As the *Enola Gay* neared the Japanese islands, Captain Parsons began to arm the bomb. Captain Lewis continued his letter as the plane approached its target:

Captain Parsons has put the final touches on his assembly job. We are now loaded. The bomb is alive. It is a funny feeling knowing it is right in back of you. Knock wood. . . . We have set the automatic. We have reached proper altitude. . . . Not long now, folks. . . .[3]

Meanwhile, on board the U.S.S. *Augusta*, President Truman listened to the ship's radio for news of the atomic attack.

Back in the White House was a sign on Truman's desk that read "The buck stops here." Nothing illustrated that slogan better than Truman's decision to drop atomic bombs on Japan. Yet that decision in many respects had already been made before Vice-President Truman became president on April 12, 1945, when President Franklin Delano Roosevelt died.

Harry S Truman had been vice-president for only three months when the President died; before then he had been a relatively unknown senator from Missouri. He knew nothing about the Manhattan Project prior to becoming president. He did not know that the United States had spent nearly $2 billion on atomic research by April 1945. Indeed, most members of Congress were equally in the dark; President Roosevelt had successfully concealed the project's budget in otherwise ordinary spending bills.

On April 24, 1945, Secretary of War Stimson sent a note to President Truman:

Dear Mr. President,

I think it is very important that I should have a talk with you as soon as possible on a highly secret matter.[4]

Truman asked Stimson to come see him the following day. The secretary of war decided to bring along General Groves, who entered Truman's office by the side door so that even the President's appointments secretary would not suspect anything unusual. Stimson told Truman that "the most terrible weapon ever known in human history" would probably be ready for use within four months.[5]

Truman told Stimson and Groves that he believed it was absolutely necessary to continue development of the atomic bomb. After the meeting Truman spoke with a member of his staff: "I have just gotten some important information. I am going to have to make a decision which no man in history has ever had to make." Truman paused. "I'll make the decision, but it is terrifying to think about what I will have to decide."

The original reason for developing an atomic weapon had been to obtain the bomb before Nazi Germany. Within a month of Truman's assumption of the presidency, Germany was collapsing and its surrender was imminent. Yet there is no evidence that President Truman ever considered halting the Manhattan Project. Under Secretary of War Robert P. Patterson sent a message to all Manhattan Project employees that reflected both the thinking within the U.S. government and the intensity of feeling against the Japanese. It read in part:

The importance of this project will not pass away with the collapse of Germany. We still have the war against Japan to win. The work you are doing must continue without interruption or delay, and it must continue to be a military secret. . . .

You know the kind of war we are up against in the Pacific. Pearl Harbor—Bataan—Corregidor—Tarawa—Iwo Jima—and other bloody battles will never be forgotten.

We have begun to repay the Japanese for their brutalities and their mass murders of helpless civilians and prisoners of war. We will not quit until they are completely crushed. You have an important part in their defeat. There must not be a letup![6]

On June 11, 1945, several Manhattan Project scientists sent a secret report to Secretary of War Stimson that argued against dropping atomic bombs on Japan and warned of the danger of a future atomic weapons race. There is no evidence that this message, known as the Franck Report, ever reached the president or was seriously considered by Stimson.

The overriding concern of the top U.S. officials was to end the war as soon as possible. A massive invasion of Japan by Allied troops was planned for early November 1945. But U.S. military commanders were deeply concerned about the number of casualties that could result from such an invasion; in the Philippines and other Pacific islands, the Japanese had fought almost to the last man. Truman was informed on June 18, 1945, that the assault upon Japanese forces on the islands of Leyte, Luzon, Iwo Jima and Okinawa had resulted in 109,700 U.S. casualties (including wounded and missing) and in the death or capture of 340,000 Japanese. U.S. officials assumed that the Japanese would be even more determined in defense of their homeland. Stimson received estimates that an Allied invasion of Japan could result in 250,000 to 1,000,000 American casualties. There was no telling how many Japanese would die.[7]

Japan had not approached the United States with any offer of a peace settlement, and after years of terrible conflict wartime emotions ran extremely high. Like many other Americans, President Truman believed that the Japanese could not be trusted after their surprise attack upon Pearl Harbor in 1941, which sank or badly damaged eighteen U.S. Navy ships and caused 3,581 American casualties. Distrust of the Japanese ran so deep that 120,000 U.S. citizens of Japanese descent were ordered by the U.S. government to leave their homes and businesses and relocate to "internment camps" where they could be watched.

Facing the prospect of a bloody invasion of Japan, Truman and his advisors looked to the atomic bomb as an alternative. Secretary Stimson said later, "At no time, from 1941 to 1945, did I ever hear it suggested by the President, or by any other responsible member of the government, that atomic energy should not be used in the war." He pointed out that " . . . we were at war, and the work must be done . . . it was our common objective, throughout the war, to be the first to produce an atomic weapon and use it."[8]

British Prime Minister Winston Churchill wrote that the decision to use the bomb "was never an issue." "To avert a vast, indefinite butchery, to bring the war to an end, to give peace to the world, to lay healing hands upon its tortured peoples by a manifestation of overwhelming power at the cost of a few explosions seemed, after all our toils and perils, a miracle of deliverance."[9]

Of course, the exact effects of the bomb in a combat situation were unknown. Some U.S. military officials did not believe that it would be as powerful as the scientists claimed. Others, among them General George C. Marshall, felt that the bomb could be used primarily to protect American troops during an invasion. "We knew that the Japanese were determined and fanatical," said Marshall. "So we thought the bomb would be a wonderful weapon as a protection and preparation for landings. But we didn't realize its value to give the Japanese such a shock that they could surrender without complete loss of face."[10]

When Japan rejected the Potsdam Declaration on July 29, the decision to use the bomb was sealed. But there was still one alternative to dropping it on a Japanese city. Some scientists and officials recommended that the United States invite neutrals or Japanese observers to witness a second atomic test; they hoped that the demonstration of an atomic explosion would convince the Japanese to surrender.

Several arguments convinced Truman not to follow this course of action. The United States had only enough material to produce two more bombs before the end of August, and there was fear of wasting even one of the scarce weapons. For even if a demonstration should result in an explosion as powerful as the one at Alamogordo, there was still no guarantee that it would convince the Japanese military to surrender. After all, while they had been pushed back from many Pacific strongholds, the main forces of the Imperial Japanese Army had not been defeated in battle. Furthermore, if the demonstration were a dud, it would be humiliating and counterproductive for the United States. The Japanese might believe that the Americans were bluffing and stiffen their resistance.

Isidor I. Rabi later explained the difficulties he perceived in using a demonstration to induce a Japanese surrender. The Japanese would need to send a scientist who understood atomic physics; the Americans would have to tell the Japanese observer which instruments to bring to measure the force of the explosion and where to stand to take the measurements. Such communication was very unlikely in the midst of a bitter war. After the explosion, the Japanese government still could argue for months over the proper course of action for Japan. Rabi concluded:

And what would President Truman say to the American people afterward? How could he explain to them that he had had a weapon to stop the war, but had been afraid to use it, because it employed principles of physics that hadn't been used in wartime before?[11]

At 8:15 A.M. on August 6, the bombardier of the *Enola Gay* put the debate to rest forever as he released the atomic weapon 31,600 feet over Hiroshima. The bomb descended, attached to parachutes visible to the Japanese on the ground. Multiple devices built into the bomb ensured detonation. Two thousand feet over the city, the atomic bomb exploded.

Through his goggles, Captain Lewis saw a brilliant flash of light behind and below the plane. Then he and his fellow crew members were jolted by shock waves. Almost instantly, a fireball shot upward amid purple clouds. Within three minutes, a mushroom-shaped cloud reached an altitude of 30,000 feet. The heat generated by the explosion reached 1,000,000° F on the ground. Fires broke out instantly over the area within two miles of "ground zero."

At least 78,000 Japanese who were later identified were killed instantly or soon thereafter by the blast, by fires and by radiation. Another 37,000 inhabitants of Hiroshima simply disappeared.

The blast was so destructive that it cut off all communications between Hiroshima and the Japanese capital of Tokyo, 500 miles away. The Japanese Government did not receive complete reports about the extent of the devastation for nearly three days.

On board the U.S.S. *Augusta*, President Truman declared, "This is the greatest thing in history." At Los Alamos, Oppenheimer called the staff together and raised his hands over his head in a victory sign. Soviet Premier Stalin told U.S Ambassador Averell Harriman on August 8 that the secret of atomic energy "would mean the end of war and aggressors—but the secret would have to be well kept."

Truman had authorized the military to drop "atomic bombs" on Japan, and the Army Air Corps soon had a second weapon ready on Tinian. Groves noted that forecasters predicted good weather over Japan for August 9, with several days of poor weather following. Since visual aiming was important for accuracy, plans proceeded for use of the second bomb on the 9th.

There were alternate targets this time: Kokura, the primary target, had an arsenal that was, according to Groves, "one of the largest war plants in Japan"; Nagasaki, the secondary target, was "one of Japan's largest shipbuilding and repair centers."[12]

At 3:50 A.M. on August 9, another trio of B-29s took off from Tinian. One plane, named *Bock's Car* after Fred Bock, one of the pilots, carried the second atomic bomb. This weapon was different in design from the bomb dropped on Hiroshima. It was heavier; it had a plutonium instead of a uranium core; and unlike the Hiroshima bomb, which was armed as the *Enola Gay* approached its target, this weapon was armed on the ground at Tinian. If the heavy B-29 crashed during takeoff, the device might explode. Both the aircrew and those on the ground were relieved when *Bock's Car* took off safely.[13]

Seated in another plane was William Laurence, a reporter from *The New York Times* who had been selected to accompany the mission. On August 6 the skies had been clear over Hiroshima, but on the 9th the weather was beginning to cause difficulties. As the planes approached Japan, Laurence wrote that the final choice of targets "lies with destiny":

The winds over Japan will make the decision. If they carry heavy clouds over Kokura, that city will be saved, at least for the time being. Its inhabitants will not know that a wind of a benevolent destiny had passed over their heads. But that same wind will doom Nagasaki.

Our weather planes ahead of us are on their way to find out where the wind blows. Half an hour before target time we shall know what the winds have decided.[14]

The third plane, assigned to take photographs of the bombing, strayed off course. When the two remaining planes reached Kokura, thick clouds obscured the city. The planes circled repeatedly, searching for a break in the cloud cover that would enable a visual drop. During the third pass over the city, antiaircraft fire and approaching Japanese fighter planes convinced the pilots to proceed to Nagasaki.

Thick clouds obscured Nagasaki as well, and an unexpected problem with the fuel-supply system left *Bock's Car* with sufficient fuel for only one pass over Nagasaki if the plane was to get back to its return base on Okinawa. As the plane completed its pass, a slight opening appeared, and at 11:02 A.M., the second—and last—atomic bomb to be used in a war was dropped on Nagasaki. As the 10,000-pound device dropped from the bomb bay, the aircraft jerked upward. Fifty-two seconds later the bomb exploded. Laurence reported that a giant flash broke through their dark arc-welder's lenses and flooded the cabin with intense light.

After the first flash we removed our glasses, but the light lingered on, a bluish-green light that illuminated the entire sky all around. A tremendous blast wave struck our ship and made it tremble from nose to tail. This was followed by four more blasts in rapid succession. . . .

Observers in the tail of our ship saw a giant ball of fire rise as though from the bowels of the earth, belching forth enormous white smoke rings. Next they saw a giant pillar of purple fire, ten thousand feet high, shooting skyward with enormous speed. . . . It was a living thing, a new species of being, born right before our eyes. . . .

Then, just when it appeared as though the thing had settled down into a state of permanence, there came shooting out of the top a giant mushroom that increased the height of the pillar to a total of 45,000 feet.

The mushroom top was even more alive than the pillar, seething and boiling. . . . [15]

The bomb missed its target point by a mile and a half. Unlike Hiroshima, Nagasaki lay in a series of valleys and ridges, a topography that limited the destruction and protected some of the inhabitants. Nevertheless, over 40,000 Japanese were killed and 25,000 more were injured. The city burned for over twenty-four hours. General Groves wrote later, ". . . the damage was not nearly so heavy as it would have been if the correct aiming point had been used. I was considerably relieved when I got the bombing report, which indicated a smaller number of casualties than we had expected, for by that time I was certain that Japan was through and that the war could not continue for more than a few days."[16]

After Hiroshima, there had been no reconsideration of Truman's original order to drop "atomic bombs" on Japan. On August 10, after the second bomb was dropped on Nagasaki, Groves wrote to General Marshall informing him that a third weapon would be available for use after August 24. Marshall sent Groves's communication back within twenty-four hours, with a handwritten note at the bottom: "It is not to be released over Japan without express authority from the President."

At a Cabinet meeting on August 10, Truman suspended further atomic bombing of Japan. According to the diary of Henry A. Wallace, Truman's secretary of commerce, "Truman said he had given orders to stop the atomic bombing. He said the thought of wiping out another 100,000 people was too horrible. He didn't like the idea of killing, as he said, 'all those kids.' " Despite the stated target criteria, the vast majority of victims of Hiroshima and Nagasaki were civilians.[17]

That same day the Japanese offered to surrender on the basis of the Potsdam Declaration on the condition that they retain Emperor Hirohito as sovereign ruler. On August 11 the United States replied that if the emperor cooperated with the Allied commander who would be stationed in Japan, the Americans would accommodate the Japanese request. Negotiations dragged on for several days. On August 14 U.S. planes armed with conventional bombs made their heaviest attack of the entire war on Japanese targets. The Allies accepted a formal Japanese surrender later that day.

Afterward there was considerable debate about whether the Japanese would have surrendered before Hiroshima—or at least before Nagasaki—if they had known that their emperor would be allowed to retain his traditional role. General Dwight D. Eisenhower, commander of Allied forces in Europe, believed that Japan might have surrendered if the United States had given the Japanese government more time to consider its position. Those who disagree cite the fact that Japanese militarists, who wanted to keep fighting, tried to assassinate Emperor Hirohito to prevent his announcing Japan's surrender.[18]

The evidence remains inconclusive. Edward Teller, a scientist at Los Alamos who would play a major role in developing the hydrogen bomb, asked later, "Could we have avoided the tragedy of Hiroshima? Could we have started the atomic age with clean hands?" His answer was "No one knows. No one can find out."[19]

It is a sad and disturbing fact that people continue to suffer and die from the long-term radiation and blast effects of the bombs dropped on Hiroshima and Nagasaki.

Since hardly anyone in the world knew of the existence of atomic bombs before their use on the Japanese cities of Hiroshima and Nagasaki, most people wondered how this development had come about. What scientific breakthroughs led to the bomb? Who were the scientists involved? President Truman's announcement of the Hiroshima bombing referred to the "harnessing of the basic power of the universe," but it was unclear then, as it still is to many today, just what this new weapon was, and how it could have been built.

In addition to scientific questions concerning the bomb, many people thought back to the political events that had led to World War II. Could the war and its consequent death and destruction have been avoided? Many facts relevant to these scientific and political questions were classified Top Secret for years after World War II ended. That veil of secrecy has now largely been lifted. The chapters that follow describe the events and discoveries that led to the development of the atomic bomb, to the decision to use it and to the advent of the nuclear age.

THE MARCH TO WORLD
WAR II

The German form of life is definitely determined for the next thousand years!

> Nazi Proclamation,
> Nuremberg Rally,
> September 4, 1934

Italy! Italy! Entirely and universally Fascist. The Italy of the black shirt revolution, rise to your feet. . . .

> Benito Mussolini,
> International Radio Broadcast,
> October 2, 1935

Japan cannot remove the difficulties in Eastern Asia unless she adopts a policy of blood and iron. . . .

> Japanese Premier Tanaka,
> July 25, 1927

Nuremberg, in southern Germany, was a quiet, dignified city, the birthplace of the sixteenth-century painter Albrecht Dürer and a center of the arts. First mentioned in official records in the year 1050, by 1934 Nuremberg was almost one thousand years old. In early September 1934, flags, banners and posters decorated the city for the annual rally of the German Nazi Party. The Nazi symbol, a twisted cross—the swastika—was displayed everywhere. Marching bands led 30,000 Nazis dressed in brown and black uniforms in a snakelike procession through narrow streets toward a huge auditorium. Enthusiastic crowds sang and shouted slogans.

German Chancellor Adolf Hitler, in brown military uniform and leather boots, mounted the stage and faced the packed auditorium. Flanked by uniformed aides and bodyguards, he stood silent as the crowd thundered "Heil Hitler!" and cheered wildly. There was a call for silence, and to the romantic strains of a Beethoven overture 500 Nazi standards were solemnly paraded. Heads were bowed as a speaker read the names of Nazi party members killed in Hitler's struggle for power.

Hitler spoke intensely and persuasively of Germany's former national glory and of Nazi efforts to recover it. He called for vengeance against those he claimed were Germany's enemies, singling out Jews in particular but condemning other minority groups as well. His rhetoric overwhelmed the audience; by the end of his speech, most were prepared to follow "der Führer" (the leader) wherever he led. [1]

The Nuremberg rally lasted for days. Most speeches began at 8:00 P.M.; at that hour, Hitler believed, "man's suggestibility was high, and his resistance at its lowest ebb." [2] Spectacular searchlight displays and triumphant music enhanced the hypnotic effect of Hitler's speeches. In addition to the official parades, speeches and meetings, Nazi rallies were occasions for celebrating and drinking. Unlike many of his followers, Hitler was a strict nondrinker and a vegetarian.

The high point of the 1934 Nuremberg rally occurred on September 6. German "labor squads" carrying shovels marched smartly onto the field of a huge outdoor stadium. Suddenly they broke into a high-kicking military "goose step" and shouldered their shovels like rifles. Hundreds of thousands of spectators went wild with enthusiasm. With this demonstration, Hitler disclosed to German citizens and to the world that he was secretly training a new German army.

What was the meaning of the goose-stepping "labor squads" and why did they have such great appeal to the Germans? How did German militarism and similar trends in Italy and Japan lead to World War II—and eventually to Hiroshima and Nagasaki? Though these questions are still debated, the development and use of the first atomic bombs cannot be understood without a clear appreciation of the origins and events of World War II.

Fifty-five million people died in World War II as a consequence of failed attempts to preserve peace. Less than 1 percent of those deaths were caused by the atomic bombs dropped on Hiroshima and Nagasaki. This does not lessen the horror of the first atomic bombings, but the devastation they caused should not be viewed in isolation. Hiroshima and Nagasaki were the culmination of the unprecedented escalation of violence that characterized the two World Wars fought in the first half of this century. Today there are more than 50,000 nuclear weapons in world arsenals. With today's supersonic missiles and aircraft, the total casualties of World War II could occur in the course of minutes rather than years. In this nuclear age, it is essential to grasp what led human beings to a war that culminated in the use of nuclear weapons. It is imperative that insights be gained so that such weapons will never be used again.

*   *   *

One day President Roosevelt told me that he was asking publicly for suggestions about what [World War II] should be called. I said at once "the Unnecessary War." There never was a war more easy to stop than that which has just wrecked what was left of the world from the previous struggle.

Winston S. Churchill
The Gathering Storm

The "previous struggle," World War I, was fought and won by France, Great Britain, the United States, Italy and others against Germany and Austria-Hungary between 1914 and 1918. It was an agonizing conflict fought for the most part by soldiers who lived— and often died—in muddy trenches. "No-man's-land," the area between the opposing trenches, was a place of craters dug by exploded artillery shells, of blasted tree stumps, barbed wire and bodies.

World War I battlefield casualties were horrible. France alone lost 1,500,000 soldiers. Many deaths were caused by the machine gun and poison gas, two of the latest weapons. People hoped that it had been "the war to end war," but less than 30 years later "the Great War" (as it was once called) had to be renamed World War I after being surpassed in violence and bloodshed by a second World War.[3]

Immediately following World War I, national leaders sought to establish international laws and a world organization to prevent future conflict. U.S. President Woodrow Wilson, in a statement known as the Fourteen Points, called for an association of nations to guarantee world peace. In 1919, in response to this call, thirty-three nations formed the League of Nations to "promote international cooperation and to achieve international peace and security by the acceptance of the obligations not to resort to war. . . ."

United States membership in the League of Nations hinged on the approval of the U.S. Senate. Article II of the U.S. Constitution requires that the Senate ratify by a two-thirds majority all proposed treaties with foreign governments. Although President Wilson had inspired the League's formation, the Senate fell back on a long-standing tradition of isolationism in world affairs and refused to permit the United States to join. Several Senators quoted from George Washington's Farewell Address of 1796: "Foreign influence is one of the most baneful foes of republican government . . . it is our true policy to steer clear of permanent alliances. . . . Our detached and distant situation invites and enables us to pursue a different course." George Washington, living in another era, believed that the United States would be more likely to prosper if it kept its political distance from European affairs and other "mischiefs of foreign intrigue."[4]

American isolationists felt that a formal association with Europe could involve the United States in a war that it had no part in starting nor any interest in fighting. The policy suggested by George Washington—that the United States use the great distance provided by the Atlantic Ocean to insulate, or even isolate, itself from Europe—had been largely successful for over a century. This tradition prevailed over President Wilson's efforts to establish an international order. The United States' refusal to join the League of Nations undermined the new organization.

Early in 1919, the leaders victorious in World War I met at Versailles, near Paris, to decide what conditions to impose upon the vanquished. The Treaty of Versailles reflected the victors' determination that Germany should never again become a military threat. Germany was virtually disarmed: Its army was disbanded (aside from 100,000 troops to maintain internal order); its fleet of large ships was sunk; its air force was destroyed.

The treaty also reflected the anger of the victors. It included a "war guilt" clause that forced Germany to formally acknowledge sole responsibility for the outbreak of World War I. It also required that Germany make territorial concessions to other countries. Finally, Germany was ordered to pay an enormous sum of money as "reparations" for damages sustained by the Allies—as if the war's destruction could be calculated in dollars and cents. These provisions of the Treaty of Versailles created tremendous resentment among the defeated Germans.

Deteriorating economic conditions aggravated German frustration. In the early 1920s, the cost of living in Germany rose drastically. Prices rose daily—sometimes twice a day—until a wheelbarrow full of German currency was needed to buy a loaf of bread. Even the victorious nations suffered economic hardship, as the Great Depression took its toll in unemployed, hungry and dispossessed people. In 1929 the American stock market collapsed, bankrupting many U.S. businesses, banks and farms, and disrupting the entire world economy.

In Germany, frustration and fury were vented at the postwar democratic government known as the Weimar Republic. Viewed by many Germans as an imposition of the enemy, this new government was held responsible for accepting the terms of the Treaty of Versailles. Beset by serious economic, social and political turmoil, the Weimar government failed to capture the trust of the German people and eventually crumbled. The consequences of its failure were summarized by Winston Churchill, whose books about this period and the Second World War that followed earned him the Nobel Prize for Literature:

. . . a gaping void was opened in the national life of the German people. . . . Mighty forces were adrift; the void was open, and into that void after a pause there strode a maniac of ferocious genius, the repository and expression of the most virulent hatreds that have ever corroded the human breast—Corporal Hitler.[5]

Adolf Hitler, a corporal in World War I, rose to power by condemning the terms of the Treaty of Versailles and blaming Germany's "betrayal" and defeat on his political opponents and racial minorities. During the 1920s Hitler became the leader of the German National Socialist (Nazi) party. After the Nazis gained enough votes to secure Hitler the office of chancellor on January 30, 1933, they promptly burned books that did not support their versions of history and science. The next month the first concentration camps were set up to detain political dissenters.[6]

The Nazi program boasted of Germanic supremacy over all other peoples. A mystical notion that Germans were a "master race" incited fervent national pride and provided a rationale for blaming Germany's problems on others. "Those responsible" were persecuted with a vengeance. Jews, gypsies, Catholics, socialists, communists and all who dissented or resisted the Nazis were violently suppressed.

Unchecked racial, religious and political persecution escalated in the 1930s and 1940s into an actual program for a "final solution" that involved the complete elimination—in plain terms, the murder—of people they considered inferior. The Nazis built extermination camps equipped with poison-gas showers and ovens to kill and cremate their victims. More than 6,000,000 Jews, gypsies, Poles, Soviet prisoners of war, religious and political dissenters, homosexuals, as well as the mentally and physically handicapped, were systematically murdered in what is now known as the Holocaust.

One of the miserable questions of the twentieth century, and of human history, is how the civilized German people could have been led to participate in such barbarism and butchery.

We must also ask how the peace-seeking statesmen of the world could have misread or ignored the many signs pointing to another war. They deluded themselves into believing that Hitler could be appeased, but their attempts to preserve peace at almost any cost only encouraged his aggression.

After the carnage of World War I, well-meaning people everywhere wanted to avoid conflict. Some considered Hitler a bigoted crackpot who could do no real harm. When Field Marshal Paul von Hindenburg, Germany's president from 1925 to 1934, met Hitler for the first time, he is said to have remarked: "That man as chancellor? I'll make him a postmaster and he can lick stamps with my head on them."[7]

But not everyone took Hitler so lightly. Winston Churchill warned the British throughout the 1930s that Hitler was reorganizing and rearming Germany to wage another war. William L. Shirer, an American newspaper correspondent stationed in Berlin, repeatedly warned Americans about Hitler's intentions. He characterized the 1930s as the "nightmare years."

Hitler's "labor squad" parade at Nuremberg in September 1934 signaled his contempt for the Treaty of Versailles. Within six months, by March 1935, several thousand airplanes had been built in secret, and Hitler proudly announced the existence of a new German air force. One week later compulsory national military service was declared, eventually increasing the German army from the 100,000 men allowed by the Treaty of Versailles to over

3,000,000. Soon afterward, Germany disclosed that it had strengthened its navy by building two battleships, each more than twice the permitted size. Although these open violations of the treaty created tremendous concern, most political leaders, wishing to prevent a confrontation, chose to look the other way.

On March 7, 1936, emboldened by the growing strength of his military forces and by the compliant attitude of France and Britain, Hitler ordered 35,000 troops to march into the Rhineland. This largely German-speaking area between France and Germany had been "demilitarized" after World War I. The occupation violated both the Treaty of Versailles and the Treaty of Locarno (1925), which bound Germany to keep all military forces out of the Rhineland. As the German troops marched in, Hitler confused world opinion by claiming that his action was merely "symbolic." Again seeking to avoid confrontation, Europeans and Americans registered only verbal protests.

The French at this time had the largest army in Europe; it was well equipped and more than a match for the German forces. In fact, German military commanders carried sealed orders to retreat immediately at any sign of French resistance. None materialized. Most of Hitler's generals doubted that he would win the Rhineland gamble. After this success the German military increasingly accepted Hitler's judgment, and the German people became even more supportive of his policies.

The precarious political stability of Europe was further shaken when Benito Mussolini, dictator of Italy since 1922, abandoned Italy's World War I allies to join forces with Hitler. On October 21, 1936, Mussolini and Hitler signed a secret protocol that outlined a common foreign policy for their two countries. A few days later Mussolini publicly referred to this agreement without divulging its details. On November 1 he spoke of a "Rome–Berlin

Axis" around which other European powers "may work together." Germany had grown more aggressive, but at least it had stood alone. Now that too had changed.

The political philosophies of Mussolini and Hitler had much in common. Mussolini called himself a "Fascist": the word derives from the Latin *fasces,* which refers to a symbol—an axe attached to a bundle of rods; historically this was an ancient Roman sign of authority and unity. The Fascist movements in Italy and Germany emphasized the supreme authority of the leader and the state over the rights of the individual. When combined with total control of mass media and unrestrained use of propaganda, fascism provided a convenient rationale for leaders willing to employ any means to gain and retain power.

Like Hitler, Mussolini was a charismatic leader who wore military uniforms and enthralled his followers with dramatic speeches and extravagant promises. On special occasions Mussolini would don the black-shirted uniform of the *Arditi,* the daredevil Italian soldiers made famous in World War I. Although Italy had fought with the victors in the Great War, Italians felt slighted by the Treaty of Versailles; they had not been conceded all the territory they wanted for expansion. Mussolini exploited this desire; he made it a major goal to acquire a "new empire" for Italy.[8]

To this end, in October 1935 the Italian army, navy and air force attacked Abyssinia (now Ethiopia) in North Africa. The Ethiopians had no navy or air force and were equipped only with primitive weapons. They were no match for the Italian forces, who attacked on several occasions with poisonous mustard gas. After five months of lopsided struggle Mussolini proclaimed to a cheering crowd of 400,000 in Rome that Italy had won its empire.

Hitler was encouraged by his Rhineland success and by his new alliance with Mussolini. In March 1938, with strengthened forces,

German troops invaded and occupied Austria, again meeting little resistance. By this act Hitler (born in Austria) achieved the imperative printed on the first page of his autobiography *Mein Kampf* (My Struggle): "German Austria must return to the Great German Motherland." Germany annexed Austria, subjecting all citizens to conscription in the German military and to the anti-Jewish racial laws.

Later in 1938 Hitler demanded that the Sudetenland, a highly industrialized, largely German-speaking area of Czechoslovakia, be transferred to Germany. French and British leaders, still hoping to avoid war, traveled to Munich, a city in southern Germany, to assure Hitler that they would not oppose this takeover. They made this concession without consulting Czechoslovakia, a nation with which France had been allied since 1925. In exchange, Hitler assured the leaders of France and Britain that "this is the last territorial claim I have to make in Europe." British Prime Minister Neville Chamberlain returned to London and proclaimed, "I believe it is peace for our time."

At war crimes trials held in Nuremberg eight years later, German Field Marshal Wilhelm Keitel was asked: "Would [Germany] have attacked Czechoslovakia in 1938 if the Western Powers had stood by Prague?" Keitel answered: "Certainly not. We were not strong enough militarily. The object of Munich was to . . . gain time and to complete the German armaments."[9]

On May 22, 1939, Hitler and Mussolini publicly signed an agreement creating a new military alliance. The two dictators called it their "Pact of Steel." The wording of this agreement was bluntly aggressive: It declared that the two nations ". . . united by the inner affinity of their ideologies . . . are resolved to act side by side and with united forces to secure their living space." The next day Hitler held a meeting with his military chiefs. This remark by Hitler is excerpted from the minutes of that meeting:

We are presently in a state of patriotic fervor, which is shared by two other nations—Italy and Japan. . . . There is . . . no question of sparing Poland, and we are left with the decision: to attack Poland at the first suitable opportunity.[10]

At dawn on September 1, 1939, Hitler's army invaded Poland, supported by his new air force, the *Luftwaffe*. Hitler falsely accused the Poles of attacking Germany so that he could claim he was acting in self-defense. He further justified the invasion by claiming that the growing German nation needed "living space" in the east. Much weaker than Germany, Poland did not stand much chance against the Nazi invaders, but nonetheless resisted. In some battles Polish horse calvalry and bicycle troops fought German tanks and fighter aircraft.

Prior to the Polish invasion, to prevent Russian interference, Hitler secured a "nonaggression pact" with the Soviet Union. (Later, when it suited his purposes, Hitler would ignore this pact and attack the Soviet Union.) But Britain and France were finally pressed beyond the limits of their tolerance. Honoring their prior commitments to Poland, they declared war on Germany. But in the United States isolationist sentiments prevailed in the debate about America's participation. For now, the United States would stay out of this latest European war.

*   *   *

Halfway around the world, Japan was pursuing its own course of territorial expansion through military aggression. During this period and throughout the Second World War, Emperor Hirohito was nominally the supreme ruler of Japan. Japanese tradition held that he be viewed as a "descendant of heaven" who would reign gently and benevolently. Japan had adopted a constitution in 1895 that established a two-house congress, or diet, but the government was in reality controlled by militarists in the powerful and fast-growing Japanese army and navy.

Japan was overpopulated and lacked natural resources, and the worldwide economic depression generated political unrest. The military took advantage of the unstable situation to appropriate power for itself and to seize by force the territory and resources of its Asian neighbors. On September 18, 1931, a date that many historians mark as the real beginning of World War II, the Japanese army launched a full-scale invasion of Manchuria, a province of China. By the end of 1931, the Japanese had installed a puppet government to rule the province, which they renamed "Manchukuo." Although the Japanese government had claimed to be acting in self-defense, a League of Nations investigation ruled that this justification was unfounded. When the League announced its findings in February 1933, the Japanese delegation promptly walked out of the assembly. In March Japan resigned from the League of Nations; Germany followed suit in October.[11]

During the next few years the Japanese army invaded other Chinese provinces, adopting a "scorched-earth" policy of burning or otherwise destroying everything in its path. Nanking, the Chinese capital, fell on December 13, 1937, and the Japanese army went berserk, killing and raping thousands of Chinese civilians.

Japanese military aggression should have come as no surprise to the United States. Several years earlier, on December 27, 1934, U.S. Ambassador to Japan Joseph C. Grew had cabled his appraisal of the situation to Washington. According to an official

U.S. State Department document, Ambassador Grew observed that the Japanese were "constantly boasting that their destiny was to subjugate and rule the world." Ambassador Grew reported that a "swashbuckling temper" influenced by military propaganda "could lead Japan during the next few years to any extreme unless the saner minds in government were able to cope with it and to restrain the country from national suicide."[12]

On September 27, 1940, Germany, Italy and Japan signed a far-reaching treaty of alliance. This "Tripartite Pact" provided that Japan would recognize and respect the leadership of Germany and Italy in their establishment of a new order in Europe; that Germany and Italy would recognize and respect the leadership of Japan and its establishment of a new order in Greater East Asia; and that the three countries would assist one another if any one was attacked by a power not then involved in the European conflict. U.S. State Department officials believed that the last provision was aimed directly at the United States.

While Hitler, Mussolini and the Japanese militarists were marching Europe and Asia into World War II, scientists seeking to understand the inner workings of the atom discovered an amazing phenomenon involving the element uranium. As World War II began, however, hardly anyone understood the significance of uranium, much less the wartime role it was destined to play.

IV

A WALK IN THE WOODS

Origin of the word "atom": Derived from the Greek words a (not), temnein (to cut). First used by the Greek philosopher Democritus in the fifth century B.C. to denote the idea that matter was composed of units so small they could not be divided.

We all know that [the uranium atom] can't really burst asunder. . . .

Excerpt from a letter written by Otto Hahn to Lise Meitner, dated December 12, 1938 (twenty-four centuries later)

In late December 1938 Lise Meitner and her nephew took a walk through snow-laden woods in southern Sweden. Meitner, who had just celebrated her sixtieth birthday, boasted to thirty-four-year-old Otto Frisch that she could walk as fast as he could ski. As they moved side by side through the woods, often the only sounds that they could hear were the crunch of Meitner's boots in the snow and the soft hiss of Frisch's skis cutting new tracks.

The serenity of this winter setting and the absence of distractions helped Meitner and Frisch concentrate on a riddle of atomic physics that was perplexing them and eluding other scientists. Their answer built on years of work by physicists from many nations. Lise Meitner and Otto Frisch could hardly have foreseen that the solution they reached that day would lead directly to the development of the atomic bomb seven years later.[1]

Lise Meitner was a very determined, soft-spoken Austrian physicist and a leading expert on radioactive substances. Her work was highly respected, and she was the first woman appointed to a professorship at the University of Berlin. But in spite of her extraordinary competence and fine reputation she was fired from her university post because Adolf Hitler had decreed that Jews were forbidden to hold positions of such importance. Several German scientists tried to persuade Hitler to make an exception in Meitner's case, but Hitler was adamant. As Nazi anti-Semitism led to increased repression and violence, Meitner realized that she had to flee Germany to avoid arrest, imprisonment or death. She fled to Sweden, whose neutrality made the country a haven for political refugees.[2]

Meitner's nephew, Otto Frisch, another physicist, had also fled Hitler's Germany. He now worked with the world-famous Niels Bohr in Copenhagen, Denmark. Dr. Bohr had been awarded the Nobel Prize for Physics in 1922 for his theories on the structure and behavior of atoms. Since 1933, when Hitler had come to power, Bohr had been finding positions for many eminent scientists whose lives and work were threatened by Nazism; he had encouraged Lise Meitner's escape, and had arranged work for her in Sweden.[3]

Only days before her walk with Frisch, Lise Meitner had received a puzzling letter from Germany. Otto Hahn, her trusted colleague for over thirty years, and his assistant, Fritz Strassmann, described a carefully prepared experiment that had produced astounding results. The experiment suggested that when atoms of the element uranium were bombarded with neutrons they somehow turned into atoms of other substances.

Uranium, named after the planet Uranus, was discovered in Czechoslovakia in 1789. A second, more abundant source of this rare metal was later found in the Belgian Congo (now Zaire); Bateke tribesmen there smeared the uranium-rich mud on their skins to

make themselves glow like ghosts in the forest night. Their enemies, convinced that the Bateke possessed magical powers, were
terrified.[4] The phenomenon described by Hahn and Strassmann
also seemed supernatural, and reminiscent of alchemists' efforts
in the Middle Ages to turn lead into gold. The report of uranium
being transformed into other elements smacked of charlatanism or
sloppy research. But Meitner knew Hahn to be rigorous and unlikely to make careless mistakes. Although she was baffled, she
believed there must be some clear scientific explanation. Meitner
and her nephew Otto Frisch took their walk to ponder Hahn's
experimental results.

Otto Frisch usually spent the holidays with his aunt, and he
had arrived this Christmas in Sweden just as she received Hahn's
message. Hahn and Strassmann had difficulty believing that the
uranium atom could split to yield lighter elements such as barium.
Atoms were thought to be indivisible; there was no known set of
principles to explain such an unexpected phenomenon. "We all
know," Hahn wrote Meitner, "that [the uranium atom] can't really
burst asunder. . . ." Hahn concluded by urging Meitner to "put
forward some fanciful explanation for it all."[5]

They all knew that an atom consists of a minute but dense
central core called the nucleus, made up of protons (which are
positively charged) and neutrons (which are electrically neutral).
Protons and neutrons are held together in the nucleus by a powerful
"binding energy." Due to its protons, the nucleus carries a positive
charge.

Negatively charged electrons orbit the nucleus at very high
speeds. Electrons are held in their orbits because their negative
charges are attracted to the positive charge of the nucleus. Most
atoms are stable because the number of positive protons equals
the number of negative electrons. While the electrical charges of

protons and electrons offset each other in a stable atom, their weights do not. Each proton (and each neutron, which weighs about the same as a proton) is more than 1,800 times heavier than an electron. Thus the nucleus contains almost all the mass of the atom.

Despite its mass, the nucleus is actually only $\frac{1}{10,000}$ (0.0001) the size of the entire atom. Most of the atom is simply empty space. For example, an atomic nucleus magnified to the size of a marble would have its electrons moving in paths reaching the ceiling and walls of a classroom.

As we have seen, atoms are stable because they have an equal number of protons and electrons. This number is unique and characteristic of each element. Hydrogen, for example, has one electron and one proton, helium has two of each, lithium three of each, and so on through the table of elements to uranium, which has 92 of each. This characteristic is called the atomic number. All existing substances can be broken down into one or some combination of the 92 elements. Artificially produced elements, the so-called "transuranics" (beyond uranium), have more than 92 protons and electrons. Transuranics do not occur in nature under normal conditions.

Atoms that have an unequal number of protons and electrons are unstable, and are rarely found in nature. They tend to emit particles in order to stabilize their electrical charge, and these emissions cause them to be "radioactive." The emissions also cause the atoms to change, or transmute, into atoms of other substances. New Zealand physicist Ernest Rutherford had discovered that radioactive substances decay at certain rates. He measured the "half-life" of each radioactive substance (the time it takes half of any amount of that substance to decay) but Rutherford hesitated to claim that the atoms of one substance had changed into atoms of another. Transmutation was then considered impossible, and his colleagues warned him not to make a fool of himself.[6]

When Meitner and Frisch took their walk in the woods to ponder the Hahn-Strassmann experiment, they brought with them both an awareness of Rutherford's findings and knowledge of over forty years of discovery in atomic physics. They were building upon research that dated from New Year's Day, 1896, when the German scientist Wilhelm Roentgen distributed a pamphlet describing his discovery of mysterious rays, which he called "X rays." Roentgen claimed they could penetrate flesh and even more solid materials. To prove this, his pamphlet included amazing and disconcerting photographs of the bones of his own hand. Within weeks, laboratories all over Europe began to turn out X-ray images of hands, feet, arms, legs, skulls, and other body parts—even some with bullets visible in them.[7]

Meanwhile, in France, Henri Becquerel and his father had been studying a phenomenon called fluorescence, the ability of certain substances to glow after being exposed to sunlight. Becquerel's curiosity was piqued when he learned of Roentgen's discovery, and he immediately turned his attention to X rays. Becquerel had already been using uranium in his experiments concerning fluorescence. He discovered that even when uranium had <u>not</u> been exposed to sunlight, it spontaneously gave off X rays that could pass through wrapping paper and expose a photographic plate. It was a tremendous discovery, though for the time being the nature of the rays and the reason for their emission remained a mystery.

Enter Marie Sklodowska Curie, a Polish-born student of physics living in Paris and the wife of the French physicist Pierre Curie. Marie Curie was a scientist of great intelligence and extraordinary stamina. Focusing her doctoral thesis on "the new phenomenon" discovered by Becquerel, she set out to examine every known element to determine whether any substances other than uranium emitted the mysterious, penetrating X rays. After an exhaustive search, she found that thorium spontaneously emitted rays "similar to those of uranium." Marie Curie then coined the term "radioactivity" to denote the ability of certain substances to emit energy on their own.

Marie Curie persuaded her husband to set aside his own projects in order to pursue with her this new field of radioactive substances. Not only did they find that certain minerals were even more radioactive than uranium; they also identified two new radioactive elements: One was polonium, which they named after Marie Curie's native Poland; the other was radium, which in its pure form is about 1,000,000 times more radioactive than uranium. For this last discovery, the Curies shared the Nobel Prize for Physics with Henri Becquerel in 1903.

At this time, scientists were largely ignorant of the nature of radiation and its health hazards. We now know that radiation consists of protons, neutrons, electrons and other subatomic particles that shoot through space at speeds up to 100,000 miles per second. Some of this radiation occurs naturally, in the form of cosmic rays from outer space and uranium and thorium in the ground (most brick, stone, and other building materials are slightly radioactive as a result). Radioactive particles can penetrate the human body. They can strike and damage cell tissue, potentially causing cancer in individuals and genetic defects in later generations.

The human body can repair much naturally occuring radiation damage: Experiments have shown that chromosomes broken by low levels of radiation can grow back together. But higher doses received over short periods—whether they be from excessive exposure to X rays, a nuclear reactor accident or the detonation of a nuclear weapon—raise the probability that the body's recuperative powers will be overwhelmed, and that cancers and genetic defects will result. High levels of radiation exposure cause fever, vomiting, hemorrhaging and, eventually, death.

At the time of their Nobel Prize, the Curies began to suffer from a series of strange and hard-to-diagnose diseases. (Becquerel also suffered—from skin burns—because he often carried a piece of uranium in his pocket.) In 1906 Pierre was struck and killed by a horse-drawn cart in a Paris street. Marie lived to the age of 67, but she was ill for a long time and eventually died of a blood disease caused by excessive exposure to radiation. Marie Curie rarely left her laboratory except to sleep and cook for her family at home; her cookbooks were found to be radioactive fifty years after she had used them.[8]

Lise Meitner and others were intrigued by the discoveries of Roentgen, Becquerel, the Curies and Rutherford, and devoted themselves to working with radioactive substances. Before Meitner fled Germany, she and Otto Hahn had experimented with ways to use the emissions of radioactive substances to probe the atom. In the 1930s, one approach was to bombard one element after another with particles from known radioactive elements. The problem with using charged protons and electrons to bombard atoms is that both tend to be deflected either by the positive charge of the atomic nucleus or by the negative charge of its electrons.

Then, in 1932, James Chadwick at Cambridge University proved the existence of the electrically neutral particle, the neutron. Enrico Fermi, a young physicist in Rome, thought to use neutrons to bombard atoms. By aiming many neutrons at atoms with large nuclei, Fermi found that the number of collisions could be vastly increased. He also found that slowing or "moderating" the speed of the neutrons increased the likelihood of collisions. Fermi's wife later wrote, "This slow neutron will have a much better chance of being captured by a . . . nucleus than a fast one, much as a slow golf ball has a better chance of making a hole than one which zooms fast and may bypass it."[9]

Fermi successfully bombarded a whole series of elements with "slow neutrons." Then, when uranium was the target, puzzling radioactive substances were produced. Fermi's colleagues and other scientists believed that he had created a new element, one heavier than uranium; that is, they thought that the uranium nucleus had captured an additional neutron, thus increasing its weight. Although Fermi, uncertain as to what had actually occurred, would not make this claim, he was awarded the Nobel Prize for Physics in 1938 "for his identification of new radioactive elements produced by neutron bombardment and for his discovery of nuclear reaction effected by slow neutrons." Ironically, just as Fermi was receiving the Nobel Prize, Otto Hahn and Fritz Strassmann were conducting the experiments in Berlin that disproved this interpretation of Fermi's results.

While walking in the woods, Lise Meitner and Otto Frisch had discussed Niels Bohr's theory that an atomic nucleus was more likely to act like a liquid drop than like a brittle solid. Bohr's idea precipitated their breakthrough: if the heavy uranium nucleus resembled a very large and wobbly drop, then it might capture a neutron, elongate, and split into two new nuclei whose combined weights nearly equal the weight of uranium. This was a revolutionary idea about the behavior of atoms, which were long thought to be indivisible.[10]

Since each of these new nuclei would be positively charged, they would repel each other with great force. The binding energy that had held them together would be released as heat and radiation. Meitner and Frisch sat down on a tree trunk and asked themselves, "Where could all that energy come from?"

The formula that Lise Meitner used to answer the question is part of physicist Albert Einstein's theory of relativity, which describes the relationship—specifically the interchangeability—of matter and energy. The equation expressing Einstein's assumption— $E = mc^2$ —says that E (energy) is equal to m (mass) multiplied by c (the speed of light) squared. This constant c is a very large number (the speed of light is 186,000 miles per second); and so the equation suggests that most of the energy of the universe is locked up within matter—indeed, within the nucleus of the atom. Meitner calculated that $\frac{1}{10}$ of 1 percent (0.1%) of the original mass of the uranium nucleus had "disappeared" in the Hahn-Strassmann experiment.

This very slight decrease in mass is the source of tremendous energy. Applying Einstein's equation, the mass lost is multiplied by the speed of light squared (186,000 × 186,000 = 34,596,000,000). So even minute quantities of matter can be transformed into enormous amounts of energy, which are measured in units called MeV, or million electron volts. Splitting a single uranium nucleus liberates sufficient energy to cause a grain of sand to jump. The mass of a paper clip converted into energy would provide all the heat, light and power a small town could use in a day.

To put this force into a slightly different perspective: Before the advent of atomic weapons the most powerful energy release was produced by exploding trinitrotoluene, commonly known as TNT. When atomic weapons were developed, their explosive power was quantified in kilotons (thousands of tons) or megatons (millions of tons) of TNT. A 1-megaton atomic weapon contains approximately

100 pounds of uranium or plutonium. When it explodes, the energy released is equivalent to that produced by exploding enough TNT to fill a freight train 300 miles long.[11]

After his walk in the woods with Lise Meitner, Frisch returned to Copenhagen to conduct experiments that confirmed her conclusions. Frisch presented the results to Niels Bohr, who struck his head with his palm, exclaiming, "Oh, what fools we have been! We ought to have seen that before."

By telephone, Meitner and Frisch quickly prepared a thousand-word report, introducing the term "fission" to describe the splitting of the uranium nucleus. (In Copenhagen, Frisch had asked a young American biologist named William Arnold what he called the phenomenon of cell division. "Fission," he replied.)[12]

On January 26, 1939, just one month after Meitner and Frisch's walk in the woods, Niels Bohr announced the discovery of nuclear fission to a conference of scientists at George Washington University in Washington, D.C. The news generated frenzied activity. Physicist Leo Szilard said that the Physics Department of Princeton University was like "a stirred-up ant heap."[13] One physicist excited by Bohr's report was the young American J. Robert Oppenheimer, later chief scientific director for the Manhattan Project, the group that would apply this discovery to the design and production of the first atomic weapon.

The discovery of nuclear fission by Hahn and Strassmann was an example of how the international scientific community could cooperate to solve problems of great interest and complexity. The relatively small group of atomic scientists met frequently at universities and international conferences to explain their experiments and theories. They were a tightly knit mosaic of nationalities, including Germans, Austrians, Italians, French, Danes, Hungarians, British, Canadians and Americans who sought, for reasons of intellectual and scientific interest, to unlock the mysteries of the atom.

With the onset of World War II, scientific research was redirected toward military applications. Some Allied scientists feared that if Adolf Hitler became the first to harness the energy of the atom and build an atomic bomb, Nazism could dominate the world. What began as an innocent exploration of the atom, and a walk in the woods, would soon develop into a race to build the first atomic bomb. The political and military leaders of the warring nations were still unaware of the significance of uranium and nuclear fission, but they were not to stay ignorant for long.

V

EARLY WARNING

That night there was very little doubt in my mind that the world was headed for grief.

> Physicist Leo Szilard,
> after learning that surplus neutrons
> are emitted by the fission of uranium nuclei,
> March 1939

Pa, this requires action!

> President Franklin Roosevelt,
> to his attaché, General Edwin "Pa" Watson,
> after being informed of recent uranium experiments,
> October 1939

The ruthless momentum of Hitler's aggression troubled Leo Szilard and Eugene Wigner, Hungarian physicists who had been conducting advanced atomic research in Germany before emigrating to the United States. The German occupation of the Rhineland, the anti-Jewish laws, and the invasions of Austria and Czechoslovakia convinced Szilard and Wigner that Hitler would stop at nothing to achieve world domination. They understood the implications of the Meitner-Frisch report and feared that if Nazi scientists developed atomic bombs, Hitler would surely use them. These two physicists were acutely aware that nuclear fission had first been discovered by Hahn and Strassmann in Berlin, and that

51

the Germans had the sophisticated physicists, the highly developed industry and, now that they occupied Czechoslovakia, the uranium mines to support an atom bomb project.

Driven by their concerns, Szilard and Wigner sought to alert U.S. President Franklin Roosevelt to the recent discoveries in atomic physics and to the destructive potential of an atomic bomb. In the summer of 1939 they drafted a letter advising him to support U.S. physicists in their experimental work as a safeguard against ongoing atomic research in Germany. To capture the president's attention, Szilard and Wigner asked Albert Einstein, who shared their concerns, to send the letter under his name.

Leo Szilard, the individual primarily responsible for initiating this historic communication, was a lively, witty man as well as a respected physicist. Earlier in 1939, he had designed an experiment to determine whether, when a uranium nucleus splits apart, the fission process releases surplus neutrons. If so, these neutrons would be available to split other uranium nuclei, releasing more neutrons to split even more nuclei, and so on. Szilard realized that initiating a "chain reaction" in a sufficient quantity of uranium could result in "the large-scale liberation of atomic energy" and lead to the possibility of developing an atomic bomb.

On March 3, his preparations complete, Szilard threw a switch, sat back and watched a screen. Flashes of light would indicate that surplus neutrons were being emitted from the uranium; this would confirm the possibility of a chain reaction. After the switch was thrown, flashes streaked across the screen. Szilard watched them awhile, then turned everything off and went home. He wrote later, "That night there was very little doubt in my mind that the world was headed for grief."[1]

For years Szilard had worried about the misuse of uranium in the event that a chain reaction were proven possible. Now that his

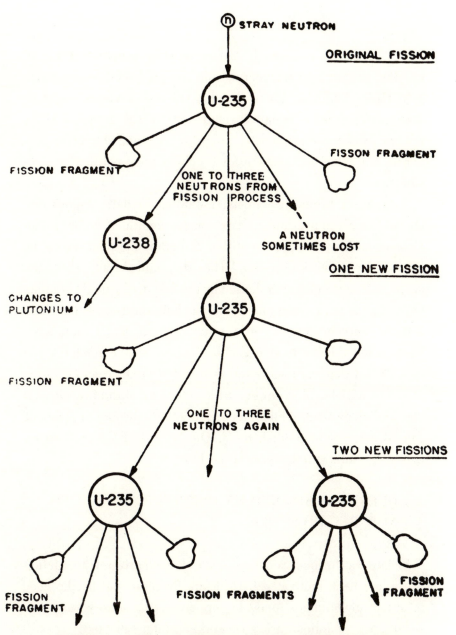

Schematic diagram of a fission chain reaction. In an explosive reaction the number of neutrons multiplies indefinitely. In a controlled reaction the number of neutrons builds up to a certain level and then remains constant.

theory had been confirmed, Szilard actively sought to keep all uranium research secret, fearing that any published results might help Hitler build an atomic bomb. Although findings might be discussed privately among a small and trusted group of U.S., French and British physicists, Szilard felt nothing should be published. But other scientists did not feel the same political responsibility.

A group of French scientists, including Frédéric Joliot-Curie (Marie Curie's son-in-law), independently confirmed Szilard's conclusions and wrote a paper entitled "Liberation of neutrons in the nuclear explosion of uranium." They determined that, on the average, 3.5 neutrons were released by the fission of a single uranium nucleus, enough to start and sustain a chain reaction. If the chain reaction were to begin in a large enough amount of uranium— later called the "critical mass"—so many atomic nuclei would split so fast that the energy released would produce an explosion of almost unbelievable power.[2] Szilard learned of the French findings and made several attempts by letter and telegram to persuade Joliot-Curie not to publish them. On April 6, 1939, Szilard received the following telegram from France:

QUESTIONS STUDIED MY OPINION IS TO PUBLISH
NOW REGARDS JOLIOT.

Szilard was furious. Some scientists claimed privately that Joliot-Curie had been motivated by a desire for fame and by the need to attract government funds to support his laboratory. Lew Kowarski, one of Joliot-Curie's co-workers, later reflected:

To be first to achieve the chain reaction was like achieving the philosopher's stone. It's far more than a Nobel Prize. We were perfectly aware of that. Whether it was disinterested glow of scientific curiosity or sordid interest of self-exaltation, I don't know—mixed motives, human nature.[3]

Motives aside, Szilard was certain that the article would open the starting gate for a race to develop atomic bombs.

The French publication did indeed precipitate extensive international discussion about how a uranium chain reaction might lead to the development of a new powerful explosive. More than fifty research articles on uranium fission appeared in journals in Germany, France, England and the United States. One article in particular, published in Germany in June 1939, demonstrated an extensive understanding of atomic fission and its potential use as an explosive.

This state of affairs led Szilard and Wigner to approach Albert Einstein with their letter warning President Roosevelt, which Einstein signed on August 2, 1939. To ensure its delivery to the president, the letter was entrusted to Alexander Sachs, a friend of both Einstein's and Roosevelt's. It read:

Sir:

Some recent work by E. Fermi and L. Szilard, which has been communicated to me in manuscript, leads me to expect that the element uranium may be turned into a new and important source of energy in the immediate future. Certain aspects of the situation which has arisen seem to call for watchfulness and, if necessary, quick action on the part of the Administration. I believe therefore that it is my duty to bring to your attention the following facts and recommendations:

In the course of the last four months it has been made probable— through the work of Joliot in France as well as Fermi and Szilard in America—that it may become possible to set up a nuclear chain reaction in a large mass of uranium by which vast amounts of power and large quantities of new radium-like elements would be generated. Now it appears almost certain that this could be achieved in the immediate future.

This new phenomenon would also lead to the construction of bombs, and it is conceivable—though much less certain—that extremely powerful bombs of a new type may thus be constructed. A single bomb of this type, carried by boat and exploded in a port, might well destroy the whole port together with some of the surrounding territory. However, such bombs might very well prove to be too heavy for transportation by air.

Einstein advised Roosevelt to secure a supply of uranium for the United States and to establish permanent contact between the U.S. government and physicists working on chain reactions. He also asked the president to obtain financial support "to speed up the experimental work." Einstein's letter ended with a lightly veiled warning:

I understand that Germany has actually stopped the sale of uranium from the Czechoslovakian mines which she has taken over. That she should have taken such an early action might perhaps be understood on the ground that the son of the German Under-secretary of State, von Weizsäcker, is attached to the Kaiser-Wilhelm-Institut in Berlin where some of the American work on uranium is now being repeated.[4]

In this period of extreme international tension, Sachs had difficulty arranging an appointment with the president. He finally delivered the letter on October 13, six weeks after Hitler's invasion of Poland, an event that strengthened the impact of its message. The discussion between Roosevelt and Sachs led to the initiation of the Allied atom bomb project, and merits repetition:

SACHS: *All I want to do is tell you a story. During the Napoleonic wars the young American inventor Robert Fulton came to the French emperor and offered to build a fleet of steamships with the help of which Napoleon could, in spite of uncertain weather, land in England. Ships without sails? This seemed to the great Corsican so impossible that he sent Fulton away. In the opinion of the English historian Lord Acton, this is an example of how England was saved by the shortsightedness of an adversary. Had Napoleon shown more imagination and humility at that time, the history of the nineteenth century would have taken a very different course.*[5]

Sachs then spoke about the potential peaceful applications of the atom for energy production and medicine before turning to the prospect of "bombs of hitherto unenvisaged potency." He meant to illustrate what he saw as "the two poles of good and evil" embodied in the discovery of uranium fission. Concluding his presentation to Roosevelt, Sachs read from a prescient 1936 lecture by British physicist Francis Aston, emphasizing the last two sentences: "Personally I think there is no doubt that sub-atomic energy is available all around us, and that one day man will release and control its almost infinite power. We cannot prevent him from doing so and can only hope that he will not use it exclusively in blowing up his next door neighbor."

Sachs finished speaking, and the president remained silent for several minutes. Then he scribbled on a scrap of paper and handed it to an aide, who promptly left the room. The man returned with a parcel, and at a sign from Roosevelt unwrapped a bottle of French brandy dating from the Napoleonic era. The bottle had been held by the Roosevelt family for many years. The president asked that two glasses be filled. Then he raised his own and drank to Sachs.

Roosevelt asked: "Alex, what you are after is to see that the Nazis don't blow us up?"

"Precisely."

Roosevelt then called in his attaché, General Edwin M. "Pa" Watson. Pointing to Sachs's documents, Roosevelt declared:

"Pa, this requires action!"[6]

The "action" ordered that day began rather slowly. A distinguished group of U.S. scientists was asked to form an "Advisory Committee on Uranium" ("Uranium Committee") to determine the feasibility of building an atomic bomb. However, government funding for the committee was minimal; by the spring of 1940 only $6,000 had been granted. After all, the United States remained technically neutral, and the war was being fought far from home. Two years marked by momentous events would pass before serious work began on the bomb.

While the Uranium Committee pondered its task, war raged throughout Europe. Poland was conquered in September 1939. In May 1940 Hitler invaded France, which fell in only eight weeks. In July 1940 Hitler launched an all-out bombing campaign against England. Although the Battle of Britain was a nightmare for the English—particularly for citizens living in London, where the bombing raids were heaviest—their resistance was the first effective defense against the Nazi juggernaut.

In June 1941, frustrated by his inability to defeat the British, Hitler turned east with a massive attack on the Soviet Union. The Soviets eventually lost 20 million people in their fight against Hitler—more than any of the other Allies. Their contribution to the overall war effort in Europe cannot be overestimated.

On Sunday morning, December 7, 1941, Japanese torpedo planes attacked the U.S. Navy fleet at Pearl Harbor, Hawaii, without warning. Convinced that war with the United States was inevitable, Japan hoped that the surprise attack would destroy the large U.S. Pacific Fleet. The United States declared war on Japan the following day, and President Roosevelt was directed by Congress to employ the military forces of the U.S. and "all the resources of the country" to bring the war against Japan to a "successful termination." Four days after the attack on Pearl Harbor, Germany declared war on the United States.[7]

Two years had passed since Einstein's letter warned President Roosevelt about the potential for a Nazi atomic bomb. During that period, U.S. atomic research had dawdled. Now the United States was at war with both Germany and Japan, and about to commit itself to a crash program to build an atomic bomb.

VI

THE MANHATTAN PROJECT

Most of us considered it a major tragedy when Mr. Oppenheimer put the finger on Los Alamos. It is sad to see this beautiful ranch, which had perhaps 80 people on it at most during the school period, now covered with a modern city of 20,000 or more people.

John S. Reed,
former Chairman of the Atchison,
Topeka & Santa Fe Railroad,
and former student at the Los Alamos Ranch School

The Manhattan Project was a gigantic gamble—the President of the United States indeed said it was—a 2 billion dollar gamble which we won.

Ernest A. Lawrence,
to the American Society of Mechanical Engineers,
Los Angeles, California,
July 26, 1946

Los Alamos sits on an isolated plateau 7,000 feet above sea level, beneath the rim of the Jemez mountain range in New Mexico. *Jemez* is an Indian word that means "place of the boiling springs," and the name fits the demonic topography. As one account described it, "Even to an untrained eye, thick layers of volcanic ash, heaps of burned rock, cone-shaped hills and fumaroles, and bubbling hot sulfur springs all give unmistakable evidence of an open passage to the underworld in the not-too-distant past."[1]

Long after volcanic activity ceased, Los Alamos had become the site of an exclusive ranch school for boys. The school's brochure promised a rigorous education, strict discipline and an "altitude which promotes deep breathing and a bountiful pulse." The students, aged twelve to eighteen, wore shorts year round and slept on open, unheated porches even in subfreezing temperatures. Students such as John Reed and Roy Chapin, who later became chairmen of major corporations, found the school to be a rigorous experience that built character. Author Gore Vidal, however, speaks of spending a "grim year on the mesa," and another writer, William S. Burroughs, recounted: "Far away and high on the mesa's crest, I was forced to become a Boy Scout, eat everything on my plate, exercise before breakfast, sleep on a porch in zero weather, stay outside all afternoon, and ride a sullen, spiteful, recalcitrant horse twice a week and all day on Saturday. We had to stay outdoors, no matter what, all afternoon. They even timed you in the john. I was always cold, and I hated my horse, a sulky strawberry roan."[2]

Unlike Burroughs and Vidal, J. Robert Oppenheimer enjoyed outdoor life in the Los Alamos area. He was not a student at the Ranch School, but as a young man he often vacationed nearby. Oppenheimer told his friends: "My two great loves are physics and New Mexico. It's a pity they can't be combined."

Oppenheimer was born in New York City. His father imported men's suit linings and his mother was a painter. As a child he spent hours collecting, cataloguing and polishing mineral samples. At age eleven he was elected to the New York Mineralogical Club; at age twelve he delivered his first scholarly paper. He went on to complete a four-year chemistry course at Harvard University in three years and then to study theoretical physics at several European universities, where he impressed many physicists. In 1939 he turned down eleven other teaching positions to accept a professorship at the University of California at Berkeley. His scientific colleagues nicknamed him "Oppie."[3]

In 1939 President Roosevelt ordered the Uranium Committee to determine the feasibility of an atomic bomb, and the committee later recommended a major effort to build the weapon. Oppenheimer, who had been conducting atomic research at Berkeley under Nobel Prize-winning physicist Ernest Lawrence, was selected as scientific director of the project.

World War II still seemed very far away from the Jemez mountains. Then, in the summer of 1942, unexpected and strange attention came to the remote desert mesa. As the Ranch School's summer program began, school officials noticed "low-flying aircraft that seemed to study the area. Cars and military vehicles appeared on the crest of the road that led up to the valley."[4] As a light snow was falling one afternoon in late November, several unmarked automobiles made their way up the Los Alamos dirt road, circling around several boys playing soccer. In one car rode Oppenheimer and General Leslie Groves, military director of the newly authorized U.S. atomic bomb project, code-named "Manhattan Project" because its original offices were in New York. Oppenheimer and Groves were looking for a place to establish their headquarters; Oppenheimer had remembered the Ranch School and suggested to Groves that it might be suitable for their laboratories and meet their housing and security requirements. As soon as Groves saw it, he said, "This is the place."

On December 7, 1942, the first anniversary of Pearl Harbor, school officials received a message from the secretary of war: "You are advised that it has been determined necessary to the interests of the United States in the prosecution of the War that the property of Los Alamos Ranch School be acquired for military purposes."[5]

Groves and Oppenheimer chose Los Alamos for a number of

reasons. The Ranch School had adequate housing for a small group of scientists, sufficient cleared land for the quick construction of additional buildings and enough surrounding uninhabited desert (54,000 acres that could be bought secretly by the government) to distance potentially dangerous experiments from residences and laboratories. Furthermore, Los Alamos was far enough from both the Atlantic and Pacific coasts not to be immediately vulnerable should the United States be attacked or invaded by the Germans or the Japanese.

Leslie Groves had earned his reputation supervising the construction of the Pentagon, the national headquarters of the U.S. armed forces, in Washington, D.C. Groves was hardly beloved by those who worked for him; he pushed his subordinates unmercifully. On the other hand, he often got things done ahead of schedule and below cost—to the delight of his superiors. Senior military and civilian officials believed that Groves's forceful personality was needed if the Manhattan Project was to have any chance of succeeding.

Work at Los Alamos was supported by laboratories of the University of Chicago, Columbia University, and the University of California. The responsibilities of approximately 150,000 employees were divided between military personnel and civilians. Electrical and mechanical engineers, metallurgists, physicists and other civilian scientists developed basic research and design principles and reported to Oppenheimer. The U.S. Army, under Groves, coordinated the logistics and civil engineering. His people negotiated industrial contracts for materials and managed personnel; they constructed roads and put up housing and support facilities, including plants to process uranium. Groves was responsible for maintaining secrecy, both from outsiders and from insiders who had no "need to know" the Project's ultimate aim.[6]

Manhattan Project scientists faced several problems, some of which had been identified by the now-defunct Uranium Committee. One was to determine the quantity of uranium required to build a bomb. Laboratory experiments had produced fission in minute quantities of uranium, but these quantities were well below the "critical mass"—the amount necessary to sustain a chain reaction and produce an explosion. That is the reason Otto Hahn and Fritz Strassmann had survived the effects of their experiments and lived to tell about their work.

Another problem involved the type of uranium to use. In nature, 99.3 percent of all uranium exists as U-238 (with 92 protons and 146 neutrons); only .7 percent exists as U-235 (with 143 neutrons). Experiments had shown that U-235 atoms were less stable and therefore more likely to fission when bombarded with neutrons; creating an explosive chain reaction would require a much higher ratio of U-235 to U-238 atoms than is found in nature. Two complicated separation techniques were developed, based on the slight weight difference between U-235 and U-238 atoms, and enormous plants were built at Oak Ridge, Tennessee, to enrich the uranium to "weapons-grade" purity. The scientists also developed processes to remove impurities that would absorb rather than release neutrons: the presence of virtually any other element would slow or stop the chain reaction, preventing an explosion.

The problem of calculating critical mass remained: What quantity of U-235 would be needed to produce an explosion? A pile of uranium interspersed with 400 tons of graphite moderator was constructed to allow the physicists to test their theories and calculations. This involved the dangerous assembly of enough uranium to initiate a chain reaction, but not so much as to result in a catastrophic explosion. The physicists did not know whether a chain reaction, once started, could be controlled.

From September to November 1942, the pile was constructed in a squash court under the stands of the football stadium at the University of Chicago. Enrico Fermi was the scientist in charge. The test was scheduled for December 2, 1942. An artist's conception of the scene is on the following page.

The three men atop the pile are the "suicide squad" whose job was to flood the pile with a cadmium solution if the reaction got out of hand. (Cadmium is an effective neutron absorber, and would slow down or stop the chain reaction.) There was also a cadmium rod at the base of the pile. A man stationed there was to pull out the rod by hand—very slowly—so that the chain reaction would take place gradually. Fermi stands on the balcony checking meters and gauges and giving orders.

As the control rod was removed, scientists watched neutron counters, which resembled clocks. A clicking sound would indicate the release of neutrons and the beginning of a chain reaction. Herbert Anderson, a scientist present at the squash court, described what happened:

At first you could hear the sound of the neutron counter, clickety-clack, clickety-clack. Then the clicks came more and more rapidly, and after a while they began to merge into a roar; the counter couldn't follow any more. . . . Again and again, the scale of the recorder had to be changed to accommodate the neutron intensity, which was increasing more and more rapidly.

Grasping his slide rule, Fermi raised his hand and announced, "The pile has gone critical." They had produced the first controlled self-sustaining nuclear chain reaction. Then he ordered, "Zip in!" and the neutron-absorbing control rod was dropped into the pile.[7]

Since the discovery of uranium fission in 1938, physicists had

speculated that other yet unidentified elements would split and chain-react after neutron bombardment. In June 1940, scientists pursuing this possibility at the University of California at Berkeley proved the existence of a ninety-third element, which they called "neptunium" after the planet Neptune. In early 1941, Glenn T. Seaborg, a twenty-eight-year-old nuclear chemist also at the University of California, produced the first measurable quantities of Element 94, named "plutonium" after the farthest planet from the sun. According to one journalist, Seaborg apparently was unaware that the planet Pluto was named after the Roman god of death and the Greek lord of the underworld.[8]

The discovery of plutonium was particularly important to the development of the atomic bomb because it is fissionable and avoids the very difficult U-235/U-238 separation problems. A second secret facility—this one to produce plutonium—was built in the desert town of Hanford in Washington state. (Today, a significant proportion of U.S. nuclear weapons contain plutonium.)

Theoretical predictions of the critical mass needed for a bomb were checked experimentally at Los Alamos by Louis Slotin, a Canadian physicist. Slotin built a device he called the "guillotine." A slug of fissionable material was dropped between two larger pieces. For a fraction of a second the neutron count would shoot up, and the mass would go critical, but not long enough to cause an explosion. In another experiment Slotin pushed two hemispheres of uranium toward each other and measured the rising neutron count. "Tickling the dragon's tail," as this was called, was a tricky business, but there was no other way to determine the exact critical mass of the fissionable materials. (Tragically, Slotin later lost control over a similar experiment and two hemispheres of fissionable material came together. Courageously he tore them apart with his bare hands, thereby saving the lives of

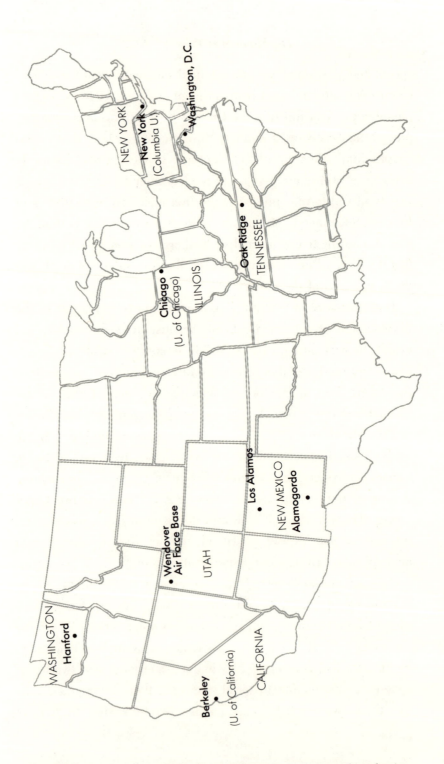

The Manhattan Project stretched from coast to coast. Industrial production at Oak Ridge and Hanford was backed by theoretical work at the Universities of Columbia, Chicago, and California. The bomb was designed at Los Alamos, tested at Alamogordo, and dropped by crews trained in Utah.

seven others in the room. But nine days later Slotin died in agony from the massive dose of radiation he had received.)[9]

The Ordnance Division at Los Alamos had the difficult assignment of designing and engineering the actual bomb. Two ways to achieve a critical mass had been proposed. One was called the "gun"— basically just a big gun barrel. At one end there would be a pie-shaped piece of fissionable material; at the other a smaller, wedge-shaped piece. TNT would drive the wedge into the pie, achieving critical mass.

The second technique proposed was more complicated, but more efficient—a greater percentage of atoms in the mass would split. It was based on the principle of "implosion"—the opposite of explosion. A ball of fissionable material, not dense enough to be critical, would be surrounded by conventional explosives arranged in such a way that the force of their explosion would be directed inward. The resulting shock waves would compress the core into a critical mass.

From thirty scientists and a small support staff, the Manhattan Project grew enormously over the course of the war. The physical site mushroomed like the old western "boom towns" whose interests focused on gold or oil rather than uranium and plutonium. Buildings were hastily constructed and bulldozers droned constantly, leveling ground for new roads running up and around the mesa. The Los Alamos grocery store was enlarged ten times between 1943 and 1945. The project's growth was also reflected in its secret funding: By 1942, $16 million had been spent; by 1943, $344 million; by late 1944, spending had skyrocketed to $100 million per month.[10] Appropriations, as mentioned earlier, were concealed in various spending bills and even kept secret from members of Congress.

Secrecy produced a whole range of personal difficulties for scientists and their families accustomed to open academic environments. The scientists themselves were forbidden to talk even to their spouses and children about their work. They had been informed that they would be relocated "somewhere in the Southwest"; they would stay there "until the end of the war." Once moved, families were not allowed to divulge their exact whereabouts to relatives, friends or former neighbors. Los Alamos was code-named "Site Y" and everyone's mail went to the same Santa Fe, New Mexico, address: Post Office Box 1663.[11]

The Manhattan Project has been described as the most secret operation of World War II. Security procedures in effect at Los Alamos were also enforced at Oak Ridge and Hanford. All incoming and outgoing mail was opened and inspected by government censors. Regulations distributed to everyone stated, in part: "Correspondence may be conducted in English, French, German, Italian and Spanish. Permission to use any other language must first be secured from the Post Commander. Codes, ciphers or any form of secret writing will not be used. Crosses, X's or other markings of a similar nature are equally objectionable. . . ." Letters could not discuss the location of the project (except that it was in New Mexico), the nature or any details of work conducted, the number of people employed, any opinions or rumors concerning the project, or any information regarding censorship regulations.[12]

Referring to themselves half jokingly as the "Lost Almosts," civilian residents of the mesa often felt ridiculously and unnecessarily confined by the Army's security regulations. Nonetheless, they voluntarily adopted a lifestyle quite different from what they were accustomed to. University professors signed pledges not to publish any research results until after the war. Military authorities kept every branch of research secret and "compartmentalized," so that most departments did not know what others were doing.

Scientists' wives at Los Alamos (most of the scientists were male) were required to adapt to the routine of an Army post in an environment resembling a frontier mining camp. Lacking most modern amenities, life for homemakers at Los Alamos was less than ideal. One wife has written:

We occupied the sidelines of history and our role was not easy. It was up to us to see that our men were fed and loved and kept serene, so that they could give their full attention to the Bomb, the still-winged ant queen who reigned in the Technical Area.[13]

Manhattan Project scientists were driven by fears of a Nazi atomic bomb and by their own inner motivations to succeed at an endeavor described by Oppenheimer as "technically sweet."[14] Those scientists who had fled the Nazis had the keenest personal reasons for wanting to beat them to the bomb. As we will show, however, fears of a Nazi atomic bomb were largely, but not entirely, unfounded.

VII

THE URANIUM SOCIETY

The moment may come when we use a weapon which is not yet known and against which there is no defense.

Adolf Hitler,
Speech at Danzig,
September 19, 1939

It was from September 1941 when we Germans saw the open road ahead of us, leading to the atomic bomb.

Werner Heisenberg,
Nobel Laureate in Physics and
Director of German Wartime Uranium Research

NAZI FIELD MARSHAL ERHARD MILCH: *How large a uranium bomb would be needed to destroy a large city like London?*
WERNER HEISENBERG: *About the size of a pineapple.*

Meeting at the Harnack House,
Berlin, June 4, 1942

In March 1939, only two days after the appearance of the French article describing how to produce surplus neutrons from uranium fission, the German War Office received a letter from Dr. Paul Harteck, a prominent German physicist. The letter was remarkably similar to the one that would be delivered seven months later to President Roosevelt. It read as follows:

We take the liberty of calling your attention to the newest development in nuclear physics, which, in our opinion, will probably make it possible to produce an explosive many orders of magnitude more powerful than conventional ones. . . . That country which first makes use of it has an unsurpassable advantage over all others.[1]

The letter was forwarded to the Army Weapons Department, which immediately took steps to begin secret research into the "special qualities" of uranium.

Almost simultaneously, a group of atomic physicists who were to form the core of a secret German "Uranium Society" independently urged another Nazi government department, the Reich Ministry for Science and Education, to support uranium research. At their first meeting in Berlin, almost six months prior to the Sachs-Roosevelt meeting, they agreed that all stocks of uranium should be secured from the recently captured mines in Czechoslovakia, that a ban should be placed on the export of all uranium compounds, and that qualified scientists should be recruited for a "U project."[2]

With its members draft deferred from combat duty, this Uranium Society grew in size; many distinguished German physicists pledged to work in secrecy on the Nazi project. Dr. Werner Heisenberg, who led the Uranium Society, later described its origins, which mirrored those of the Manhattan Project:

In view of the possibility that England and the United States might undertake the development of atomic weapons, the Army Weapons Department created a special research group whose task it was to examine the possibilities of the technical exploitation of atomic energy.[3]

Members of the Uranium Society were unaware that Professor Harteck's group had already cornered all available uranium through the Army Weapons Department. Competition for resources and professional prestige developed between the two groups; although an agreement to share uranium and exchange research results papered over their differences, a rivalry persisted that seriously hampered Nazi efforts to develop a bomb.

By September 26, 1939, the Uranium Society had developed a detailed research plan to determine whether power could be obtained from uranium to yield an explosive. They also decided to enforce an absolute ban on German publications describing atomic research.[4] By the spring of 1940, the Allies had developed a similar policy of censorship. Before it went into effect, Enrico Fermi and American physicist Herbert Anderson had prepared, but not published, an article speculating that pure carbon would almost certainly be the perfect neutron moderator, slowing neutrons to a speed that increased the likelihood of uranium fission.[5]

Shortly thereafter, German physicist Walther Bothe conducted a fission experiment using an impure batch of carbon. The impurities absorbed rather than slowed neutrons, and Bothe incorrectly concluded that carbon was not a good moderator. As a result of this sloppy experiment, the Uranium Society decided to rely on an alternative neutron moderator called "heavy water." Heavy water is naturally present in tiny quantities in all water, but its extraction involves a painstaking process requiring large amounts of electricity. One hundred thousand gallons of normal water had to be processed to extract a single gallon of heavy water. Only one factory in the world, located in Norway, was then capable of producing it. After occupying Norway, the Nazis controlled this plant, but heavy water remained in short supply during the war.

A British commando attack on the Norwegian plant made it even more scarce.[6]

By July 1940 the Uranium Society had built a small wooden laboratory in a Berlin suburb to house a nuclear reactor. A sign reading "Virus House" was posted outside to keep unwanted visitors away. Almost a year and a half later, and one year prior to Fermi's experiment at the University of Chicago, Heisenberg had designed and built the world's first atomic pile. However, even though the Germans eventually were able to produce surplus neutrons, they never attained a self-sustaining chain reaction.[7]

By September 1941, three months before Pearl Harbor and the U.S. declaration of war, Heisenberg felt that the Uranium Society "had, by and large, grasped the physical problems involved in the technical exploitation of atomic energy. . . . we Germans saw the open road ahead of us, leading to the atomic bomb."[8] Heisenberg confided to a colleague, "All in all, I think we may take it that even American physicists are not too keen on building atom bombs. But they could, of course, be spurred on by the fear that we may be doing so."[9]

Heisenberg, awarded the Nobel Prize for Physics for 1932, attracted several invitations to emigrate to the United States. Dr. Samuel A. Goudsmit, a Dutch physicist working at the University of Michigan, extended such an offer in 1939. Goudsmit had fled to the United States in the early 1930s after Hitler assumed power. Goudsmit had known Heisenberg for many years; in fact, the Dutchman was personally acquainted with many German atomic physicists. He offered Heisenberg a chance to escape Germany, but his invitation was turned down. Goudsmit was certain that Heisenberg had refused him because of loyalty to the German nation: "He was so convinced of the greatness of Germany, that he considered the Nazis' efforts to make Germany powerful of more importance than their excesses . . . near the end of the war, when visiting Switzerland, he said, 'How fine would it have been if we had won this war.' "[10] In the summer of 1939, Enrico Fermi also invited Heisenberg to live and work in the United States. Heisenberg included his response to Fermi in his memoirs, entitled *Physics and Beyond*:

Every one of us is born into a certain environment, has a native language and specific thought patterns, and if he has not cut himself off from this environment very early in life, he will feel most at home and do his best work in that environment. . . . People must learn to prevent catastrophes, not run away from them. . . . We have to decide for ourselves and cannot tell in advance whether we are doing right or wrong. Probably a bit of both. . . . [11]

By September 1941, realizing that atomic weapons could be built, Heisenberg sought the counsel of his former professor and mentor, Niels Bohr, with whom he had worked for three years in Denmark. Heisenberg's protégé, Carl Friedrich von Weizsäcker, had urged this: "It might be a good thing if you could discuss the whole subject with Niels Bohr in Copenhagen. It would mean a great deal to me if Niels were, for instance, to express the view that we are wrong and that we ought to stop working on uranium."[12] Heisenberg arranged to give a lecture in Copenhagen and Bohr agreed to attend. But now that Bohr's native Denmark was occupied by the Nazis, the cooperative prewar atmosphere at the Copenhagen Institute had deteriorated: the Allies were speculating about a German bomb project, and Bohr was skeptical about the intentions of Heisenberg's visit.

In Copenhagen the two physicists went for a stroll under a clear night sky. Heisenberg asked, "Do you think it's right for physicists to devote themselves in a war to the uranium problem?" Bohr answered with his own question: "Do you really think that uranium fission can be used for the construction of weapons?" "In principle, yes," replied Heisenberg. Shocked and frightened, Bohr soon broke off the conversation; a silence fell between the two men.

As Heisenberg later described it, he asked Bohr quite sincerely how he felt about the morality of working on scientific research that could produce an atomic weapon. But Bohr was left with the impression that the Germans were working very hard on the uranium problem, that Heisenberg thought its solution might decide the outcome of a prolonged war, and that the Germans had sent Heisenberg to learn what Professor Bohr knew about fission. Heisenberg floated the suggestion that all scientists agree not to work on projects aimed at producing an atomic weapon; Bohr believed this was an attempt to curtail U.S. and British research.[13] In her book *Inner Exile*, Heisenberg's widow said: "Yes, secretly he even hoped that his message [to Bohr] could prevent the use of an atomic bomb on Germany one day. He was constantly tortured by this idea."[14] Bohr came to the United States two years later as part of the British atomic bomb project. He neither saw nor talked with Heisenberg for the rest of the war.[15]

Bohr had good reason to distrust Heisenberg. Heisenberg's ambivalence about the morality of his work could not hide the fact that he was the director of Adolf Hitler's atom-bomb project. Unlike most Germans, Heisenberg had opportunities to escape the Nazi regime—but he did not leave. Heisenberg knew many of the scientists who had to flee for their lives from his very own institute—but he did not protest. He willingly chose to work on a project that, if successful, would have been used to crush Hitler's enemies in a ruthless effort to dominate the world. Nobel Prize or not, Heisenberg's choices cannot be easily forgotten or forgiven.

On June 4, 1942, Heisenberg met in Berlin with Albert Speer, Reich Minister for Armaments, and other high-ranking Nazi military officers. Two months earlier Hitler had issued a general decree forbidding funding of research programs that would not yield quick results for the war effort; Speer alone could decide whether any particular program deserved special consideration. In light of this decree, top German atomic scientists assembled to discuss the potential military applications of nuclear fission.

At the meeting, Field Marshal Erhard Milch asked, "How large a uranium bomb would be needed to destroy a large city like London?" Gesturing with his hands, Heisenberg replied, "About the size of a pineapple." Nonphysicists present at the meeting were stunned; uneasy excitement buzzed through the room.[16] Speer then asked Heisenberg how nuclear physics could be applied to the manufacture of atomic bombs. Speer recalls Heisenberg's answer that "the scientific solution had already been found . . . [but] the technical prerequisites for production would take years to develop, two years at the earliest even provided that the program was given maximum support."[17]

Nevertheless, Speer decided to continue funding the Uranium Society. In his memoirs, *Inside the Third Reich,* Speer said: "I am sure that Hitler would not have hesitated for a moment to employ atom bombs against England." He remembered viewing a newsreel with Hitler: "The film ended . . . showing a plane diving towards the outline of the British Isles. A burst of flame followed, and the island flew into the air in tatters. Hitler's enthusiasm was unbounded. 'That is what will happen to them!' he cried out, carried away. 'That is how we will annihilate them!' "

The Allies were largely ignorant of the Germans' organizational and scientific problems. General Groves wrote: "I could not help but believe that the Germans, with their scientific capacity and their extremely competent group of first-class scientists, would have progressed at a rapid rate and could be expected to be well ahead of us." Some scientists thought that the "secret weapon" brandished in Nazi propaganda reports alluded to an atomic weapon, although in fact Hitler was referring to the development of long-range V-1 and V-2 rockets.[18] Concerns about Nazi atomic research beset Allied military leaders planning the invasion to liberate Europe. They feared that Hitler would spread radioactive dust or drop atom bombs on French beaches to stop the Allies; they speculated that the reinforced concrete bunkers on the coast of France were built by the Germans to withstand the explosions of nuclear warheads.

On April 8, 1944, at General Groves's suggestion, U.S. commanding General Dwight D. Eisenhower was apprised of the possibility that the Germans were prepared to use radioactive materials. As a precaution, "Operation Peppermint" was planned; it called for radiation detection equipment—Geiger counters and photographic film—to go ashore with the invading troops. On June 6, 1944, "D-Day," the United States, Great Britain and Canada launched "Operation Overlord," landing troops, tanks and equipment from England on the Normandy beaches of France. No radiation was detected.[19]

On the heels of Overlord, a joint Anglo-American secret intelligence team was charged to "follow immediately in the wake of our armies in the invasion of Europe, for the purpose of determining precisely how much the Germans knew about the atomic bomb and how far they had progressed in its construction."[20] This team of over a hundred men was code-named "Alsos," which in Greek means "grove" (after General Leslie R. Groves). They were to seize Nazi documents concerning nuclear research and any related production facilities. Alsos was also directed to capture, question and detain German atomic scientists. The military director of Alsos, Colonel Boris T. Pash, carried a document signed by the U.S. secretary of war ordering that the colonel be accorded "every facility and assistance" to complete his mission.[21] Dr. Samuel A. Goudsmit was appointed scientific chief for the mission.

The Alsos mission found that the Uranium Society was far behind the Manhattan Project. Heisenberg said later that the physicists were afraid to ask for the substantial amounts of money and materials needed to build a bomb. If they failed to produce one, German science would be tainted, and Hitler's vengeful temper might well lead him to imprison or execute the culprits or pack them off to the Eastern Front to fight the Russians.[22] It was not until 1945 that the Germans discovered their mistake about carbon's suitability as a neutron moderator; by then it was too late— their research had been set back severely. Had Fermi and Anderson published their article as they were initially inclined to do, the Germans could have overcome one of their significant obstacles.

After the war Goudsmit wrote:

More than two years have passed since the war's end, and still today not merely the man in the street, but many of our scientific and military experts as well, believe that we were engaged in a desperate race with the Germans for the secret of the atom bomb, and it was only by a miracle, by a hair's breadth, that we got there first. . . . To be sure we were engaged in such a race, but that race, as we now know, was rather a one-sided affair and the situation was not nearly so desperate as we supposed. The plain fact of the matter is that the Germans were nowhere near getting the secret of the atom bomb.[23]

When he had determined that the Uranium Society did not pose any danger to the Allies, Goudsmit was hesitant to risk the lives of his men. He asserted, "not one more broken Allied ankle should be risked on the Alsos project." He was not the only refugee who felt sorry that so much had been made of so little. Albert Einstein later commented on his signing of the letter to Roosevelt: "Had I known that the Germans would not succeed in developing an atomic bomb, I would have done nothing for the bomb."

After the war, an Alsos-type mission was dispatched to investigate the status of Japanese atomic research. According to one scholar, John W. Dower, "it seems indisputable that the scale of Japan's wartime work on the uranium bomb was so small as to be virtually meaningless."[24] Japanese atomic research was never a factor in the American effort to build the first atomic bomb.

VIII

DEJECTION, GRIEF, JUBILATION

I believe the reason why we didn't do it was that all the physicists didn't want to do it, on principle. . . . If we had all wanted Germany to win the war, we could have succeeded.

Carl Friedrich von Weizsäcker,
participant, German A-bomb Project at Farm Hall, England,
August 6, 1945

Why is it night already? Why did our house fall down? What happened?

Myeko Nakamura, age five, to her mother,
from John Hersey's *Hiroshima*

WAR-WEARY WORLD AT PEACE: ECLIPSE OF THE RISING SUN BRINGS JOY TO NATION

The Atlanta Constitution,
August 14, 1945

DEJECTION

At 6:00 P.M. on August 6, 1945, the British Broadcasting Company (BBC) announced that an atomic bomb had been dropped on Hiroshima that morning. British listeners learned that this single blast had the power of 2,000 of their own 10-ton bombs. For the first time, President Truman disclosed that the Germans had at-

82

tempted and failed to build their own atomic weapon. The Allies had beaten them to it.

The BBC broadcast was also heard at Farm Hall, an English country house near the town of Godmanchester, 50 miles north of London. Farm Hall was being used as a special internment camp for ten former members of the German Uranium Society. Captured by the Alsos special intelligence mission in April–May 1945, they were being held in England largely to avoid capture by the Soviets. Although British and American diplomats, politicians and military commanders publicly continued to applaud Soviet war efforts, by this time, late in the war, they believed that communism would be the next threat to democracy.

Free to move about the house and grounds, the German scientists enjoyed the good life at Farm Hall. Professor Walther Gerlach, Nazi Party liaison for nuclear physics, tended a rose garden. There were books in three languages and daily newspapers. Tennis courts were available. Professor Otto Hahn took long runs around the estate. Professor Heisenberg played Beethoven piano sonatas in the living room. Five German prisoners of war were detailed to cook for the physicists; they gathered mushrooms for omelettes in the English countryside, and everyone gained weight.[1]

On August 6, just before supper, British Major T. H. Rittner took Hahn privately into his office to tell him that a bomb had been dropped on Hiroshima. Professor Hahn said later, "I was shocked and depressed beyond measure. The thought of the unspeakable misery of countless innocent women and children was something I could scarcely bear." Overwhelmed by the knowledge that his uranium research had culminated in this event, he told Rittner that he felt personally responsible for the death of thousands.[2]

Meanwhile, the other nine German scientists gathered in the

dining room for the BBC 7:00 P.M. broadcast. Because British and U.S. intelligence agencies were concerned that they had not gleaned all critical information about the German bomb project through direct interrogation, they had bugged the entire estate; the conversation this evening was particularly intriguing. General Groves excerpted parts of a verbatim transcript of it in his book of memoirs, *Now It Can Be Told*.

Heisenberg suggested that the Hiroshima announcement was a bluff—when he had been taken prisoner three months earlier, he had asked Goudsmit whether the Americans were working on an atomic bomb and Goudsmit had assured him to the contrary. Heisenberg had stayed with Goudsmit in America in 1939, and he simply refused to believe that his fellow physicist had lied to him.[3]

Rejoining the others and fortified by several stiff drinks, Hahn said that he hoped Heisenberg was right. But Hahn was distressed, and perhaps wishing to inflict this on the group, he taunted his good friend: "If the Americans have the uranium bomb, then you're all second-raters. Poor old Heisenberg!" Heisenberg asked quickly, "Did they use the word 'uranium' in connection with this 'atomic' bomb?" "No," said Hahn. "Then it's got nothing to do with atoms," retorted Heisenberg. Perhaps the Allies' bomb used some new chemical concept.

Drs. Horst Korsching and Karl Wirtz speculated that the Americans had perfected a uranium separation technique that the Germans themselves had considered. Heisenberg regretted that the V-1 and V-2 rocket programs had received more government support than his atomic research. Dr. Wirtz said, "I'm glad we did not have [the bomb]." Von Weizsäcker agreed: "I think it's dreadful for the Americans to have done it. I think it is madness on their part." From across the dinner table, Heisenberg intervened: "One can't say that. One could equally well say that it's the quickest way of ending the war. . . ." "That," said Hahn, "is what consoles me." But then he added, "I think we'll bet on Heisenberg's suggestion that it is a bluff."[4]

At nine o'clock they all clustered around the radio in the drawing room to hear a more complete broadcast. "A tremendous achievement of Allied scientists—the production of an atomic bomb. . . . One has already been dropped on a Japanese army base. . . . Reconnaissance aircraft couldn't see anything hours later because of the tremendous pall of smoke and dust that was still obscuring the city of once over 300,000 inhabitants." Then they learned that American Secretary of War Henry Stimson had announced that uranium had been used to build the bomb.[5]

The Germans felt dejection, horror and disbelief. "Goudsmit has led us up the garden path!" lamented Dr. Erich Bagge. Some bitter conversation ensued. Heisenberg recalled later, "That night we said many ill-considered things."[6]

Dr. Korsching remarked that the American scientists had obviously been able to cooperate better than they. "That would have been impossible in Germany. Each one said the other was unimportant." Von Weizsäcker disagreed: "I believe the reason why we didn't do it was that all the physicists didn't want to do it, on principle. If we had all wanted Germany to win the war, we could have succeeded." Said Bagge, "I think it is absurd for von Weizsäcker to say he did not want the thing to succeed: that may be so in his case, but not for all of us." Just the fact that "others had succeeded" distressed Heisenberg: "How have they actually done it? I find it is a disgrace if we, the professors who worked on it, cannot at least work out how they did it."[7]

Their first guess was that the Allies had dropped a whole uranium pile on Hiroshima. They wondered aloud why Otto Hahn wasn't credited with the discovery of fission. Why did the papers emphasize Lise Meitner's role, and why did they stress that she was Jewish?[8] Then von Weizsäcker spoke of possible international repercussions of the bomb: "Stalin certainly has not got it. If the Americans and the British were good imperialists, they would attack Stalin with the thing tomorrow, but they won't do that. They will use it as a political weapon. Of course, that is good, but the result will be a peace which will last until the Russians have it, and then there is bound to be war."[9]

Sometime after 1:00 A.M., Max von Laue confided to Bagge: "When I was a boy I wanted to do physics and watch the world make history. Well, I have done physics and I have seen the world make history. I will be able to say that to my dying day." He went off to bed but could not sleep. At 2:00 A.M. he awoke Bagge: "We must do something. I am very worried about Otto Hahn; the news has shocked him terribly, and I fear the worst." They opened the door to Hahn's bedroom, where he lay agitated and sleepless. Hahn admitted later that he had contemplated suicide. Von Laue and Bagge relaxed only when they saw him drift off to sleep.[10]

GRIEF

On August 11, 1945, two days after the bombing of Nagasaki, and one day after the Japanese offered to surrender under the terms of the Potsdam Declaration, General Leslie Groves ordered the Manhattan Project to investigate the effects of the atomic bombs. An "Atomic Bomb Investigating Group" of U.S. and British scientists and physicians was immediately dispatched to Japan.

Part of the group flew by seaplane, landing in the Nagasaki harbor. The aircrew opened the doors and were met by vast and total silence, broken only by water lapping the seaplane pontoons. On the shore, nothing moved. There was complete desolation: No person or dog or tree was in sight, no birds chirped, no leaves rustled in the wind. The scientists' first reaction was to grip their guns in fear.

After completing their investigation, they wrote a report entitled *The Atomic Bombings of Hiroshima and Nagasaki,*[11] describing the effects of the two bombs, the casualties and destruction. Parts of the report read as follows:

The damage to man-made structures and other inanimate objects was the result in both cities of the following effects of the explosions:

a. Blast, or pressure wave, similar to that of normal explosions.

b. Primary fires, i.e., those fires started instantaneously by the heat radiated from the atomic explosion.

c. Secondary fires, i.e., those fires resulting from the collapse of buildings, damage to electrical systems, overturning of stoves, and other primary effects of the blast.

d. Spread of the original fires (b and c) to other structures.

The casualties sustained by the inhabitants of both cities were due to:

a. "Flash" burns, caused directly by the almost instantaneous radiation of heat and light at the moment of the explosion.

b. Burns resulting from the fires caused by the explosion.

c. Mechanical injuries caused by collapse of buildings, flying debris, and forceable hurling-about of persons struck by the blast pressure waves.

d. Radiation injuries caused by the instantaneous penetrating radiation (in many respects similar to excessive X-ray exposure) from the nuclear explosion. . . .

The report summarized the damage to Hiroshima and Nagasaki:

In both cities the blast totally destroyed everything within a radius of one [1] mile from the center of the explosion, except for certain reinforced concrete frames as noted above. The atomic explosion almost completely destroyed Hiroshima's identity as a city. Over a fourth of the population was killed in one stroke and an additional fourth seriously injured, so that even if there had been no damage to structures and installations the normal city life would still have been completely shattered. Nearly everything was heavily damaged up to a radius of three [3] miles from the blast, and beyond this distance damage, although comparatively light, extended for several more miles. Glass was broken up to twelve [12] miles.

In Nagasaki, a smaller area of the city was actually destroyed than in Hiroshima, because the hills which enclosed the target area restricted the spread of the great blast; but careful examination of the effects of the explosion gave evidence of even greater blast effects than in Hiroshima. Total destruction spread over an area of about three [3] square miles. Over a third of the 50,000 buildings in the target area of Nagasaki were destroyed or seriously damaged. The complete destruction of the huge steel works and the torpedo plant was especially impressive. The steel frames of all buildings within a mile of the explosion were pushed away, as by a giant hand, from the point of detonation. The badly burned area extended for three [3] miles in length. The hillsides up to a radius of 8,000 feet were scorched, giving them an autumnal appearance.

The report concluded with the following observation:

Aside from physical injury and damage, the most significant effect of the atomic bombs was the sheer terror which it struck into the peoples of the bombed cities. This terror, resulting in immediate hysterical activity and flight from the cities, had one especially pronounced effect: persons who had become accustomed to mass air raids had grown to pay little heed to single planes or small groups of planes, but after the atomic bombings the appearance of a single plane caused more terror and disruption of normal life than the appearance of many hundreds of planes had ever been able to cause before. The effect of this terrible fear of the potential danger from even a single enemy plane on the lives of the peoples of the world in the event of any future war can easily be conjectured.

The British summarized their observations in the following statement: "The impression which both cities make is of having sunk, in an instant and without a struggle, to the most primitive level."[12]

Although the Manhattan Project investigators were not sent to describe the pain and suffering of the Japanese, it affected them greatly. Several of the physicians were overwhelmed by the number and extent of blast and burn injuries, and by the prolonged agony of radiation victims.

The grief of the victims is perhaps best conveyed by the testimony of Japanese who survived:

I climbed Hijiyama Hill and looked down. I saw that Hiroshima had disappeared. . . . I was shocked by the sight. . . . What I felt then and still feel now I just can't explain with words. Of course, I saw many dreadful scenes after that—but that experience, looking down and finding nothing left of Hiroshima—was so shocking that I simply cannot express what I felt. I could see Koi [a suburb at the other end of the city] and a few buildings standing. . . . But Hiroshima just didn't exist.

History professor, quoted in Robert Lifton,
Death in Life: Survivors of Hiroshima

*Everything I saw made a deep impression—a park nearby covered
with dead bodies waiting to be cremated . . . very badly injured
people evacuated in my direction. . . . The most impressive thing
I saw was some girls, very young girls, not only with their clothes
torn off but with their skin peeled off as well. . . . My immediate
thought was that this was like the hell I had always read about. . . . I
had never seen anything which resembled it before, but I thought
that should there be a hell, this was it—the Buddhist hell, where
we were taught that people who could not obtain salvation always
went.*

Young sociologist, quoted in Lifton,
Death in Life: Survivors of Hiroshima

*Dr. Sasaki worked without method, taking those who were nearest
him first, and he noticed soon that the corridor seemed to be getting
more and more crowded. Mixed in with the abrasions and lacer-
ations which most people in the hospital had suffered, he began to
find dreadful burns . . . wounded people supported maimed people;
disfigured families leaned together.*

from John Hersey, *Hiroshima*

*An old woman lay near me with an expression of suffering on
her face; but she made no sound. Indeed one thing was common
to everyone I saw—complete silence. . . . Miss Kado [a nurse] set
about examining my wounds without speaking a word. No one*

spoke. . . . Why was everyone so quiet? . . . It was as though I walked through a gloomy, silent motion picture.

Dr. Hachiya, quoted in Lifton,
Death in Life: Survivors of Hiroshima

In general, then, those who survived the atom bomb were the people who ignored their friends crying out in extremis; *or who shook off wounded neighbors who clung to them, pleading to be saved. . . . In short, those who survived the bomb were, if not merely lucky, in a greater or lesser degree selfish, self-centered, guided by instinct and not civilization . . . and we know it, we who have survived. Knowing it is a dull ache without surcease.*

Takashi Nagai, quoted in Lifton,
Death in Life: Survivors of Hiroshima

The suffering moans of people who had barely managed to hang onto life filled the place. "I wish they would stop the war, I wish they would stop the war." I recalled all that my child had said the night before—how he wished that war would be banished from earth. Those are not the words of a fourteen-year-old child; they are words of God, I thought.

From then on I have never failed to look up at the starry sky. It seemed to me that the spirit of Hirohisa, his friends of the First Middle School who died with him, and the countless people of Hiroshima who died that day, have all gone up to the heavens and turned to stardust, and are softly looking down at us every night, so that such a catastrophe will never be repeated on earth.

Toshie Fujino,"The Stars are Looking On" in *Give Me Water: Testimonies of Hiroshima and Nagasaki,* March 1972

JUBILATION

At 4:27 A.M. on August 14, 1945, D. Reginald Tibbetts, a San Francisco electrical engineer, was in his bedroom amid a clutter of radio equipment. He was listening to the Morse code as it came from the Japanese Domei news agency: Japan was officially offering to surrender. In Portland, Oregon, the news was picked up by a Federal Communications Commission monitor. It was officially "Victory Over Japan" or "V-J" day. ("V-E" or "Victory in Europe" day had been celebrated several months earlier after Germany's surrender, but the feeling was not quite the same with the war still being fought in the Pacific.)

At 10:20 A.M., bulletins were posted on the Times Tower building in Times Square, New York City, and the celebration that followed far surpassed any New Year's Eve bash. New York City hosted a party of unparalleled proportions. World War II and its years of unremitting bloodshed had ended; American troops could finally come home to their families and loved ones. Manhattan garment workers threw tons of paper and cloth shreds into the streets. Fourteen hundred sailors, most of whom had been scheduled for redeployment from the Atlantic to the Pacific, arrived at Staten Island piers just before the announcement of Japan's surrender. Upon hearing the news, they literally danced down the gangplanks, singing as they went.

In St. Louis crowds beating pans and blowing whistles persuaded a priest to open his church for 2:00 A.M. services. In Miami, hundreds of motorists tied down their auto horns, blaring their joy and relief. Baton Rouge had to close its bars to preserve some civil order, but citizens cheered themselves hoarse in the streets. In Salt Lake City thousands snake-danced in the pouring rain. In Indianapolis a parade of tooting automobiles surrounded the city's Monument Circle. In Milwaukee a man told the following story:

"You know the old lady who runs the laundry. She weighs at least 300 pounds. Tonight when the whistles started to blow, she grabbed me and kissed me so hard she broke three teeth in my lower jaw. 'Don't worry, I'll pay for it because I've wanted to kiss you all my life,' she told me."[13]

In Washington, D.C., in front of the offices of *The Washington Post*, a soldier and a woman got out of a taxi and started to take off their clothes to the encouragement of an enthusiastic group of well-wishers. The couple stripped completely, then each dressed in the other's clothes; the woman put on shorts, pants and shirt while the soldier struggled into bra, panties, slip and dress, to the applause of the bystanders.[14]

San Franciscans went completely wild. They built bonfires on Market Street, ransacked liquor stores, commandeered trolley cars, and skinny-dipped in the public fountains. Anything that would make a noise was blown, pounded or beaten. San Francisco was a main port of embarkation for the war in the Pacific, and when the good news arrived, thousands of men were awaiting orders to invade Japan. Pacific Telephone and Telegraph Co. assigned all its personnel to the long-distance lines so that soldiers could call home to tell their families they had been spared. One woman commented, "When I was going home on the trolley car, some Navy guy gave me a whole fistful of shoe ration stamps, sort of symbolic of the war's end. . . ." In Pearl Harbor, fireworks and colored flares were shot from every ship. At Los Alamos, an ordnance expert pushed a button detonating explosives he had wired together. Manhattan Project scientists cheered and drank to peace.[15]

From coast to coast, church bells pealed.

After the initial jubilation, other reactions set in. There was a somber realization that mankind now possessed the means to destroy itself. President Harry Truman said, "I realize the tragic significance of the atomic bomb . . . [it] is too dangerous to be loose in a lawless world . . . we must constitute ourselves trustees of this new force—to prevent its misuse, and to turn it into the channels of service to mankind . . . it is an awful responsibility which has come to us."[16]

Newsweek magazine headlines read: "Victory! The Warsick World Hails It Wildly With Jap Broken by Shock of Cosmic Weapons; But Grave Problems Loom in the Coming Peace." And *Time* magazine commented, "The race had been won, the weapon had been used by those on whom civilization could best hope to depend; but the demonstration of power against living creatures instead of dead matter created a bottomless wound in the living conscience of the race. . . . Was man equal to the challenge? In an instant, without warning, the present had become the unthinkable future. Was there hope in that future, and if so, where did hope lie?"

Dawn of the nuclear age: zero hour plus .006 seconds at Alamogordo, July 16, 1945.

Zero plus .016 seconds.

Zero plus .025 seconds. The growing fireball acquires a skirt of radioactive dust.

Zero plus 2.0 seconds. Thousands of tons of dust and debris explode into the atmosphere.

The world's first mushroom cloud.

J. Robert Oppenheimer (left) and Leslie R. Groves inspecting the remnants of the bomb tower two months after the Alamogordo test.

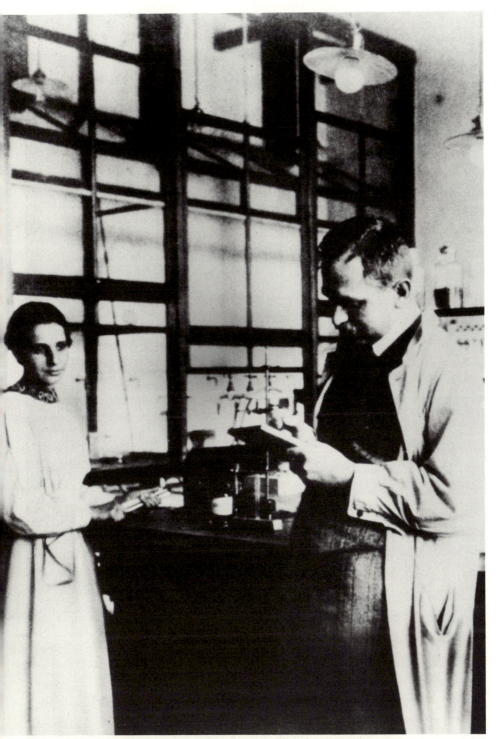

Lise Meitner and Otto Hahn in their Berlin laboratory, 1913.

ARBEITSTISCH VON OTTO HAHN

The worktable used by Otto Hahn and Fritz Strassmann in the discovery of uranium fission.

Albert Einstein (left) with J. Robert Oppenheimer.

Students playing ice hockey on the pond at the Los Alamos Ranch School.

The Manhattan Project scientists and their wives enjoy a social event at Los Alamos.

Werner Heisenberg (left) and Niels Bohr in a photograph taken in Denmark before World War II.

A Japanese soldier walks through a leveled Hiroshima.

IX

JOE I

A single demand of you, Comrades. Provide us with atomic weapons in the shortest possible time. You know that Hiroshima has shaken the whole world. The equilibrium has been destroyed. Provide the bomb—it will remove a great danger from us.

Soviet Premier Josef Stalin,
to the People's Commissar of Munitions,
August 1945

We are here to make a choice between the quick and the dead. . . .

Bernard M. Baruch,
U.S. Representative to the
United Nations Atomic Energy Commission,
June 14, 1946

At the end of the war, when Europe and Japan lay in smoldering ruins, there was widespread enthusiasm for the United Nations, the charter of which was signed while the war was still being fought. The terrible destruction of modern war was deeply etched in people's minds, and this awareness had been keenly accentuated by the atomic bombs dropped on Hiroshima and Nagasaki. The United Nations Charter stated: "Twentieth-century man has become increasingly aware that world government is a necessary corrective to the dangers of aggressive nationalism, and that only cooperative international control can save man from his own destructive genius."

Many Americans felt that one important function of the United Nations should be to control atomic energy. On June 11, 1945—in a report to the U.S. Secretary of War—James Franck, Leo Szilard and seven other Manhattan Project scientists went on record to oppose dropping atomic bombs on Japan and to urge that they be subjected to international controls. Though this advice regarding Japan was disregarded, after the war the United States did make an attempt to place atomic weapons under the United Nations' authority. The Franck Report had warned:

Nuclear bombs cannot possibly remain a "secret weapon" at the exclusive disposal of this country for more than a few years . . . the scientific facts are well known to scientists of other countries. Unless an effective international control of nuclear explosives is instituted, a race for nuclear armaments is certain to ensue. . . .[1]

In response to a U.S. initiative, the United Nations organized an International Atomic Energy Commission. On June 14, 1946, Bernard M. Baruch, the American representative, presented a plan to establish a permanent international authority to control, inspect and license all atomic reactors and materials to ensure their use for peaceful purposes only. The "Baruch Plan" proposed to destroy all U.S. atomic bombs when international controls, including enforcement provisions to punish violators, were agreed upon. Baruch pleaded:

We are here to make a choice between the quick and the dead. . . . That is our business. . . .
Behind the black portent of the new atomic age lies a hope which, seized upon with faith, can work [to] our salvation. If we fail, then

we have damned every man to be the slave of Fear. Let us not deceive ourselves: We must elect World Peace or World Destruction.[2]

Five days later, Andrei Gromyko, the Soviet representative to the United Nations, countered the Baruch Plan with a proposal to prohibit the use of atomic weapons and to destroy all American weapons within three months. He objected to the Baruch Plan's verification measures; specifically, the Soviets refused to permit U.N. inspections of Soviet territory. Gromyko did not want his country "invaded" by international inspectors with rights of free and unhampered travel, and he insisted that inspections be subject to Soviet veto. Disagreements over "verification procedures"—that is, how to ensure that an agreement is kept—remain to this day one of the most troublesome issues in arms control negotiations.

But the U.S. government may have inadvertently torpedoed the possibility for international control of atomic energy. Just after the war the U.S. Navy had asked permission to conduct tests to evaluate the effects of atomic bombs on warships. Truman approved the request on January 10, 1946—apparently giving little thought to how such tests could negatively affect the Baruch Plan in particular and U.S.–Soviet relations in general.

On March 29, Senator Scott W. Lucas of Illinois proposed that Truman cancel the Navy tests. "If we are to outlaw the use of the atomic bomb for military purposes, why should we be making plans to display atomic power as an instrument of destruction?" Alluding to the Soviets, Lucas continued: "Suppose the U.S. had a big army but little or no air power, no fleet and no atomic bombs. Would the Senate rest unperturbed should some other power undertake a nuclear display in the Atlantic or Pacific?" The proposal fell on deaf ears.[3]

Bikini Atoll, located in the Marshall Islands in the western

Pacific Ocean, was chosen as the site for the test series, designated "Operation Crossroads." Bikini (population 167) was evacuated, and naval personnel moved in. Operation Crossroads involved 42,000 men, 242 ships, 156 airplanes, 25,000 radiation recording devices, and, for various experiments, 5,400 rats, goats and pigs. The target fleet of ninety vessels would have comprised the world's fifth-largest navy. Unlike the bomb test at Alamogordo, this one was no secret: Members of Congress, scientists, foreign observers (including a Soviet representative) and an entire shipload of accredited journalists were invited to witness the blast; Truman even postponed the test from May 15 to July 1 so that more observers could attend.[4]

The first postwar atomic test took place only 16 days after the Baruch Plan was presented to the United Nations. This two-track approach—testing the bomb and at the same time proposing international controls—continued throughout 1946 and left the United States wide open to the criticism that it was conducting "atomic diplomacy." This seemingly contradictory approach continues to this day as the United States, the Soviet Union and other nations build and test nuclear weapons, all the while advocating arms control. We have no hard evidence that the Baruch Plan and Operation Crossroads were coordinated as a deliberate strategy. But for the Soviets, the concurrence of events was evidence enough; the official Soviet newspaper *Pravda* charged that the United States "aimed not at restricting but perfecting atomic weapons" and that Americans sought to maintain their monopoly as an instrument of international blackmail. The Bikini test, *Pravda* argued, was timed to influence arms control deliberations in progress at the United Nations.

On July 26, President Truman instructed Baruch in steadfast terms: "We should not under any circumstances throw away our gun until we are sure the rest of the world can't arm against us."[5] U.S.–Soviet differences over atomic controls have never been resolved, and the United Nations has never become a supranational authority for controlling the atomic bomb. This failure signified an emerging rivalry between the United States and the Soviet Union, known as the "Cold War." This term, coined by *New York Herald Tribune* columnist Walter Lippmann, referred to the tense, cold relations—short of hostilities—that had been developing between the United States and the Soviet Union since World War II.[6] With the defeat of Germany and Japan, and the decline of the British and French empires, the United States and the Soviet Union had emerged as the two major competitors for world power.

The Cold War between the new "superpowers" involved ideological, economic and political differences. Since the Russian Revolution of 1917–1918, the U.S. and Soviet governments had been at odds because their systems of government and basic philosophical beliefs were in conflict. It was democracy, individual freedom, and capitalism versus strict government control and communism.

Communist ideology derives from the writings of Karl Marx, a German born in 1818, who predicted that workers in industrial countries would eventually overthrow capitalism, abolish private property, and create societies in which everything would be owned by the state. Nikolai Lenin, a Russian born in 1870, was a forceful advocate of Marx's theories. In November 1917 Lenin led a group of Communist revolutionaries (the Bolsheviks) who overthrew the government and seized power in Russia: They renamed their nation the Union of Soviet Socialist Republics (U.S.S.R.) and established a radically new system of government that continues today.

Power in the Soviet Union is vested in the Communist Party,

yet only about 6 percent of the Soviet population are members. At the top of the Communist Party hierarchy is the twenty-one-member Politburo, which sets policy, and a nine-member Secretariat, which is the executive branch of the party. The Soviets also have a 1500-member legislature, the Supreme Soviet, which meets in the Kremlin (a walled fortress in Moscow) for two to four days twice a year to adopt legal codes and statutes. These features of Soviet government imply a dedication to the principle of collective leadership that, in theory, is designed to guarantee that power is shared. In practice, however, power usually lies with one man who heads both the Communist Party and the Soviet government.[7] From 1924 to 1953, that man was Josef Stalin.

The West grew to fear Stalin and the Communist ideology he represented. Stalin was capable of ruthless cruelty; he consolidated and maintained his power by jailing or murdering his political opponents, dissenters and anyone else who stood in his way. George F. Kennan, former U.S. Ambassador to Moscow and a respected Sovietologist, described him in scornful terms: "[Stalin had] an insatiable vanity and love of power . . . an inordinate touchiness, an endless vindictiveness, an inability ever to forget an insult or a slight, but great patience . . . in selecting and preparing the moment to settle the score. . . . This was a man of incredible criminality, of a criminality without limits; a man apparently foreign to the very existence of love, without pity or mercy; a man in whose entourage no one was ever safe; a man whose hand was set against all that could not be useful to him at the moment."[8]

President Roosevelt had considered the Soviet Union to be an "ally of necessity" in World War II. But after the defeat of the Nazis, many felt that Stalin had replaced Hitler as an archvillain and the chief enemy of democracy. Tensions between the United

States and the Soviet Union re-emerged. They were aggravated by the existence of atomic weapons, and particularly by the fact that Americans had them and the Soviets did not.

Since their efforts had been critical to winning the war, and their casualties so great, the Soviets felt that they had earned certain concessions from the Western Allies: the Soviets were particularly anxious to create a buffer zone of satellite nations between their territory and the West. At a conference at Yalta late in the war, Stalin secured what he considered a "sphere of influence" over Eastern Europe. Accordingly, Soviet troop strength in Eastern Europe was not substantially reduced after the war. Many Western officials feared that the Soviets wanted to eventually expand their influence to dominate Western Europe as well. Some argued that the continued presence of the Soviet Red Army in Eastern Europe was Stalin's counter to the U.S. atom bomb.

Although the United States was deeply disturbed by the Soviet occupation and by the imposition of communism upon the nations of Eastern Europe, it seemed that another war was the only way to drive the Soviets out. But the American people wanted both to "bring the boys home" and to reduce defense expenditures. In the immediate postwar period, Europeans and Americans were almost in a "peace at any price" mood; another war was simply unthinkable. So the United States in effect left Eastern Europe to the Soviets, and adopted a strategy of "deterrence" to prevent Soviet aggression against Western Europe and the United States. Rather than concentrate large numbers of American troops, tanks and artillery in Europe to counter the huge and well-equipped Soviet Red Army, the United States threatened to use atomic bombs against the Soviet homeland if the Soviets attacked.

Overt hostilities in Europe were avoided, but increasing tensions led to a "war of words." On February 9, 1946, Stalin announced that war was inevitable as long as capitalism existed. The content and tone of Stalin's speech shocked U.S. Supreme Court Justice William O. Douglas, a noted liberal, who said it represented a "declaration of World War III."[9] On March 6, 1946, ex-Prime Minister Winston Churchill proclaimed that an "Iron Curtain" had descended across the continent of Europe. To the east were nations increasingly subjected to totalitarian control by Moscow.

Beyond the rhetoric, the United States did formulate policies to stop the expansion of Soviet influence outside Eastern Europe. Ambassador Kennan wrote that the United States should commit itself to a "long-term, patient but firm and vigilant containment of Russian expansive tendencies."[10] Accordingly, on March 12, 1947, President Truman announced the "Truman Doctrine" proposing American economic assistance for Greece and Turkey, where Communist insurgents were fighting against U.S.-backed governments. In May 1947 the U.S. Congress agreed to send $400 million in civilian and military assistance to the two countries. Truman believed that stable economies led to stable governments that could better resist Soviet influence.

The hoped-for economic recovery of Europe was not materializing. Historian Charles L. Mee, Jr., described the disastrous situation:

Nations were in shambles everywhere. . . . Bridges and roads were gone. . . . Unexploded bombs and shells lay in the fields . . . post war inflation whipsawed the survivors . . . disastrous harvests all across the continent would leave Europeans hungry, and, in some places, even starving.[11]

The Europeans' plight caused the Truman Doctrine to evolve into a program to rebuild Europe. In June 1947, Secretary of State

George C. Marshall laid down the principles of a European Recovery Program. "Marshall Plan" aid was also offered to the Soviets, but they refused.

Two crises in Eastern Europe inflamed Cold War animosities. On February 24, 1948, the Communist Party leader of Czechoslovakia eliminated all independent political parties; Soviet armies camped on the border as a new Communist government assumed control on February 25. Truman said that the coup "sent a shock throughout the civilized world." He privately felt that "we are faced with exactly the same situation which Britain and France faced in 1938–39 with Hitler."[12]

The second crisis involved the German capital of Berlin, 110 miles inside the Soviet-occupied Eastern Zone of Germany. After World War II, the United States, Great Britain, France and the Soviet Union had divided Germany into four zones of occupation; in addition, Berlin itself was subdivided into four sectors. The three Western zones of Germany, occupied by the United States, Great Britain and France, would become the Federal Republic of Germany, usually called "West Germany," today with 62 million inhabitants. The Eastern Zone, including the Eastern or Soviet-occupied sector of Berlin, was occupied by the Soviet Union; it would become the German Democratic Republic, usually called "East Germany," now with a population of approximately 18 million. France, Britain, and the United States were guaranteed access to the Western sectors of Berlin by ground transportation and by three twenty-mile-wide air corridors.

In June 1948 the Western Allies devised a new economic plan for West Berlin, including a currency reform, that reintroduced the principle of "supply and demand" common to Western free-market economies. The Soviet Union opposed the currency reform, fearing that establishment of an economic system fundamentally different from the Communist model would unify the three Western zones. Then, on June 24, 1948, in a surprise action, the Soviets blockaded all roads, rails and waterways leading from the West into Berlin. Since Berlin was almost entirely dependent upon the West for food and other supplies, Berliners were threatened with starvation. With the overthrow of democracy in Czechoslovakia fresh in mind, Western public opinion favored taking a stand: immediately, the United States, Great Britain and France organized an airlift, nicknamed "Operation Vittles." By mid-July 1948, 150 U.S. Air Force transport aircraft were flying in approximately 1,500 tons of food, medicine and other supplies every day.

In a show of resolve, President Truman ordered two groups of B-29 bombers to fly from the United States to England. According to U.S. government press releases, the B-29s were "atomic capable."[13] In 1947, the year before the Berlin blockade, the United States had thirteen atomic weapons; by 1948 the number had grown to fifty, and by 1949 the U.S. stockpile contained nearly 250 atomic bombs.[14] The U.S. Atomic Energy Act of 1946 had placed custody of all U.S. atomic weapons and fissionable materials in the hands of a civilian Atomic Energy Commission (AEC). Later in the 1950s, when nuclear weapons were deployed to Europe, custody shifted to the military. But no military officer could authorize the use of atomic weapons—only the president had (and still has) that authority.

During the Berlin crisis, President Truman claimed to be ready to use atomic weapons again if he had to. When the Soviet Union began its blockade, Truman assured his secretaries of both state and defense that although he prayed the bomb would not have to be used, "if it became necessary, no one need have a misgiving but that [I] would do so."[15] David E. Lilienthal, Chairman of the AEC, reported that Truman said that "the atomic bomb was the mainstay and all he had; that the Russians would have probably taken over Europe a long time ago if it were not for that."[16] Leading newspaper publishers agreed that if war broke out because of Berlin, the American people would expect the atomic bomb to be dropped.

Fortunately, the Soviets chose not to precipitate a war. They stopped obstructing ground traffic on May 15, 1949, almost a year after their blockade began. By the time the last relief plane had flown into West Berlin, 2,325,000 tons of supplies had been air-lifted in 277,569 flights.

The Berlin crisis and the occupation of Czechoslovakia galvanized the formation of a formal military alliance among Western democratic nations. On April 4, 1949, the North Atlantic Treaty Organization (NATO) was created to defend against Soviet expansionism. Article V of the Treaty declares that "an armed attack against one or more of the Parties shall be considered an attack against all the Parties." The North Atlantic Treaty was signed in Washington by the foreign ministers of Belgium, Canada, Denmark, France, Iceland, Italy, Luxembourg, the Netherlands, Norway, Portugal, the United Kingdom and the United States. Later Greece, Turkey, West Germany and, most recently, Spain joined the alliance.

NATO's military force was predicated primarily on the U.S. monopoly on atomic weapons, and the Soviets were determined not to leave this monopoly in American hands. On September 23, 1946, Soviet Premier Stalin told a British reporter for the *Sunday Times* of London that "monopolist possession of the atomic bomb cannot last long." In May 1947 Andrei Gromyko told the United Nations that "the idea of an American monopoly of atomic energy production is an illusion."[17]

As early as February 1943 Stalin had established a small atomic research program under the direction of physicist Igor Kurchatov. During the war, this group conducted small-scale but highly productive experimental work with uranium. When the Red Army captured the German atomic research centers at Berlin and Leipzig in 1945, Soviet agents seized scientists, equipment and atomic research reports. Shortly after the bombing of Hiroshima, Stalin ordered his military officials to "provide us with atomic weapons in the shortest possible time. You know that Hiroshima has shaken the whole world. The equilibrium has been destroyed. Provide the bomb—it will remove a great danger from us."[18]

Just after Hiroshima and Nagasaki the United States released the Smyth Report, an official account of the Manhattan Project that provided scientific and technical data about the bomb. The report had been released to meet the demands of the U.S. and world press, which were clamoring for information about the Manhattan Project. By January 1946 the Soviets had translated the report, and 30,000 copies were distributed in the Soviet Union. What had been intended by the United States as a gesture of openness and candor may have been useful to the Soviets in the development of their atomic program.[19]

Though American scientists were certain that the Soviet Union would develop an atomic bomb within a few years, U.S. military and political leaders scoffed at Soviet capabilities. General Groves, for example, told a congressional committee late in 1945 that without help from others Russia would need 15 or 20 years to make an atomic bomb; even with help, it would be five to seven years. In 1946, President Truman told a press conference that he doubted that the Soviet Union would ever have the "know-how" to make atomic weapons.

Less than three years later, however, American and British planes equipped with air-sampling and Geiger-counter-type devices gathered evidence of the first Soviet atomic blast. On September 3, 1949, a specially equipped aircraft collected radioactive air samples while on patrol from Japan to Alaska. Flying across the Pacific on September 5, a second plane also reported intense radioactivity. By the following week, American scientists had determined that a large amount of uranium had been present in the explosion that produced these radioactive air samples; either an atomic bomb test or an accident at an atomic energy research and production plant was responsible. The U.S. Air Force asked for a second report from a panel of scientists including Oppenheimer and Admiral William S. Parsons, the Manhattan Project explosives expert who had armed the Hiroshima bomb.

The panel concluded that the evidence was indeed "consistent with the view that the origin of the fission products was the explosion of an atomic bomb whose nuclear composition was similar to the Alamogordo bomb and that the explosion occurred between the 26th and 29th of August" somewhere over Siberia. Truman was informed on September 19, but he decided to delay a public announcement.

Shortly before 11:00 A.M. on Friday, September 23, 1949, White House aide Myrtle Bergheim called reporters into the office of Charles G. Ross, Truman's press secretary. As the last reporter entered Ross's office the door was closed. A Secret Service guard was posted to keep it shut. Ross announced that he had a statement to distribute and that no one was to leave the room until everyone had a copy. Suddenly someone shouted, "Russia has the atomic bomb!" When the door opened, reporters rushed wildly to grab telephones in the nearby press room. According to *The New York Times*, one correspondent hurrying out was from Tass, the official Soviet news agency.

Simultaneously, Truman informed his Cabinet that the United

States had recently detected evidence of a Russian atomic explosion. And on Capitol Hill, having spoken to Truman the previous day, Senator Brien McMahon of Connecticut, Chairman of the Joint Congressional Committee on Atomic Energy, brought his committee members the news. Oppenheimer was with McMahon to confirm the scientific evidence. Truman's press release read:

We have evidence that within recent weeks an atomic explosion occurred in the U.S.S.R.

Ever since atomic energy was first released by man, the eventual development of this new force was to be expected. This probability has always been taken into account by us. . . .

Truman's reference to "an atomic explosion" conveyed some doubt that the Soviet Union actually had a bomb; even several years later he maintained that the explosion might have been an accident at a Soviet atomic research facility.[20]

Senator McMahon's committee met immediately to assess the implications of the first Soviet test, which American officials called "Joe I" after Soviet Premier Josef Stalin. The committee's first reaction was surprise and horror: Why had the United States been caught unawares? Was there any chance that the Soviets would attack the United States? As anxious members of Congress talked vaguely about possible military reprisals, storm clouds gathered in the skies over the U.S. Capitol. A thunderclap startled the legislators in their seats and someone exclaimed, "My God, that must be Number Two!" Laughter momentarily eased their tension.[21]

A number of U.S. government officials quickly assured each other and the public that there was no need to panic. Secretary of State Dean Acheson insisted that the news had not come as a shock. General Eisenhower recalled past predictions that others would eventually solve the secret of atomic energy: "I see no reason why a development that was anticipated years ago should cause any revolutionary change in our thinking or in our actions."

Nevertheless, the United States had lost its atomic monopoly. Ambassador George Kennan had written, "There could be no greater protection for our own people against atomic attack than the deterrent effect of overwhelming retaliatory power in the hands of this country."[22] On October 10, 1949, less than three weeks after the announcement of Joe I, Secretary of State Dean Acheson, AEC Chairman Lilienthal, and Secretary of Defense Louis A. Johnson told President Truman that national security required that the production of U.S. atomic weapons be accelerated. Truman agreed, and a second atomic arms race began: Unlike the first race between the Allies and the Nazis to build the first atomic bomb, this one initially focused on U.S. attempts to "keep ahead" and Soviet attempts to "catch up."

In the years after World War II, fears of communism and the Soviet Union reached a fever pitch. In the United States, the House Committee on Un-American Activities (later called the House Un-American Activities Committee, or HUAC) began in 1947 to "ferret out" Communist influence in the American labor movement, and to identify Communist sympathizers in the federal government, in educational and religious institutions and in the entertainment industry.[23] After Joe I, several events exaggerated American fears. In October 1949 eleven leaders of the American Communist Party were convicted of conspiracy to advocate the overthrow of the U.S. government by force and violence. In December 1949 the remnants of the Chinese Nationalist Government fled to the island of Taiwan, leaving China to the Communist regime of Mao Zedong. And on

February 9, 1950, U.S. Senator Joseph McCarthy of Wisconsin told a Wheeling, West Virginia, women's club:

> *. . . I have here in my hand a list of 205 that were known to the Secretary of State as being members of the Communist Party and who nevertheless are still working and shaping the policy of the State Department.*

McCarthy's inflammatory accusations were vicious and false, but his charges were widely reported and believed.[24] To many, the menace of communism never seemed greater than during the winter of 1949–1950.

Then, during that same winter, the United States discovered that the Soviets had been spying on U.S. atomic research since 1942.

X

ATOM BOMB SPIES

---

espionage—the systematic use of spies by a government to discover the military and political secrets of other nations

The American College Dictionary,
1956

General Groves had seen to it that Manhattan Project work and workers were subject to the strictest security; the possibility that the project had been infiltrated by spies was an ever-present anxiety. For most of the war the Allies' main security concern was to keep atomic secrets from the Nazis. But as Germany slid toward defeat, U.S. and British officials became increasingly concerned with preventing information about atomic research from falling into Soviet hands.

In 1946 British physicist Allan Nunn May was caught providing highly sensitive atomic secrets to the Soviets. A member of Canada's National Research Council, he had worked on the Manhattan Project and, like all others, had been sworn to secrecy. After a British investigation exposed his activities, May confessed to giving a Soviet intermediary "a written report on atomic research as known to me"; he further admitted that "at one meeting I gave the man microscopic amounts of U-233 and U-235." Although May accepted money for these acts (he claimed to have forgotten how much), he stated that his principal motivation lay in his sympathy with communism and his desire to ensure that the Soviet Union shared in atomic developments. He pleaded guilty and was sentenced to 10 years in prison; he expressed no remorse for his offenses, he refused to identify other Soviet agents and he did not appeal his conviction.[1]

The May case prompted an intensified investigation into espionage activities. A major breakthrough came in 1949, when Robert Lamphere of the Federal Bureau of Investigation's counterintelligence unit (whose business is to discover and arrest spies operating in the United States) was examining coded Soviet messages that had been intercepted and deciphered. Lamphere was startled to discover a report authored by a German-born British atomic scientist named Klaus Fuchs that described in detail the wartime progress of the Manhattan Project.

The FBI found it hard to believe that the unassuming Dr. Fuchs was or had been a spy; they thought it more likely that the Soviets had obtained the report in some other way. But an FBI background check revealed that Fuchs had been a member of the German Communist Party in the early 1930s; though the British government had known, they made nothing of Fuchs's political affiliation, since their concern at the time was to identify Nazi rather than Soviet agents. Fuchs's name and address had also surfaced in the Allan Nunn May investigation, but again, the connection had been missed. The most incriminating evidence turned up in another deciphered Soviet document referring to a British atomic spy whose sister was attending an American university. Fuchs's sister Kristel was a student at Swarthmore College in Pennsylvania during the time he worked on the Manhattan Project.[2]

Government investigators found that Fuchs had a pious, pacifist background. His father was a prominent Lutheran pastor who converted to Quakerism; he was jailed by the Nazis for his liberal political views. Fuchs, like his father, was a member of the Social Democratic Party. Later, distressed that the Social Democrats did not confront the Nazis more aggressively, he joined the German Communist Party. In January 1933 Fuchs took part in street fighting against Nazi students at the University of Kiel. The "Brownshirts" beat him up and threw him in the river.[3]

When the Nazis came to power, Fuchs was forced into hiding. After five months he was destitute, but he managed to make his way to France and then to England, where he arrived as a refugee on September 24, 1933. By 1937 Fuchs had earned a Ph.D. in mathematical physics at the University of Bristol, England. He was a superb student: meticulous, methodical and persistent. During his studies he made several trips to the Soviet Union with other students, but he did not join the British Communist Party; this decision helped Fuchs avoid security exposure when he was recruited for the British atom bomb project.

In July 1939, Fuchs applied for British citizenship, but anti-German feeling ran so high in England that the British government no longer drew a distinction between those who had fought and fled the Nazis and those who were Nazi Party members and sympathizers. All Germans in England were classified as "enemy aliens" who were to be moved to internment camps. Fuchs was shipped to Canada along with other Germans residing in England, many of whom were Nazis or Nazi supporters. For the remainder of 1940 he lived behind barbed wire wearing the uniform of a prisoner of war.

Several British scientists who respected Fuchs's research skills intervened to get him released from internment and returned to Britain. In the spring of 1941 Fuchs received a letter from Dr. Rudolf Peierls, a physicist at the University of Birmingham. Would Fuchs be interested in work of "a special nature"? It was urgent, secret and connected with the war. After an interview, Fuchs was offered the job, and he accepted. His work in Birmingham concentrated on the gaseous diffusion process of separating uranium isotopes; his research directly contributed to the British atomic bomb project (code-named "Tube Alloys"), which later merged with the Manhattan Project.[4]

Fuchs contacted the Russians soon after his arrival in Birmingham. Over the next two years, he handed over enough important information about U.S. and British atom-bomb research to convince the Soviets that they could build an atomic bomb.

On August 19, 1943, Britain, Canada and the United States signed the "Quebec Agreement," a secret accord that provided for pooling resources and scientists in a cooperative effort to conduct atomic research and produce atomic bombs. Fuchs was selected to be a member of that Anglo-American team. Most of the highly sensitive work took place in the United States, and Fuchs was initially assigned to work in New York City. Arriving in the United States, Fuchs and other members of the British team immediately traveled to Washington, D.C., to sign security agreements with the U.S. government. Since Fuchs had already been cleared by Britain, America's closest ally, no further check of his background was required.[5]

One afternoon in September Fuchs left his New York hotel carrying a tennis ball. According to a plan developed before he left Britain, Fuchs was to make contact at a specified time and place with a Soviet courier. As Fuchs recalled, the courier "would be wearing gloves and would have an additional pair of gloves in his hands, while I would have a ball in my hand." Fuchs met his contact, code-named "Raymond," at least four more times in New York between December 1943 and August 1944 to pass on what he knew about how work on the Manhattan Project was progressing.

Fuchs was reassigned to Manhattan Project headquarters at Los Alamos late in 1944. He did not tell Raymond about his new assignment, and did not show up for a scheduled meeting at the Brooklyn Museum in Brooklyn, New York. Raymond frantically tried to locate Fuchs, who may have intended to sever his connection with the Soviets—at least for a time.

Early in 1945 Raymond finally tracked Fuchs down in Cambridge, Massachusetts, where Fuchs's sister Kristel now lived. A few days later Fuchs handed Raymond written notes describing all he had been able to learn at Los Alamos, including detailed information about the plutonium bomb (only months later dropped on Nagasaki). Fuchs also identified Hanford, Washington, as the site of plutonium production and revealed what he knew of the processes used there. Fuchs and Raymond met again on June 2, 1945, in Santa Fe, New Mexico, where Fuchs turned over more written material describing the bomb's design and gave six weeks' advance notice of the Alamogordo test. Then on September 19, 1945, at his final meeting with Raymond, Fuchs handed over an extremely detailed set of notes describing the bombs that had been dropped on Hiroshima and Nagasaki. They included his eyewitness account of the test at Alamogordo.[6]

In June 1946, Klaus Fuchs left Los Alamos and returned to England to assume duties at the new British atomic energy establishment at Harwell. In early 1947, he resumed contact with the Soviets, and over the next two years apprised them of British atomic developments. His Soviet contact began to ask for information about hydrogen-bomb research; for the first and only time Fuchs accepted money in exchange for information.

Then in 1949 the FBI informed British counterintelligence about the deciphered Soviet documents that identified Fuchs as a probable Soviet agent. James Skardon, an experienced British spy catcher, was assigned to confront Fuchs with the evidence, obtain a confession and persuade Fuchs to divulge the names of other spies. British intelligence wanted to avoid repetition of the case of Allan Nunn May, who had gone to jail without naming other agents or accomplices.

Skardon questioned Fuchs gently and reassuringly, leading him to believe that in spite of his espionage activities, he might be able to continue his work at Harwell. When Fuchs finally confessed, after several meetings with Skardon, even the veteran spy catcher was startled by the nature and extent of Fuchs's espionage activities. Fuchs had begun spying for the Soviets about the middle of 1942 and had continued for seven years—a period covering the inception, construction and explosion of the first atomic bomb. [7]

Fuchs's confession and subsequent arrest made major headlines all over the United States and Europe. At Los Alamos particularly, many were astounded. One of Fuchs's co-workers at New York, a physicist named John M. Corson, cabled Fuchs immediately:

NATURALLY DO NOT BELIEVE THE ACCUSATIONS
STOP IF CAN BE OF ANY SERVICE CALL ON ME STOP

CORSON

To which Fuchs replied:

THANK YOU STOP THERE IS NOTHING YOU CAN DO
STOP THE EVIDENCE WILL CHANGE YOUR MIND

FUCHS

Fuchs's trial on March 1 lasted only one hour and twenty minutes. He was convicted largely by his own confession, since both

U.S. and British officials wanted to keep secret the fact that they had broken a Soviet code. The British Chief Justice, Lord Goddard, sentenced Fuchs to 14 years in prison.

Reaction in the United States was swift and vehement. Senator Brien McMahon said he was "shocked" when he heard of Fuchs's arrest, and later "having read his confession, including those parts which had not been made public for reasons of security, I was still shocked." Several politicians expressed outrage at Fuchs's "light" sentence, among them Representative Richard M. Nixon of California, a member of the House Un-American Activities Committee (HUAC), who called for a "full-scale Congressional investigation of atomic espionage."

The FBI particularly wanted to apprehend Raymond, Fuchs's courier to the Soviets. But even Fuchs had no clue as to Raymond's real identity.

Fuchs described Raymond as an American about forty years of age, about five feet ten inches tall, with a "broad" build and a round face. Fuchs guessed that Raymond was a chemist by profession. The FBI dragnet eventually focused on two suspects. One was Harry Gold, a chemist working at Philadelphia General Hospital. Two FBI agents tracked him down at work. Gold nonchalantly answered questions for approximately five hours; he said later that at the time he was terrified. Months before, he had been warned by a Soviet agent of Fuchs's impending arrest, but he had decided against leaving the United States.

The FBI agents came back for a nine-hour interview. Gold gave them samples of his handwriting and printing, allowed them to take motion pictures of him and invited them to search his house the following week. (They needed Gold's permission because they did not have sufficient evidence against him to obtain a search warrant.) Gold knew his home contained incriminating evidence, which he intended to destroy immediately. For some reason he procrastinated. He woke up at 5:00 A.M. on the morning of the search and frantically began ransacking his drawers and closets, ripping up evidence and flushing it down the toilet.

The FBI agents searched Gold's belongings with painstaking thoroughness. They examined every page of every notebook as well as clothing labels and other items Gold had not thought twice about. Gold had quick answers for most questions about his papers and other effects, but his luck did not hold: The agents found a street map of Santa Fe. Gold knew it would lead the FBI back to his meeting with Fuchs. This time he had no quick answer. In Gold's words:

. . . *"Give me a minute," I said as I sunk down on the chair. . . . I accepted a cigarette and then, after a few moments, said the fatal words: "Yes, I am the man to whom Klaus Fuchs gave the information on atomic energy."*[8]

Shortly thereafter, Klaus Fuchs identified Harry Gold as Raymond on the basis of FBI photographs and movies, and Gold made a full confession.

Harry Gold immediately linked others to espionage activities. Gold told his interrogators he had contacted a soldier living in Albuquerque, New Mexico. The soldier was paid $500 for information he gave Gold about Los Alamos. Gold recalled meeting the soldier's wife: "Her name may have been Ruth, although I am not sure." FBI agents in New Mexico identified a soldier living in Albuquerque whose wife's name was Ruth. The soldier's name was David Greenglass; a week later, Gold positively identified his photograph, and the most controversial spy case of the century was about to unfold.[9]

At about this time, in New York City, a number of close friends and acquaintances of Julius Rosenberg, an electrical engineer, mysteriously disappeared. Rosenberg was a committed Communist; his wife, Ethel, was the sister of David Greenglass. David Greenglass was now out of the Army and living in New York City. Rosenberg excitedly warned Greenglass that Greenglass and his family might have to flee the country soon. Thinking that Rosenberg was overreacting, Greenglass decided not to worry his wife.

On February 2, 1950, Fuchs was arrested in England and Rosenberg advised Greenglass to flee to Mexico. Rosenberg spelled out the facts and his conclusion: Harry Gold, whom Fuchs had dealt with, was the same courier to whom Greenglass had delivered atomic secrets in Albuquerque; Greenglass was likely to be implicated soon. Rosenberg produced an envelope stuffed with ten- and twenty-dollar bills. He promised more money once Greenglass and his family were in Mexico. Greenglass now discussed the situation with Ruth; they decided that Rosenberg "must have been reading too much science fiction."[10]

During the afternoon of June 15, 1950, several hours after Harry Gold identified a photograph of David Greenglass, four FBI agents appeared at the Greenglass apartment in New York City. With David Greenglass's permission they spent hours searching his place and then took him downtown for questioning.

Informed that Gold had identified him as the person who had been paid $500 for secret Manhattan Project data, Greenglass broke down and confessed. He insisted that he "did not furnish the information for the money, but for the cause." David and Ruth Greenglass had been active for years in a group called the Young Communist League.

That night Greenglass provided the FBI with a signed statement implicating both his wife and Julius Rosenberg. In later testimony

Greenglass named his sister Ethel, Julius's wife, as another participant in Soviet espionage activities. Specifically, Greenglass admitted that while he was working as a machinist on the atombomb project, he and Ruth had provided Julius Rosenberg with a description of the Los Alamos facilities, the names of scientists working on the project, a list of people at Los Alamos whom Greenglass thought might be recruited for the Soviet cause and a description and sketches of explosive lenses used in experiments to determine how to detonate a plutonium bomb. David Greenglass also gave Rosenberg a detailed description (including a drawing of a cross section) of the bomb that was dropped on Nagasaki.

Greenglass's testimony and the subsequent arrests of Julius and Ethel Rosenberg created an overnight sensation. American members of Congress demanded further investigation into Communist infiltration and prompt revenge against all atom-bomb spies. But between the arrest and the trial of the Rosenbergs, there was significant legal maneuvering. Attorneys for David and Ruth Greenglass offered government prosecutors the Greenglasses' testimony against the Rosenbergs in exchange for leniency. The prosecutors estimated that the Greenglasses' full cooperation would be necessary to convict the Rosenbergs, whom they viewed as more important to Soviet espionage activities. They agreed not to indict Ruth Greenglass at all, and to recommend a "lighter" sentence for David Greenglass once the Rosenbergs' trial was concluded.

The trial of Julius and Ethel Rosenberg for conspiracy to commit espionage began in New York City on March 6, 1951. They were tried along with an alleged associate and close acquaintance, a thirty-three-year-old electrical engineer named Morton Sobell, who had fled to Mexico after Klaus Fuchs's confession. Presided over by Judge Irving R. Kaufman of the United States District Court for the Southern District of New York, the trial attracted extraordinary attention. Each day's testimony and events were described, and often sensationalized, in newspaper headlines and in radio and television reports.

Julius and Ethel Rosenberg each testified on their own behalf; they claimed to be entirely innocent of the charges brought against them. They attacked the testimony of David and Ruth Greenglass, charging that the Greenglasses' hostility toward them stemmed from a family feud over business matters, and that David and Ruth had agreed to cooperate with the government to make scapegoats of the Rosenbergs and save their own skins. When they were cross-examined by prosecutors about their sympathy with Communist ideology and their affiliation with the Communist Party, the Rosenbergs hedged or invoked their Fifth Amendment right against self-incrimination. Although this is a constitutional right available to any defendant, it made a poor impression on the jury. Martin Sobell, believing that the evidence against him was minimal, chose not to testify at all.[11]

When the proceedings were complete, the jury retired to deliberate the fate of the defendants. The jurors argued late into the night, returning the next day with a unanimous verdict: All three defendants were found guilty as charged. The judge set sentencing for April 5, 1951.

The Rosenbergs' sentence was to prove more controversial than almost any other aspect of the case. On April 5, Judge Kaufman stated: "The issue of punishment in this case is presented in a unique framework of history. It is so difficult to make people realize that this country is engaged in a life-and-death struggle with a completely different system." Describing the defendants' crime as "worse than murder," Judge Kaufman charged that

. . . putting into the hands of the Russians the A-bomb years before our best scientists predicted Russia would perfect the bomb has already caused, in my opinion, the Communist aggression in Korea, with the resultant casualties exceeding 50,000 and who knows but what that millions more innocent people may pay the price of your treason. Indeed, by your betrayal, you undoubtedly have altered the course of history to the disadvantage of our country.

The judge went on to state that in his view Julius Rosenberg had been the "prime mover" in the conspiracy; Ethel was a "full-fledged partner." He had searched his conscience for reasons why he should show mercy and had found none. He then sentenced the Rosenbergs to die in the electric chair. Sobell received 30 years in prison and the next day David Greenglass was sentenced to 15 years.

The controversy did not end with the sentencing. Attorneys for the Rosenbergs and Sobell filed appeals alleging that there had been various errors in the conduct of the trial; these were rejected. The appeals were then taken to the U.S. Supreme Court, which refused to hear them. Organizations were formed in the United States and Europe to "secure justice in the Rosenberg case." Many members of these organizations believed that the Rosenbergs were innocent and, further, that they had been framed by the Greenglasses and the FBI.

Some supporters claimed that the Rosenbergs were innocent victims of anti-Semitism or anti-Communist hysteria or both. Others thought that the evidence—particularly against Ethel Rosenberg—was insufficient to warrant the death penalty; they pointed to the lesser sentences given to Allan Nunn May, Klaus Fuchs, Harry Gold and David Greenglass. Still others who believed that the Rosenbergs were guilty disapproved of the prosecution's tactics in the case, particularly of the leniency extended to the Green-glasses in exchange for their testimony, and by what they thought was use of the death penalty as a "lever" to force the Rosenbergs to confess and name other members of their spy ring. But many Americans agreed with the jury that the Rosenbergs had committed a heinous crime in turning over U.S. atomic secrets to the Soviet Union. Many also felt that the U.S. government was justified in using tough tactics to catch and convict dangerous atomic spies.

After a final attempt to gain clemency from President Eisenhower, Julius and Ethel Rosenberg were electrocuted at Sing Sing Prison in New York State on Friday, June 19, 1953. Their two young sons were eventually placed in a foster home; years later they wrote a book defending their parents. [12]

The Soviets undoubtedly learned important information about the Manhattan Project from their atom-bomb spies; exactly how much they learned is not known. The knowledge they gleaned from espionage may account for Stalin's casual reaction at Potsdam to Truman's comment about "a very powerful explosive." The efforts of the spies also probably accelerated Soviet progress toward Joe I, although certainly the Soviets would eventually have developed an atomic bomb without the help of spies.

While it is not known what the Soviets learned about U.S. thermonuclear research, they were certainly aware that the United States had been thinking about a superweapon as early as 1942. This undoubtedly created deep Soviet concern and lent impetus to their own atomic research efforts, to cold-war tensions and to the arms race that followed.

The Fuchs, Gold and Rosenberg spy cases fanned anti-Soviet feeling in the United States. Combined with fear of the new Soviet atomic capability, this feeling bordered in some quarters upon hysteria. The "Red Scare" worsened relations between the superpowers and contributed to decisions to develop more and more powerful weapons.

XI

THE SUPER

We should now make an intensive effort to get ahead with the Super. By intensive effort, I am thinking of a commitment in talent and money comparable, if necessary, to that which produced the first atomic bomb. That is the way to stay ahead.

> Admiral Lewis Strauss,
> U.S. Atomic Energy Commissioner,
> October 29, 1949

We base our recommendation [against the superbomb] on our belief that the extreme dangers to mankind . . . wholly outweigh the military advantage that could come from this development. Let it be clearly recognized that this is a superweapon; it is in a totally different category from an atomic bomb.

> General Advisory Committee Report
> to the Atomic Energy Commission,
> October 30, 1949

During World War II, Edward Teller and other atomic scientists theorized that the heat generated by an exploding atomic bomb could create temperatures high enough to ignite a rare but naturally occurring heavy form of hydrogen known as "deuterium." At 100 million degrees centigrade, the deuterium nuclei would react in a process similar to that which occurs in the sun—a "thermonuclear" process called "fusion." Whereas fission involves splitting nuclei, fusion joins, or fuses, them together. Both processes release energy, but the scientists estimated that a fusion or hydrogen bomb could explode with at least a thousand times the force of the fission bombs that were dropped on Hiroshima and Nagasaki.

Teller and others believed that there were no limits to the explosive power of these weapons, which promised "more bang for the buck." In his book *Weapons and Hope*, physicist Freeman Dyson observed:

The peculiar horror of the hydrogen bomb was seen to be the fact that its cost would be almost independent of its size. Once you had built a workable bomb, you could increase its destructive power without limit by adding deuterium fuel, which would cost about sixty cents a kiloton at 1950 prices. The cost of adding the equivalent of another Hiroshima to the destructive power of a hydrogen bomb would be only about ten dollars.[1]

Among the Manhattan Project scientists, Edward Teller was the most enthusiastic about developing a hydrogen bomb. Relatively little money had been allocated to thermonuclear research, a fact which frustrated Teller. "No one was interested in developing a thermonuclear bomb," he said later. "No one cared . . . thermonuclear work was given almost no support in the last months of 1945—or in 1946, 1947, or 1948."

During World War II the critical question had been whether atomic weapons <u>could</u> be produced, not whether they <u>should</u> be produced. Now, leaving technical questions aside, an evaluation by scientists and government officials of the political and moral consequences of developing hydrogen weapons precipitated a bitter debate.

One cool and rainy morning late in October 1949, members of the Atomic Energy Commission's General Advisory Committee met at AEC headquarters in Washington to discuss the hydrogen bomb. AEC Chairman David E. Lilienthal was skeptical about the need to proceed with thermonuclear research, believing that "we are giving far too high a value to atomic weapons, little, big or biggest." AEC Commissioner Admiral Lewis Strauss argued to the contrary: the Russian test meant that "we should now make an intensive effort to get ahead with the 'Super.' By intensive effort, I am thinking of a commitment in talent and money comparable, if necessary, to that which produced the first atomic bomb. That is the way to stay ahead."[2]

Oppenheimer was chairman of the General Advisory Committee; at this time he was opposed to extensive research on thermonuclear weapons. Several days earlier he had written: "This thing appears to have caught the imagination both of the Congressional and the military people, as the answer to the problem posed by the Russian advance. . . . [To] become committed to it as the way to save the country and the peace appears to me full of dangers."[3] Oppenheimer's committee finally recommended against hydrogen-bomb research: "We believe a super bomb should never be produced. Mankind would be far better off not to have a demonstration of the feasibility of such a weapon. . . ." Two committee members, Rabi and Fermi, issued a separate report: "The fact that no limits exist to the destructiveness of this weapon makes its very existence and the knowledge of its construction a danger to humanity." The committee hoped that U.S. restraint would encourage reciprocal restraint on the part of the Soviets.

Oppenheimer relayed the committee's conclusions to Secretary of State Dean Acheson, who felt their idealism was quite unrealistic. Acheson said to Senator McMahon with some astonishment, "You know, I listened as carefully as I knew how, but I don't understand what Oppie is trying to say. How can you really persuade a hostile adversary to disarm 'by example'?" Several days later Teller met with McMahon, who said, "[The GAC report] just makes me sick." Teller's view, unsurprisingly, was that it was "vital to the nation's defense that we proceed with the thermonuclear work."

On January 13, General Omar N. Bradley, Truman's top military advisor, told the president that U.S. military officers approved of developing the Super because the United States should not permit the Soviet Union to gain an advantage in the nuclear arms race. They believed it was "folly to argue whether one weapon is more immoral than another," for "in the larger sense, it is war itself which is immoral. . . ." On January 19, Truman told an advisor that Bradley's counsel "made a lot of sense, and . . . he was inclined to think that was what we should do."

When the AEC had informed Truman that its members were divided on the issue, Truman had asked Acheson, Lilienthal and Secretary of Defense Louis Johnson to prepare a separate study. Admiral Strauss, vehemently in favor of H-bomb research, then met with Johnson to discuss the situation: "The Russians [are] building an H-bomb, the United States is being sold down the river, and the U.S. must proceed with an H-bomb program. . . ." On January 31, 1950, at 12:30 P.M., Truman gathered his advisory group at the White House. By this time the debate within the government was public knowledge, and public pressure required that Truman resolve the issue. In just ten minutes he did: The United States would proceed with research on thermonuclear weapons. Truman told the dubious Lilienthal that he simply could take no other course.[4]

The decision to develop the H-bomb was the second forsaken opportunity in the postwar period to curtail the strategic arms race. The first chance had been the attempts to place atomic energy under some form of international control. In hindsight, it is clear that the shock of Joe I provoked President Truman to authorize thermonuclear research rather than seek ways to ban the development of hydrogen bombs. We do not know whether the arms race could have been stopped here; what we do know is that no one with political power really tried. Truman's decision stimulated Soviet thermonuclear research and marked a major new stage in nuclear arms competition.

On the afternoon of January 31 the president's press secretary distributed a statement to reporters:

It is part of my responsibility as Commander-in-Chief of the armed forces to see to it that our country is able to defend itself against any possible aggressor. Accordingly, I have directed the Atomic Energy Commission to continue its work on all forms of atomic weapons, including the so-called hydrogen or super-bomb.[5]

One week later, Truman told an advisor that the United States must build the Super, "though none wants to use it"; "we have got to have it only for bargaining purposes with the Russians."

Senator McMahon commended Truman's decision "to create, in deliverable quantities, those chunks of the sun technically known as thermonuclear weapons." According to McMahon, the president's decision was dictated by "the severe realities of the world which we inhabit today": "American renunciation of the hydrogen bomb would mean . . . our friends abroad would shrink away from us, seeing that we had lost the power to defend the United States— much less to help defend Europe."[6]

In June 1950, the "severe realities of the world" again led the United States into war, this time in response to the Communist North Korean military invasion of South Korea. The U.N. Security

Council unanimously condemned the invasion; it called for a withdrawal of the North Koreans to the 38th parallel (the border between North and South Korea) and it authorized joint military action by member states. The Soviet Union was boycotting the Security Council to protest the United Nations' refusal to grant Communist China a seat, and was not present to veto the resolution. Under U.N. auspices, Truman ordered United States air and sea forces into South Korea.

In November 1950, Chinese Communist troops attacked U.N. forces. At a press conference several weeks later Truman mentioned that the United States "might consider" dropping atomic bombs on Chinese and North Korean troops. The French and British, who also had troops in Korea, were indignant that they had not been consulted before the United States raised this possibility in public; they feared that the Soviets, allies of the Chinese and North Koreans, might retaliate by dropping atomic bombs on Europe.

The U.S. commander in Korea, General Douglas MacArthur, acknowledged in his memoirs that he wrote a "Memorandum on Ending the Korean War," recommending that North Korea should be cleared of enemy forces "through the atomic bombing of military concentrations and installations" and that "the Soviets should be further informed that, in such an eventuality, it would probably become necessary to neutralize Red China's capability to wage modern war."[7] MacArthur's repeated efforts to expand the war beyond North Korea into Red China eventually led to his dismissal by President Truman, on grounds that he had tried to usurp the Chief Executive's control over the conduct of the war.

Meanwhile, thermonuclear research had advanced to the point of an H-bomb test. On November 1, 1952, a 65-ton hydrogen weapon, encased in a huge refrigeration device to keep the hydrogen fuel at the proper temperature, was towed by U.S. vessels to the island of Elugelab, part of Eniwetok Atoll in the Pacific Ocean, 2,400 nautical miles west-southwest of Honolulu. The hydrogen device, code-named "Mike," was set up in a shed, and all ships withdrew to positions at least forty miles away. At dawn on November 2 the device was detonated.

Mike dwarfed the Alamogordo test of July 1945. Everything within a radius of 3 miles was annihilated. The fireball rose 5 miles into the sky and extended 4 miles across. Within ten minutes the fireball was followed by a gigantic cauliflower-shaped cloud, mauve and blue and gray-green, rising 25 miles into the stratosphere. The "mushroom cap" portion of the cloud, 10 miles high, spread out over the sea for nearly 100 miles. The sight terrified even those who had seen previous atomic tests.

The island of Elugelab—formed by the top, or rim, of an extinct sea volcano—disappeared. Divers later discovered a mile-long, 175-foot canyon in the ocean floor, deep enough for a seventeen-story building. Mike's destructive power was measured at 10.4 megatons, roughly 1,000 times that of the Hiroshima bomb.[8] Norris E. Bradbury, who had replaced Oppenheimer as the director of Los Alamos, was so shocked that he briefly considered keeping the test results secret.

Shortly after Mike initiated the thermonuclear age, Dwight D. Eisenhower was elected president of the United States and so assumed the problems associated with the conflict in Korea. By February 1953 it was a stalemate, both sides fighting to gain mere yards of ground along the front. Peace talks had been going on for months but with little progress. Over 21,000 American soldiers were dead, 91,000 were wounded, and over 13,000 were missing: Korea had become the fourth-costliest conflict in American history, ranking in casualties behind only the Civil War and the two World Wars.

Eisenhower had pledged during his presidential campaign that if elected, he would "go to Korea," and that he would find some way to end the military stalemate. His memoirs describe his sense of the situation at the time: ". . . it was obvious that if we were to go over to a major offensive, the war would have to be expanded outside of Korea . . . to keep the attack from being overly costly, it was clear that we would have to use atomic weapons."[9]

When he met with his advisors on February 11, 1953, Eisenhower learned that Communist troops were assembling in an area called Kaesong, where according to arrangements made at the peace talks, they were safe from attack by U.N. forces. The U.S. commander in the field, however, was concerned that the Communists would not remain in Kaesong long before launching an attack. According to the official notes of this meeting, Eisenhower's view was that "we should consider the use of atomic weapons on the Kaesong area." "In any case," the president added, "we could not go on the way we were indefinitely."[10]

Whether or not Eisenhower was actually prepared to use atomic weapons, he clearly wanted the Communists to believe that he was. Secretary of State John Foster Dulles let India's Prime Minister Nehru know that the United States might resort to atomic weapons if that was what was necessary to break the stalemate. Nehru was in close contact with the Soviets and Chinese, and Eisenhower "felt quite sure" that such a threat "would reach Soviet and Chinese Communist ears."

Meanwhile, the president's advisors continued to deliberate the issue of using atomic weapons in Korea. At a meeting on March 27, 1953, General Lawton Collins, U.S. Army Chief of Staff, said,

"I am very skeptical about the value of using atomic weapons tactically in Korea. The Communists are dug into positions in depth over a front of one hundred fifty miles, and they are very thoroughly dug in. Our tests last week proved that men can be very close to the explosion and not be hurt if they are well dug in. . . ." (Collins was speaking of recent atomic tests involving U.S. troops in the Nevada desert.)[11]

Paul Nitze, a State Department official, told Collins that a group of special consultants hired by the Eisenhower administration believed that

> . . . *there was no unshakeable policy barrier to use of atomic weapons, but the real question was whether the advantages would outweigh the disadvantages. We had to assess whether or not atomic weapons could be effective under Korean conditions.*[12]

Nitze added that "we had to weigh the political difficulties with our allies, which would arise from employment of atomic weapons, and these difficulties would be magnified if the weapons were not in fact effective." The United States was also worried about Soviet retaliation. Collins pointed out, "Right now we [U.S. troops] present ideal targets for atomic weapons."

On May 13 the president's top military advisors agreed that there were no suitable targets for atomic weapons within Korea. They further stated that "in the event atomic weapons were used [against China or the Soviet Union to obtain a peace settlement in Korea] . . . they must be used in considerable numbers in order to be truly effective."[13]

In the final analysis, several factors kept Eisenhower from resorting to an atomic attack. The first was fear that the Soviet Union would enter the war and launch an atomic attack against the United

States or its allies. Eisenhower was astounded by MacArthur's memorandum to end the Korean War: to drop atomic bombs on Asians only seven years after Hiroshima and Nagasaki was certain to make all Asians enemies of the United States.[14] Also, U.S. allies might distance themselves from the United States if Eisenhower opened the way for atomic warfare. World opinion as well might condemn such action, further isolating the United States.

Still another factor argued for restraint. When President Eisenhower was informed by his top military advisors that "considerable numbers" of atomic weapons would be necessary to end the war, he questioned whether such numbers would not contaminate the earth so "as virtually to extinguish all human life." Eisenhower had read a report by Albert Einstein and other scientists suggesting this possibility.

Nevertheless, since the West relied increasingly on atomic weapons as a substitute for large armies, Eisenhower worried that a failure to achieve U.S. objectives would depreciate the perceived value of the U.S. strategic stockpile. During the Eisenhower administration, under a program called "The New Look," nuclear weapons were placed in artillery shells, in short-range surface-to-surface missiles, in bombs carried by short-range fighter-bombers and even in land mines (called Atomic Demolition Munitions or "ADMs"). If the "atomic equalizer" did not work as advertised, this mainstay of Western security could lose its value to deter the Soviets.[15]

At a May 20 meeting Eisenhower authorized the military to devise a plan for using atomic weapons "if circumstances arose which would force the United States to an expanded effort in Korea." The effect of the American threat was to help bring the war to an end. On July 27, 1953, a truce agreement established a new border between North and South Korea.

Korea was the first conflict after World War II in which the use of atomic weapons was considered, and the first in which more than one potential adversary could have resorted to atomic weapons—a fact that influenced political and military judgments on both sides. With the U.S. monopoly gone, the prospects of nuclear retaliation weighed heavily. Furthermore, the publicized willingness of the United States to use the bomb in Korea underscored the perception that atomic weapons represent national power. This provided further impetus for the U.S.–Soviet arms race and incentive for other nations to develop atomic weapons.

On October 31, 1951, the U.S. government announced that the Soviet Union had detonated a second atomic device, which the Americans called "Joe II." On October 6, *Pravda* printed Stalin's comment:

In the event of a United States attack on our country, the ruling circles of the United States will use the atomic bomb. Precisely this circumstance compelled the Soviet Union to have the atomic weapon in order to be fully armed to meet the aggressor.

Later that month the United States announced that it had detected evidence of a third Soviet detonation.

On August 12, 1953, the Soviets exploded "Joe IV," their first hydrogen device. Soviet thermonuclear research had begun in 1948 when Igor Kurchatov organized a group of scientists, including Andrei Sakharov, after receiving Klaus Fuchs's reports on U.S. thermonuclear research. It is possible that Fuchs's reports advanced Soviet H-bomb efforts, although we cannot gauge to what extent.

Joe I followed the U.S. fission bombs by four years, and the first Soviet thermonuclear device followed the first U.S. fusion explosion by only nine months: certainly the Soviets seemed to be catching up.

The year 1953 was a critical one for the Soviets. Several events precipitated a reassessment of their military strategy. The death of Josef Stalin ended his 29 years of iron control. For the first time, the Soviets introduced nuclear weapons into their military forces. And Soviet scientists detonated their first thermonuclear device. Before 1953 the bulk of Soviet forces were targeted at Western Europe, because they had no long-range aircraft with which to directly threaten the United States. Beginning in 1953, Soviet energies were increasingly channeled into developing bombers that could carry nuclear weapons over intercontinental distances.[16]

The rapid shift from an American atomic monopoly to the threat of mutual annihilation required that U.S. military strategy be reexamined as well. A group of civilian strategists sought to clarify how nuclear weapons, by threatening unacceptable damage to an aggressor, could deter war. Bernard Brodie's concept of nuclear deterrence is described in his book *The Absolute Weapon*. This concept has come to play a fundamental and ongoing role in relations between nuclear powers:

Thus, the first and most vital step in any American security program for the age of atomic bombs is to take measures to guarantee to ourselves in case of attack the possibility of retaliation in kind. The writer in making that statement is not for the moment concerned who will win the next war in which atomic bombs are used. Thus far the purpose of our military establishment has been to win wars. From now on its chief purpose must be to avert them. It can have almost no other useful purpose.[17]

After Stalin's death there was a struggle for power among top Soviet officials. At the same time Soviet rhetoric shifted from aggressive talk about the "inevitability of war" to something milder: War was, perhaps, after all, avoidable. In March 1954 one Party leader, Anastas Mikoyan, suggested that the danger of war had receded now that the Soviet Union possessed both the atomic and hydrogen bombs. The same day, Georgi Malenkov, Stalin's immediate successor, declared that world war in the nuclear age would mean the "destruction of world civilization." In February 1956 Nikita Khrushchev, who became the new Soviet leader, recycled Marxist theory with a twist. "Wars are inevitable as long as imperialism exists," he said, but then he modified his claim, saying that the Soviets possessed "formidable means to prevent the imperialists from unleashing war, and if they actually start it, to give a smashing rebuff to the aggressors and frustrate their adventurist plans."

To counter NATO, in 1955 the Soviets formed their own alliance, the Warsaw Treaty Organization, commonly referred to as the Warsaw Pact. Its membership comprises the Soviet Union, Bulgaria, Czechoslovakia, East Germany, Hungary, Poland and Rumania. Warsaw Pact forces are equipped with "nuclear-capable" aircraft, artillery and missiles that mirror those of NATO. The United States maintains control over nuclear weapons deployed to NATO forces; similarly, the Soviet Union is thought to exercise tight control over its nuclear weapons dedicated to the Warsaw Pact.[18]

Thus both the United States and the Soviet Union moved toward similar strategies of deterrence. (The term derives from the Latin word *deterrere*, which means "to frighten away from.") Inherent in this strategy is one of the paradoxes of the nuclear age—the perceived need to be able to use nuclear weapons in order to ensure that a nuclear war is never waged. Nuclear weapons can be said to have deterred nuclear war between nuclear nations, though they certainly have not prevented conventional wars between nonnuclear nations nor even between nuclear and nonnuclear nations.

In the years that followed, the United States and the Soviet Union sought to deter each other from attack with a wide variety of land- and sea-based nuclear forces. The three chapters that follow trace the development of the three major nuclear "delivery systems"—the bombers, missiles and submarines that make up the majority of both the U.S. and Soviet deterrent forces. After all, a stockpile of nuclear weapons cannot be effective as a deterrent unless there exist means to "deliver" them to the enemy. In the United States these three delivery systems form what is now known as the "Strategic Triad."

The next chapter focuses on the earliest leg of the strategic triad, bomber aircraft, and how the invention of the airplane and its rapid development into a bomber changed the rules and dimensions of warfare. The continuing international fascination with new technology and its military application is apparent as well in the missile and submarine chapters that follow.

XII

FROM KITTY HAWK TO STRATEGIC BOMBERS

Aviation is good sport, but for the Army it is useless.

> Pre-World War I statement by French Marshal Ferdinand Foch

. . . whatever be the views held as to the legality, or the humanity, or the military wisdom and expediency of such operations, there is not the slightest doubt that in the next war both sides will send their aircraft without scruple to bomb those objectives which they consider the most suitable.

> Sir Hugh Trenchard,
> Marshal of the British Royal Air Force,
> 1928

Peace Is Our Profession.

> Motto of the United States Strategic Air Command

On December 17, 1903, on the beach near Kitty Hawk, North Carolina, five people witnessed the first flight of a powered airplane. On that day Orville Wright piloted a 750-pound aircraft that he and his brother Wilbur had designed and built. The flight lasted 12 seconds and covered 120 feet. Over the next two years the Wright brothers built planes that could stay airborne nearly 40 minutes and travel as far as 24 miles. They thought their aircraft could be used by the U.S. Army for reconnaissance and for carrying messages, but the Army initially expressed no interest. Indeed many skeptics, having witnessed only balloon flights, refused to believe that heavier-than-air aircraft could fly at all. This disbelief was short-lived.[1]

By 1914, when World War I began in Europe, airplanes were used for reconnaissance, to spot enemy troops and direct artillery barrages. Although aerial bombing tests had been conducted before the war, early aircraft were too light to carry much explosive and so slow as to be vulnerable to ground fire. But airplane design improved steadily, and as frustration with trench warfare mounted, aerial bombing became more frequent. Many of the first "bombs" were cans filled with gasoline dropped by pilots over the sides of their cockpits. French pilots even hurled steel darts—*fléchettes*—at German foot soldiers, cavalry troops and horses.

The last two years of World War I saw the construction of larger, sturdier aircraft designed specifically for bombing. Metal construction replaced wood and cloth, and as more powerful engines were developed, the altitude, range and bomb-carrying capacity of airplanes were considerably increased. Makeshift bombs were superseded by aerodynamically shaped canisters filled with dynamite and other high explosives. Fins were attached for more predictable flight and better aim. Bombsights and bomb-release gear were introduced. By 1918, hundreds of aircraft were flying regular bombing raids. French Marshal Ferdinand Foch and others initially skeptical of "air power" became convinced that aerial bombing would be an important factor in any future war.

Anticipating this development, a 1922–23 international conference at The Hague, in the Netherlands, developed rules of conduct for aerial warfare. The "Hague Draft Rules" prohibited "aerial bombardment for the purpose of terrorizing the civilian population, of destroying or damaging private property not of a military character, or of injuring noncombatants."[2] But these guidelines did little to quell fear of aircraft as a major new instrument of war. As a result, all major nations developed their own air forces.

But how would an air force function in war? As air forces grew in size and sophistication during the 1920s and 1930s, there was considerable debate about how they would be used. In a May 1928 memorandum to the chiefs of the British Army and Navy, Sir Hugh Trenchard, chief of the Royal Air Force (RAF), argued:

It is not . . . necessary for an air force, in order to defeat the enemy nation, to defeat its armed forces first. Air power can dispense with that intermediate step, can pass over the enemy Navies and Armies, and penetrate the air defenses and attack directly the centers of production, transportation and communication from which the enemy war effort is maintained.

Trenchard maintained that by bombing the means for waging war, air power could destroy both the enemy's ability and its will to resist. He reasoned that industrial targets were usually in populated areas, where frequent heavy air attacks would panic civilian workers and thus interfere with war production. Panic would then spread to the rest of the population, eventually forcing the government to surrender.[3]

"Strategic bombing," as this concept came to be called, was widely criticized on the grounds of inhumanity and illegality, not only by pacifists and others who wanted to ban the bomber altogether, but also by military professionals strongly opposed to making war on civilians.

On September 1, 1939, the day Nazi forces invaded Poland, reports reached western capitals that the Germans were bombing

Polish cities. President Roosevelt immediately proposed that all belligerents refrain from "bombarding from the air civilian populations or unfortified cities." His appeal was promptly welcomed in an Anglo-French declaration. Although Hitler expressed his unqualified intention to comply, reports continued from Poland that cities were being bombed and that fleeing civilians were being machine-gunned from the air.

On May 14, 1940, the Germans bombed the Dutch port city of Rotterdam; British intelligence reports estimated that 30,000 civilians had been killed. Emotions ran high, and the next day the British War Cabinet decided to strike against industrial targets in Germany's Ruhr Valley. Nearly 100 heavy bombers left Britain for the German mainland that evening. This decision was part of a chain of events that led to an all-out escalation of the war. Its full implications were not appreciated at the time.

It was later determined that the intelligence estimates of casualties caused by the German attack on Rotterdam were wildly exaggerated. Not 30,000 but 980 civilians had been killed.

Although much of the Battle of Britain was fought in the air over the English Channel and over military objectives such as RAF fighter bases, London and other cities were also hit. Churchill reported, "The war cabinet were much in the mood to hit back, to raise the stakes, and to defy the enemy. I was sure they were right. . . ." The day after German bombs fell on London, British bombers attacked Berlin. They inflicted relatively little damage, but Hitler was enraged; the next day he authorized an all-out air assault on the British capital. Several days later Hitler addressed a mass rally and vowed "hundredfold vengeance" against Britain. "If they attack our cities," he roared, "we will simply rub out theirs." This marked the abandonment of restraint and the beginning of unrestricted air warfare.[4]

As he had threatened, Hitler bombed London as well as cities of no conceivable military value. The *Luftwaffe* began to drop parachute mines at night, which, since they were guided only by prevailing winds, could not be aimed at specific targets. Many had delayed-action fuses, so the British could not be sure either where or when one might explode. In retaliation, on April 30, 1942, the British mounted an unprecedented "1,000-bomber" night attack against Cologne. During the next year they launched massive air assaults on other German cities as well, including a devastating incendiary raid on the northern port city of Hamburg.

In 1943 the U.S. 8th Air Force also began to bomb German cities. At first the Americans were concerned about bombing civilians and insisted on targeting precise military objectives. "Precision bombing" required that missions be flown during daylight hours so that bomber crews could see their targets. But that visibility gave an unacceptable advantage to German antiaircraft gunners and fighter pilots. After suffering heavy losses the Americans, like the British, turned to night bombing. Because navigation was difficult and targets could only be approximated in the dark, civilians inevitably were killed.

By 1944 and 1945 the U.S. 8th Air Force was making 1,000-bomber raids of its own. In February 1945 the Americans and British combined forces for an all-out assault on the German city of Dresden. Bombing with incendiaries caused a fire storm that generated winds of well over 100 miles per hour within the city. At this time, late in the war, Dresden was swollen with German civilian refugees fleeing the advancing Russian army, and the casualties could not even be estimated.[5]

Curtis E. LeMay served as commander of a squadron of bombers that flew numerous bombing missions over Germany. Broad-chested, square-jawed and stocky, LeMay was so blunt and uncompromising in his dealings with others that his closest friends called him, with irony, "The Diplomat."[6] In July 1944 LeMay was ordered to take command of the new B-29 bombers in the war against Japan. The B-29s were much larger than earlier bombers, could carry nearly twice the bomb load and had twice the range. Built by the Boeing Corporation, B-29s could operate at 38,000 feet, cruise at over 350 miles per hour, and travel 3,500 miles with four tons of bombs.

LeMay determined that Japanese cities would be extremely vulnerable to B-29s carrying incendiary bombs. ". . . they say that 90 percent of the structures in Tokyo are built of wood. That's what Intelligence tells us, and what the guidebooks and the *National Geographic* [tell us]—they all say the same." LeMay traced his decision to drop incendiaries back to a childhood experience in Ohio. A neighborhood boy had constructed a small model village of wood and paper. "And some mean kid says, 'let's see if we can burn it down.' So you set fire to the first house. And brother they all went."[7]

To set fire to Tokyo, LeMay planned to use over 300 B-29s carrying tons of incendiary phosphorus and napalm (jellied gasoline) bombs. He would also carry a few high-explosive bombs to keep the Japanese under cover, so that they could not rush out and extinguish the first fires. LeMay realized that this raid, if successful, would kill "an awful lot of civilians." He justified these tactics on the theory that they would obviate the necessity for an invasion of Japan costing thousands of American lives—the same reason later used to justify the atomic bombing of Hiroshima and Nagasaki.

On the night of March 9, 1945, LeMay's crews dropped approximately 700,000 incendiary bombs on Tokyo. Each exploded at an altitude of 2,500 feet; each released thirty-eight pipelike canisters, which burned fiercely. Within 30 minutes the Tokyo fire chief announced that the situation in the city was "out of control." The U.S. Army Air Corps official history states: "No other air attack of the war, either in Japan or Europe, was so destructive of life and property." The updrafts from the Tokyo fires, estimated to have reached 2,000 degrees, bounced the B-29s in the sky "like Ping-Pong balls."

Forty-eight hours later, U.S. B-29s bombed the Japanese city of Nagoya. LeMay received word from the Navy that a U.S. submarine, surfacing 150 miles offshore, had reported that thick smoke from the burning city cut its visibility to one mile.[8]

By June 1945 LeMay's strategic bombing group had obliterated 66.3 square miles of Tokyo, 12.4 square miles of Nagoya, 8.8 of Kobe, 15.6 of Osaka, 8.9 of Yokohama and 3.6 of Kawasaki. Then came the atomic attacks on Hiroshima and Nagasaki, and the surrender of Japan.

After the war both the United States' new superpower status and the problems that had hampered the military's general efficiency led to a major reorganization of the defense establishment. On July 27, 1947, President Truman signed the National Security Act, which established the several organizations that still constitute the U.S. national security apparatus. The Act established a national intelligence organization, the Central Intelligence Agency or CIA, and created a new mechanism for presidential decision-making, the National Security Council or NSC. The Act detached the Air Corps from the Army; it was renamed the United States Air Force and accorded the status of an independent military service, with its own civilian leader (known as the secretary of the Air Force) and military chief of staff. The secretaries of the Army, of the Navy (who also represents the Marine Corps) and of the Air Force would henceforth serve under the direction of a new secretary of defense. The three military chiefs of staff, together with the commandant of the Marine Corps, would comprise the "Joint Chiefs of Staff," to act as principal military advisors to the president, the NSC and the secretary of defense.

The Strategic Air Command (SAC, pronounced "sack") was the bombing division of the new U.S. Air Force. In 1948 General LeMay assumed command of SAC, one of whose tasks is to deliver U.S. atomic bombs to targets if the president so orders. In the early postwar years, as we have said, U.S. defense strategy was predicated on the fact that only the United States possessed nuclear weapons. In the event of a Soviet attack, SAC aircraft would have dropped atomic bombs on cities and industrial targets in the Soviet Union. The U.S. "nuclear monopoly" was relied upon to maintain peace and freedom in Western Europe while avoiding the political problems and economic costs associated with maintaining a large army and navy overseas.

When General LeMay took command of SAC, he initiated a crash program to achieve "air mastery." This involved turning SAC into a "cocked weapon" aimed primarily at the Soviet Union. The spirit of his command turned SAC into a consciously proud and elite military unit, and his budget requests received top priority. SAC's nuclear-capable aircraft increased in number from sixty in December 1948 to over 250 by June 1950.

Another priority was safety. Many accidents occurred during SAC's first few years; on each occasion LeMay demanded that the responsible commander appear before him personally. Also, since SAC was responsible for most U.S. nuclear weapons, LeMay focused much attention on security. The mere possibility that an outsider could sabotage or even steal a nuclear weapon or a nuclear-capable aircraft appalled him.[9]

In January 1952 President Truman approved a significant increase in the production of fissionable materials for bombs. The amount of available plutonium would rise by 50 percent, the amount of U-235 by 150 percent. Consequently, the Air Force asked for additional aircraft to carry the growing stockpile of nuclear weapons. While overall U.S. defense spending decreased after World War II, Air Force budgets grew, mainly as a consequence of SAC's major new role; by 1954 the Air Force was accounting for over 40 percent of the military budget. Army and Navy critics of disproportionate budget allocations accused the Air Force of "bootstrapping": They claimed that target lists generated by the Air Force were used to justify increased nuclear weapons production, which in turn was used to justify more money for more bombers.[10]

In June 1955 the Boeing Corporation (which currently produces the majority of commercial airliners) delivered the first of 744 B-52 "Strato-fortresses" to the Strategic Air Command. This new bomber's capabilities dwarfed those of its predecessors. It could fly at an altitude of over 50,000 feet and carry enormous bombloads. A fleet of jet "Strato-tankers" was built to refuel the B-52s in midair and thus extend their range.

LeMay left SAC in 1957 to become vice-chief, and ultimately chief of staff, of the U.S. Air Force. During his tenure SAC had grown from 45,000 to almost 200,000 personnel, and its aircraft had evolved from the B-29 to the B-52. SAC now had about 2,800 aircraft, most of them "nuclear capable." Bombs had also changed: the 10,000-pound fission bombs built during 1945–1949 were superseded by the 3,000-pound thermonuclear "Mark-5," by the 2,700-pound "Mark-7," and then by the relatively compact 1,000-pound "Mark-12," which detonated with the same force as its predecessors, allowing bombers to greatly increase the destructive power of their bombloads.

While General LeMay was building SAC, the Soviet Union was rapidly expanding its own nuclear capabilities. As discussed in the preceding chapter, the Soviets exploded a thermonuclear device in 1953 and went on to develop long-range bombers to deliver their growing stockpile of weapons. With the advent of a Soviet nuclear threat, SAC's mission changed. Instead of destroying Soviet cities in retaliation for an attack on Western Europe or the United States, SAC bombers would strike the growing number of Soviet nuclear-weapons production and storage facilities, fuel storage sites and airfields from which a Soviet nuclear strike might be launched.

In 1965 Curtis LeMay published his perspective on U.S. postwar nuclear policy:

There was, definitely, a time when we could have destroyed all of Russia (I mean by that, all of Russia's capability to wage war) without losing a man to their defenses. . . .

This period extended from before the time when the Russians achieved The Bomb, until after they had The Bomb but didn't yet own a stockpile of weapons.

It would have been possible, I believe, for America to say to the Soviets, "Here's a blueprint for your immediate future. We'll give you a deadline of five or six months"—something like that—"to pull out of the satellite countries, and effect a complete change of conduct. You will behave your damn selves from this moment forth."

We could have done this. But whether we should have presented such a blueprint was not for me to decide. That was a decision of national policy.[11]

Of course, once the Soviets had developed their own stockpile of nuclear weapons and the means to deliver them, presenting them with "a blueprint for your immediate future" would have smacked of suicide.

In order to win World War II, national leaders were willing to use virtually all means at their disposal. The Hague Draft Rules limiting bombing were ignored, and Trenchard's prediction about bombing civilians came true. Long-range bombers enabled the escalation of violence from the first air raids on Rotterdam, Berlin and London to the ultimate destruction of Hiroshima and Nagasaki. By the end of the war, leaders had become so accustomed to indiscriminate mass violence that, according to Winston Churchill, the decision to drop atomic bombs "was never an issue." By 1945 it seemed reasonable to use one means of indiscriminate mass violence (the atomic bomb) to avert another (the invasion of Japan).

Some nuclear strategists assume that a future war involving nuclear weapons could be controlled or limited. Based on the World War II experience, we seriously doubt that leaders could adhere to self-imposed limitations if it meant keeping the level of violence below what in the heat of battle seemed advantageous to them.[12]

The next two chapters describe the evolution of the second and third legs of our "Strategic Triad"—land-based intercontinental ballistic missiles (ICBMs) and submarine-launched ballistic missiles (SLBMs). Both land- and sea-based missiles are armed with thermonuclear weapons and can reach their targets in minutes rather than the hours it takes bombers. Missiles greatly reduce the reaction time and decision time available to national leaders, making control of a future war even more questionable once hostilities are allowed to begin.

XIII

FROM V-ROCKETS TO INTERCONTINENTAL BALLISTIC MISSILES

From the beginning we wanted to go into space; wanted to go infinite distance; wanted unimaginable speeds. . . . [But] as so often before in the history of technology the necessity . . . forced a great invention to proceed by way of weapon development. Never would any private or public body have devoted hundreds of millions of marks for development of long range rockets for purely scientific purposes.

Walter Dornberger,
1952

A screaming comes across the sky. It has happened before, but there is nothing to compare it to now.

Thomas Pynchon,
Gravity's Rainbow,
1973

At noon on October 3, 1942, General Walter Dornberger of the German Army picked up his binoculars for a closer look at the sleek 46-foot-long rocket poised on its launch pad. Steam seethed from the rocket's liquid oxygen vents, and its lacquered aluminum skin gleamed in the sunlight. Reassured that the rocket was ready,

159

Dornberger looked up into the clear blue sky. It was a brilliant fall day over northern Germany.

Dornberger was commander of the top secret experimental rocket station at Peenemünde. The purpose of his work was to develop rockets powerful enough to carry a ton, or even tons, of high explosive for long distances. Once perfected, the rockets would be produced in great numbers to bombard allied cities such as London. This was among the most sensitive of Nazi projects.

Dornberger had been in charge of rocket research since 1932, when the German Army quietly absorbed into its organization a group of amateur inventors, mechanics and dreamers who called themselves the "Society for Space Travel." The Society was founded in 1927 by nine men and one woman in the parlor of a German tavern. By 1929 it counted 870 members, among them nineteen-year-old Wernher von Braun.[1]

The Society advanced aerodynamic designs and improved the performance of small rocket engines. In 1932 the German Army decided to subsidize the Society and hired its most outstanding members. For although the Treaty of Versailles had prohibited the development and deployment of tanks, artillery and airplanes, it had neglected to outlaw rockets. Hitler took full advantage of this omission to rebuild German military strength. He ordered Dornberger "to develop in military facilities a liquid fuel rocket, the range of which should surpass that of any existing gun and the production of which should be carried out by industry. Secrecy of the development is paramount." Dornberger immediately hired von Braun as a technical assistant; he had been impressed by the young man's "energy and shrewdness . . . and by his astonishing theoretical knowledge."[2]

Early rocket work was dangerous—experimental techniques were quite primitive, and several scientists and technicians died in explosions. Igniting a rocket engine involved no more than holding a small can of flaming gasoline at the end of a wooden pole. Dornberger himself was seriously injured when a rocket ignited as he was taking it apart with a hammer and chisel. A spark lit the rocket propellant, and thousands of tiny black-powder particles struck his face. Removing them involved a year of hospital visits, in which an orderly rubbed Dornberger's face with butter and then set to work with a pair of tweezers.

By 1939 rockets were advanced enough to require a long test range, preferably over water, so the Germans built a new rocket station on a remote island off the Baltic coast at the site called Peenemünde. Hundreds of millions of German marks were poured into the rocket project. Hitler had demanded that his scientists produce *"Wunderwaffen"*—wonder weapons—that would bring victory to Germany.

As of 1942, however, the results of the rocket project were still inconclusive. Two test launches had failed. Hitler was becoming uncertain about the military usefulness of these long-range weapons: He had doubts about their range, their accuracy and whether enough rockets could be produced in time to affect the outcome of the war.

The rocket poised at Peenemünde on October 3, 1942, represented one of Hitler's major hopes to change the course of the war. Dornberger believed that if this test failed, the missile project would likely be canceled. As launch time approached and the final countdown began, Dornberger and his top aides retreated to the safety of a concrete bunker to watch on closed-circuit television and through periscopes built into the roof.

A loudspeaker rumbled "X minus three"—three minutes to go. The final minutes before rocket ignition had become known as "Peenemünde minutes" because they seemed so long. Finally, at the moment of ignition, sparks shot from the rocket's nozzle. Then came "a jutting jet of reddish-yellow combustion gases." Seconds later, the 13.5-ton rocket lifted off its pad. It accelerated, according to Dornberger, to a speed "corresponding to that of a falling stone":

I kept my eyes glued to the binoculars . . . it was an unforgettable sight. In the full glare of the sunlight the rocket rose higher and higher. The flame darting from the stern was almost as long as the rocket itself. . . . The air was filled with a sound like rolling thunder. . . .[3]

One minute into the launch, Dornberger began to weep with joy. Then he and his assistants spontaneously "yelled and embraced each other like excited boys."

The rocket worked perfectly, remaining stable in flight and achieving a speed close to 3,500 miles per hour, an altitude of 340,000 feet and a range of 120 miles. Bags of bright-green dye broke on impact, marking its point of entry into the Baltic Sea. Dornberger estimated that the force of impact was equal to fifty railroad engines simultaneously hitting a wall at 60 miles per hour.[4] Hitler viewed films of the launch, which were accompanied by von Braun's forceful description of the weapon's destructive effects. Afterward, Hitler bestowed upon von Braun the honorary title of Professor. He said to Albert Speer, Minister of Armaments, "The [missile] is a measure that can decide the war. And what encouragement to the home front when we attack England with it!"[5]

Before this rocket could be perfected, the Germans had another weapon ready for use. At 4:00 A.M. on June 13, 1944, an observer in Kent, England, saw a miniature airplane passing overhead with orange flames trailing from its exhaust. The "miniature airplane" was a long-range missile. The Germans called these "V-weapons"—"V" for *Vergeltung* (retaliation)—and they were of two types. The first to be launched against Britain was the V-1, commonly called the "buzz bomb" because of its eerie and unmistakable noise. The V-1 was a pilotless aircraft with a wingspan of 17 feet, which flew at speeds up to 400 miles per hour and had an average range of 150 miles. It carried a 2,200-pound high explosive warhead. The V-1 was powered by a small jet engine fueled by gasoline. Because jet engines, unlike rockets, are "air-breathing"—they require oxygen for combustion—the V-1 operated at relatively low altitudes of 2,000–3,000 feet.

In the 24-hour period following June 15, 244 V-1s were launched from the coast of France, 144 of which crossed the English Channel. Of these, seventy-seven dropped directly on London, inflicting many casualties. In the weeks that followed, daring Royal Air Force pilots, flying Spitfires stripped down for speed, flew alongside the V-1s making wing-to-wing contact to flip the missiles over and out of control. After weeks of practice British pilots and antiaircraft gunners were shooting down or deflecting more than 70 percent of the V-1s.

On September 8, 1944, the Germans began to bombard London and Antwerp, Belgium (a port supplying the D-Day invasion), with a second "retaliation weapon." The V-2 was a true rocket, a fully developed version of the missile tested by General Dornberger and Wernher von Braun at Peenemünde two years earlier. The V-2 carried a one-ton explosive warhead at speeds up to 4,000 miles per hour. Its propellants were liquid oxygen and a mixture of 75 percent ethyl alcohol and 25 percent water. The alcohol was derived from fermented potatoes—and was often pilfered for drinking by rocket technicians at Peenemünde and by firing units in the field. The V-2's guidance system consisted of gyroscopes, accelerometers, and a crude computer to monitor and maintain the rocket's trajectory; these instruments furnished data to position heat-resistant jet vanes that steered the rocket by deflecting its exhaust.

Since the rocket carried its own oxygen, it could fly at high altitudes, even above the earth's atmosphere; Dornberger and von Braun envisioned the V-2's eventual development into a vehicle for space exploration. Because it flew so high—over 60 miles up—and so fast—one mile per second—the weapon struck without warning; there was no defense against it. One U.S. airman stationed in London said, "At least you could hear the V-1 coming. The first you knew of the V-2 was when part of a city block disappeared." Like nighttime strategic bombing, the German V-weapons hit indiscriminately.

Despite the casualties and costly damage caused by the V-1s and V-2s, these weapons were not decisive. Had the missiles been developed earlier, they might have changed the course of the war, but by the time they were ready for use—a week after the Allied invasion of Normandy—their effect was limited.

While the V-1 and V-2 assaults were too little and too late, they caused enough casualties and damage to convince the Allies that long-range rockets would play a major role in future conflicts. Anticipating their postwar antagonism, the United States and the Soviet Union were both concerned that their respective scientists and engineers not lag behind in rocket development. As the war in Europe drew to a close, various operations were organized to capture German rockets, rocket plans and blueprints and key German scientists.

In April 1945, as the Allied armies advanced into Germany, Wernher von Braun, General Dornberger and other Peenemünde veterans concealed themselves in a country inn. They had decided to surrender to the Americans rather than be taken prisoner by the Russians, and in fact, they did manage to locate and surrender to an American patrol before the Russians found them. U.S. forces also captured 14 tons of blueprints and plans that the German rocket scientists had hidden in a mineshaft. These included 3,500 reports and 510,000 engineering drawings for the V-2 and more advanced rockets.

U.S. troops also located and captured a secret underground V-2 production facility located at Nordhausen, in what was to be the Soviet zone of occupation. Rather than hand the missiles over to the Soviets, the U.S. commanding officer, Colonel Holger Toftoy— acting against orders—directed his men to take enough missile components to assemble 100 V-2s. Toftoy's troops commandeered 360 German railroad cars; the missiles and spare parts were taken to Antwerp, then quickly transferred to sixteen ships bound for the United States. Colonel Toftoy was neither court-martialed nor reprimanded for his initiative.[6]

The Soviets also practiced wartime confiscation with determination. They commandeered scientists, technicians and skilled workers to help rebuild their war-torn country. Advancing into Poland and eastern Germany, they dismantled entire factories and shipped them back to be reassembled in the Soviet Union. Soviet radio broadcasts appealed to Peenemünde workers in particular to visit one Dr. de Pinsky in Dresden, who was organizing a new rocket project. They promised excellent pay and working conditions, and offered Wernher von Braun 50,000 marks, in bonus money, hoping to lure him over from the Americans.[7]

Von Braun did not take the bait, and several weeks later he and other members of the Peenemünde group traveled to Fort Bliss, Texas, where they were put to work developing rockets for the U.S. Army. It was a small-scale project compared to Peenemünde, and the Germans were not always well received: The commanding general at Fort Bliss was a combat soldier who had been wounded by the Germans in both World Wars.

The U.S. project to exploit the knowledge of German scientists was called "Operation Paperclip." It was meant to be temporary, but some of the 350 Germans brought to the United States, 100 of whom were rocket specialists, chose to stay in America after the Japanese surrender. They had been screened to eliminate war criminals and otherwise ardent Nazis, but because anti-German sentiment ran so high, their presence in the United States was not publicized for several months. Their wives and children were permitted to join them after one year.[8]

From 1946 to 1950 von Braun's team worked at Fort Bliss and at the nearby White Sands Proving Ground in New Mexico, which encompasses Alamogordo. During these years U.S. Army scientists and technicians fired sixty-four captured V-2s to gain experience handling and launching large rockets. One V-2 flew in the wrong direction and crashed in Mexico, provoking an international incident. Von Braun's team also contributed to the design of a rocket being developed by private industry for the U.S. Air Force. To be called "Manhattan" (after the World War II project) because it would carry a nuclear warhead, this rocket was the forerunner of the first U.S. intercontinental ballistic missile, or ICBM. (The term "ballistic" refers to the fact that once boosted outside of the earth's atmosphere, the missile is guided back to earth by gravity only.)

Rocket research in the United States slowed considerably in the early 1950s, but perked up slightly in 1954 after a panel chaired by Princeton mathematician Dr. John von Neumann reported to President Eisenhower on the feasibility of reducing the size and weight of nuclear weapons so that they could be launched from

ICBMs. Tests that confirmed the panel's findings stepped up work on a large, liquid-fueled Atlas rocket.

Placing nuclear warheads on unmanned, supersonic ICBMs had a profound impact on military strategy. The full implications of this development for the nuclear arms race between the United States and the Soviet Union, however, could not have been foreseen at the time. This theme is further developed in Chapters XVIII and XIX.

The Soviets also exploited German technology and resources, and Soviet postwar rocket development closely paralleled that of the United States. Helmut Grottrup, a chief scientist at Peenemünde, was one who chose to stay in Soviet-occupied Germany to work for the Soviets. According to his wife, there was no issue of ideology involved; Grottrup simply did not like the terms of the U.S. offer, particularly the fact that he would initially be separated from his family. Grottrup reconstructed the V-2 production facility, "stretching" the V-2 nine feet in length and increasing its thrust significantly; this first "Soviet" rocket was designated K1—it had twice the range of the V-2.

On October 21, 1946, Grottrup and his top assistants were invited by a Soviet general to a party held in the Soviet-occupied zone of Germany. The festivities lasted until 4:00 A.M., with caviar, good meats (a rare treat) and plenty of vodka. Afterward, the Soviets loaded the protesting Grottrup, with other rocket specialists and their families, onto railroad passenger cars bound for the Soviet Union. Grottrup learned later that his rocket experts were only a few of five to six thousand skilled Germans transported. All together, including families, 20,000 people were carried east into Russia. Grottrup complained often about living and working conditions in the Soviet Union, but his protests were ignored.[9]

From 1947 to 1952, German scientists designed a variety of rockets for the Soviets, including the "R14," which could carry a 6,600-pound warhead 1,800 miles, and an antiaircraft rocket. Grottrup was asked to design an "antimissile" missile, but protested that this was beyond even German technology. As the years passed, young Soviet engineers began assuming more and more of the work. Although these Germans despaired of ever returning home, Grottrup and several other rocket specialists, along with thousands of German technicians in other fields, were at last permitted to leave late in 1953, after Stalin died.[10]

Nikita Khrushchev and other top Soviet leaders were briefed on Soviet rocket development after Stalin's death by chief engineer Sergei Korolev. It seems that Khrushchev felt much as Harry Truman had when he first learned about the Manhattan Project:

. . . I don't want to exaggerate, but I'd say we gawked at what he showed us as if we were sheep seeing a new gate for the first time. When he showed us one of his rockets, we thought it looked like nothing but a huge, cigar-shaped tube, and we didn't believe it would fly. Korolev took us on a tour of the launching pad and tried to explain to us how a rocket worked. We were like peasants in a marketplace. . . . We had absolute confidence in Comrade Korolev. When he expounded his ideas, you could see passion burning in his eyes, and his reports were models of clarity. He had unlimited energy and determination, and he was a brilliant organizer.[11]

The first of Korolev's rockets exploded on ignition in the late spring of 1957. There were other failures, but then two successful launches, and Moscow announced to the world on August 27, 1957, that the Soviets had developed the first intercontinental ballistic missile. That meant it could be launched from the Soviet Union and hit the United States. Strangely, the threat posed by the new missile would not hit home until the Soviets used the rocket for a spectacular achievement in space. This will be described in Chapter XV, "Sputnik."

XIV

FROM U-BOATS TO NUCLEAR SUBMARINES

. . . The nuclear power plant is a fundamentally new means of submarine propulsion which will probably make a profound impression on submarine design and the whole art of waging undersea warfare. The advent of the true submarine, capable of unrestricted operations in a medium which covers 5/7ths of the globe, may revolutionize the entire character of naval warfare.

Report to the U.S. Chief of Naval Operations,
June 7, 1949

In World Wars I and II the Germans called submarines *Unterseeboote*, or "U-boats." At first, U-boats were considered barbaric because they refused to surface and "fight honorably" like destroyers, cruisers and battleships. Their stealth was contemptible to the sailors of the early twentieth century. Sailors' aversion to serving aboard submarines also derived from their miserable living conditions. Unlike clean, ventilated, "shipshape" surface vessels, submarines were grimy, humid and cramped. Their engines generated oppressive heat and the air stank of diesel fuel, battery acid, moldy food and body odors. Lights burned continuously, blurring the distinction between day and night.

And yet submarines were romanticized, in part because they

were so dramatically effective—because of their ability to sub-merge and silently stalk their prey, U-boats sank nearly eight thousand war and merchant ships in World Wars I and II. These sleek vessels often operated in teams called "wolf packs"; their most successful commanders frequently became national heroes. Other nations developed submarines, but for years Germany led the world in undersea warfare.[1]

Fortunately for surface ships and their crews, submarines did have their limitations. A major constraint was the need for two separate propulsion systems. Diesel engines that required air for combustion were used for their surface operations, and battery-driven electric motors powered them underwater. Not only did the electric motors drive these submarines at very slow speeds, but extended submersions were impossible because they had to surface often to recharge their batteries with the diesel engines and to get fresh air for their crews.

Also, after 1941, the Allies began to use sonar ("*sound navi-gation ranging*") to detect the presence and location of submarines. Transmitters mounted on the bottom of a surface ship sent out high-frequency sound impulses or "pings" that bounced back when they struck a submerged object. The echoes were picked up by a receiver that was monitored by a sonar operator wearing head-phones. The pings indicated the direction or bearing of a target; the time that elapsed between their transmission and reception indicated its range or distance. A change in the pitch of an echo told whether the submarine was approaching or moving away. The men in submerged U-boats could hear the pings through the hull and know they were being hunted.

Sonar and improved antisubmarine tactics caused naval experts to speculate whether submarines had become obsolete. After Hiroshima and Nagasaki, many naval leaders also wondered whether surface warships had become outdated as well. What defense could battleships, cruisers and destroyers muster against the atomic bomb? Would "push-button warfare"—which had been initiated with the V-1 and V-2 rockets—eclipse the roles of ships and other conventional weaponry?

The U.S. Navy, led by Admiral Chester W. Nimitz, a veteran submariner, had to assess these questions. Nimitz knew the limitations of submarines. If submarines were not to be easy prey, they must be able to operate submerged at high speeds for longer periods of time. Nimitz was intrigued by the idea of propelling submarines with atomic reactors. A nuclear chain reaction, requiring only a small amount of fuel and no oxygen at all, just might be the ideal source of power for future submarines.

The Navy had been the first U.S. government agency to express interest in nuclear power. After the results of the Hahn-Strassmann experiment were publicized in 1939, the Naval Research Laboratory had requested and received $1,500 to study the applications of nuclear fission to naval propulsion. The project was shelved after Pearl Harbor; the military's World War II interest in fission focused on weapons, not propulsion, and the Army's Manhattan Project took control of all available supplies of uranium for the first atomic bombs. After the war, however, the Navy pressed hard to participate in atomic research. Nimitz convinced General Groves that ". . . the most attractive use for atomic power was the military one of submarine propulsion."[2]

But the Navy had little experience with nuclear energy and needed to catch up. One of the few knowledgeable naval officers was Captain Albert Mumma, a former member of the Alsos mission. Training for the mission and tracking down members of the German

Uranium Society had given him a working understanding of nuclear technology, and he enthusiastically backed a proposal to send several naval officers to the nuclear facility at Oak Ridge, Tennessee. Selected to head the Navy's nuclear training team was a most unusual man, an engineer named Hyman G. Rickover.

Captain Rickover was born in 1900 in a small village in Poland. His father was a tailor who, fleeing religious persecution and economic hardship, emigrated to the United States with his family in 1906. They eventually settled in Chicago. During high school, Rickover delivered messages on his bicycle for Western Union, stopping frequently at the office of Chicago Congressman Adolph J. Sabath. Impressed by Rickover's industriousness and intelligence, Sabath nominated his young friend to the U.S. Naval Academy at Annapolis, Maryland. Rickover studied hard for, and passed, tough Naval Academy entrance exams. Four years later he graduated and embarked upon an extraordinarily long, influential and controversial naval career.

Rickover was exacting, demanding much of himself and others. He was often impatient and occasionally abusive. As a rule he shunned social activities. Once, ordered to attend a reception hosted by an admiral, Rickover motored to the ship, climbed the gangway on one side, paid his respects and promptly descended the gangway on the other side, returning via motorboat to his own ship for an evening of reading.[3]

Although Rickover was not the unanimous choice of officers to head the Navy's Oak Ridge team, senior officers were willing to excuse his difficult personal style because he got results. Rickover was convinced that nuclear power would revolutionize naval warfare, and he set about his new responsibilities with canny intensity.

Rickover was rigorous and persistent in addressing the technical problems that faced the Navy reactor team. He and his subordinates ferreted out any and all scientists and engineers whose knowledge and skills might prove an asset to their project. His team took copious notes and wrote detailed reports of every meeting, lecture and conversation at Oak Ridge. They boiled down massive amounts of information and identified three major problems.

The first dealt with heat transfer. Unlike a nuclear weapon, the reactor would be designed to produce heat rather than to explode uncontrollably. Heat would produce steam to provide the submarine with electricity and to turn its propellers, in much the same way that coal and oil had fueled conventional ships since Robert Fulton's day. Many substances might have been used to transfer heat from the nuclear reactor to produce steam, but Rickover narrowed the possibilities down to water and liquid sodium.

The second problem dealt with shielding. Rickover realized that crews quartered in the cramped space of a submarine would have to be protected from intense radiation. He accepted the possibility that even very low radiation levels might have long-term effects on human beings, and he insisted upon a reexamination of the standards for radiation protection that were being followed by the Manhattan Project.

The third problem involved the question of what material should be used for the reactor itself. Aluminum was the choice of many engineers because it was light; some were concerned that a reactor and its shielding would be so heavy as to sink rather than power a submarine. Rickover favored the rare element zirconium because it combined the virtues of light weight and a low rate of neutron absorption; this last factor would optimize the efficiency of the chain reaction, conserving uranium fuel. Zirconium was extremely expensive, but Rickover correctly anticipated that its price would drop to affordable levels once it was in commercial production.[4]

Rickover insisted on extensive tests of all theories and engineering concepts before they were incorporated into the first submarine reactor. A full-scale test reactor and steam plant were built in the desert of eastern Idaho for this purpose. The findings were incorporated into the actual submarine reactor, constructed at the Electric Boat Company shipyard in Groton, Connecticut. Rickover also built a full-scale wood-and-cardboard model of the first nuclear submarine, convinced that it would provide information that even experienced shipbuilders could not glean from drawings or quarter-scale models.[5]

The two figures on the next page illustrate the reactor and the propulsion plant that Rickover's group eventually designed. (Submarine reactors are smaller but similar in design to nuclear power plants designed to generate electricity.)

By the middle of March 1953 the test reactor was ready to go. Rickover was present at the Idaho site when the control rods were slowly withdrawn from the U-235 fuel elements. Several times something went wrong and the reactor automatically shut down. After considerable trouble-shooting the reactor was considered "debugged," and Rickover decided to test it rigorously with a 100-hour continuous run at full power. Rickover overruled objections that such a lengthy test was too dangerous. He posted a chart of the North Atlantic in the reactor control room, and at the end of each four-hour watch the crew marked the position of the "ship." After the test, observers calculated that the "ship" could have sailed submerged from the United States to Ireland.

The reactor was soon mounted in the first nuclear submarine, the *Nautilus*, named after Robert Fulton's experimental undersea craft of 1801 and the imaginative creation of Jules Verne in his classic novel *20,000 Leagues Under the Sea*, published in 1870.

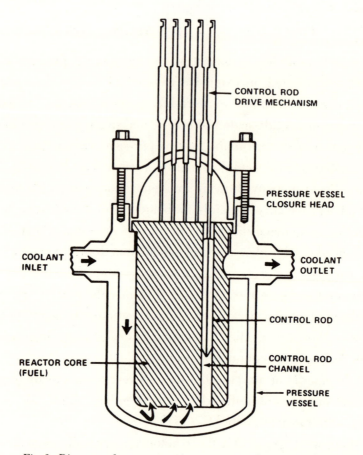

Fig. 1: Diagram of a reactor using pressurized water as the coolant.

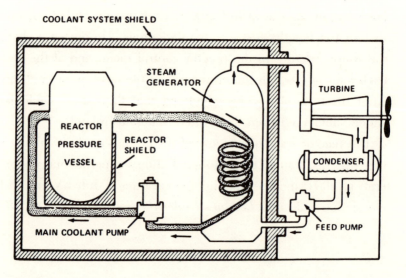

Fig. 2: Nuclear reactor and steam propulsion plant. Relative sizes are not indicated because the exact specifications are classified.

Inside the new *Nautilus* was a large mess hall that doubled as a classroom and movie theater. The ship was fully air-conditioned, and a carbon monoxide "scrubber" removed harmful gases from the atmosphere. Oxygen for the crew was obtained by the electrolysis of seawater, using electricity produced from the heat of the reactor. The *Nautilus* had ice-cream and Coke machines, and a nickel-a-play jukebox connected to a built-in sound system. If such luxury, accentuated by bright interior colors, seemed very strange to veteran submariners, one can only imagine what the old U-boat captains and crews would have made of it all.[6]

Rickover chose Eugene P. Wilkinson to command the *Nautilus.* Senior admirals in the Navy had other nominees, but Rickover prevailed as usual. Commander Wilkinson was not a Naval Academy graduate. He had graduated from the University of Southern California and taught high school mathematics and chemistry before entering the Navy. Rickover also insisted on selecting every crew member, although Navy personnel officers fumed that this was meddling in their business. Rickover personally interviewed and approved or disapproved everyone. In later years he pressed his authority further and selected the captains and crews of other nuclear submarines as well, accepting only those he judged competent to master the intricacies of nuclear technology.

In many of his interviews, Rickover posed a fictitious situation from which the submarine candidate was to extricate himself. For example, unwitting hopefuls were told to imagine that they were on a sinking boat with five other men. "The conditions are that one and only one of you can be saved. Are you resourceful enough to talk the other five into letting you be the one?" If the candidate answered yes, Rickover would call five staff members in and order the candidate to "start talking."[7]

On the morning of January 17, 1955, the *Nautilus* dropped her mooring lines and, with Wilkinson and Rickover on the bridge, pulled slowly away from the dock. As the ship cleared the break-water leading into Long Island Sound, the signalman blinked, "Underway on nuclear power." During this first sea trial, the *Nautilus* was confined to surface runs. Heavy seas rolled the submarine violently, and many of the crew were seasick, but the ship and its propulsion unit performed flawlessly. Underwater tests a few days later were more comfortable. Wilkinson reported that the results of the tests "indicate that a complete re-evaluation of submarine and antisubmarine strategy will be required. Its ultimate impact on Navy warfare should not be underestimated."[8]

Wilkinson's assessment was not overstated. In later sea trials the *Nautilus* utterly outperformed the surface ships and diesel submarines of the U.S. Atlantic Fleet. Because the *Nautilus* did not have to surface, it was nearly immune to air attack. With its high submerged speed, it could overtake a surface force and, under certain conditions, could even evade torpedo attacks.

In April 1955 the *Nautilus* cruised submerged from New London, Connecticut, to San Juan, Puerto Rico, covering 1,300 miles in 84 hours. Later it improved upon this performance, sailing from Key West, Florida, to New London at an average speed of over 20 knots, over a distance of 1,396 miles—more than ten times the distance any diesel submarine had ever traveled while submerged. Still later the *Nautilus* sailed under the Arctic ice pack, eventually reaching the North Pole. President Eisenhower awarded medals to the crew and said, "This points the way for further exploration and possible use of this route by nuclear-powered cargo submarines as a commercial seaway between the major oceans of the world."[9]

The president spoke of peaceful uses for nuclear submarines in the same manner as others had emphasized the peaceful uses of airplanes and missiles. But the impressive performance of the *Nautilus* inspired military planners to perfect it as a war machine. In June 1955, two powerful members of the congressional Joint Committee on Atomic Energy expressed regret that the *Nautilus*— the world's most advanced naval ship—was armed merely with conventional torpedoes, which had not changed much in design since World War I. Representative Melvin Price of Illinois called for nuclear submarines to carry missiles armed with nuclear warheads. In response, the secretary of the navy proposed to include a nuclear-powered guided-missile submarine in the next shipbuilding program. There were also proposals for nuclear-powered surface ships and a nuclear-powered airplane.

Building nuclear submarines that could launch missiles was attractive to the Navy—a submerged submarine would be less vulnerable to enemy attack and would provide a more stable launching platform than a surface ship. It would be necessary, however, to design smaller missiles to fit inside the hull and to use solid-fuel propellants, since volatile liquid fuels were too dangerous to carry inside an enclosed vessel. These considerations led to the development of the solid-fuel Polaris missile, 28 feet high, 60 inches in diameter and 15 tons in weight, with a range of 1,650 miles. Its development was assisted by Edward Teller, who had speculated about developing lighter nuclear warheads for the Polaris in 1956, and by the AEC's weapons laboratory, which had confirmed that a 600-pound nuclear warhead with a yield similar to one then weighing 1,600 pounds could indeed be developed.[10]

The Navy built a fleet of nuclear-powered submarines to carry and fire Polaris missiles. These were the most powerful and potentially destructive warships ever conceived. Each submarine carried sixteen missiles. Each missile was armed with a 200-kiloton warhead capable of ten times the destructive force of the Hiroshima and Nagasaki bombs. By the early 1960s, Polaris submarines had joined long-range bombers and ICBMs as the third leg of the U.S. strategic triad.

XV

SPUTNIK

Late on Friday, October 4, Soviet rocket experts announced man's greatest technological achievement since the atomic bomb flashed over the American desert.

Newsweek,
October 14, 1957

On Saturday, October 5, 1957, people all over the world were startled by banner headlines and radio and television reports announcing that the Soviet Union had launched a man-made satellite into space. The object in orbit was 22 inches in diameter and weighed 184 pounds. Named *Sputnik* (Russian for "traveler"), it circled the earth at altitudes of up to 560 miles, and traveled at a speed of 18,000 miles per hour—five miles per second. Dr. I. M. Levitt, Director of the Fels Planetarium in Philadelphia, conjectured that *Sputnik* might remain in orbit for "thousands to a million years."

The London *Daily Express* reported: The Space Age Is Here.

The London *Daily Mail* announced: Russia Launches A Moon.

Sputnik carried two transmitters that sent continuous signals to earth, and in Paris, radio listeners heard a recording of the satellite's "beep" as monitored by the Paris Observatory. Radio Moscow, which initially broke the news, listed an impressive schedule of satellite appearances over such cities as Oslo, Prague,

Rangoon, Bombay, Damascus, Manchester, Detroit, Washington, Paris, and Rome. According to William J. Jordan, an American correspondent in Moscow,

Soviet citizens made no secret of their pride in the accomplishment of their engineers and specialists. It was not so much that they had performed a wonderful scientific feat that impressed the people as that they had beaten the United States in the race to put the first earth satellite into the sky.[1]

Night after night, people around the world scanned the skies for *Sputnik*, just faintly visible to the naked eye. Amateur satellite watchers brought out binoculars and small telescopes, and radio hams with shortwave receivers tuned in to the satellite's regular beep.

Some people simply refused to believe that a man-made satellite was circling the earth. Others, who did believe it, wondered how the satellite could "stay up there" in apparent defiance of gravity. Even those who understood the scientific principles involved were surprised that the Soviet Union could accomplish such a feat.

Scientists explained that *Sputnik*'s orbit depended upon a delicate balance of its velocity, its trajectory, and the earth's reduced gravitational pull at *Sputnik*'s orbital altitude. *Newsweek* printed a simple science lesson for puzzled readers: A basic law of physics is that every object "continues in motion at constant velocity in a straight line unless acted upon by some external force. The external force that keeps *Sputnik* orbiting—rather than heading in a straight line—is gravity. Three other forces will eventually slow *Sputnik* so it can no longer offset gravity: the faint density of air in its orbit, the drag of an electrical charge, and collisions with meteors. Estimates of the life expectancy of the Russian moon now range from six days to more than a year." (*Sputnik* actually fell to earth exactly three months from the date of its launch.)

Sputnik had been propelled into orbit by a three-stage rocket of enormous thrust. Stage I had accelerated to 4,000 miles per hour before detaching, Stage II to 10,000 miles per hour, and Stage III to 18,000 miles per hour—just fast enough to counteract the force of gravity. Short of that speed the satellite would fall back to earth. Speeds up to 25,000 miles per hour would have enlarged *Sputnik*'s orbit, but speeds over 25,000 mph would have given the satellite "escape velocity," breaking it out of its orbit and into space.[2]

The fact that a Soviet satellite was passing overhead every 96 minutes provoked more than scientific inquiries. Almost immediately, partisan political charges began to fly through Congress. On Sunday, October 6, *The New York Times* reported:

Democratic Senators blamed the Eisenhower Administration's economy program today for the Soviet triumph in launching the first earth satellite.

Senators Stuart Symington of Missouri and Henry M. Jackson of Washington said that the development was further evidence of Soviet superiority in the long-range missiles field. Senator Jackson stated that the launching of the world's first artificial satellite by the Soviet Union "is a devastating blow to the United States' scientific, industrial and technical prestige in the world."

At first, the White House insisted that the launch "did not come as a surprise." News correspondents reported that upon hearing about *Sputnik*, President Eisenhower went out to play golf with George Allen, a neighbor of his Gettysburg, Pennsylvania, farm. Presidential Press Secretary James Hagerty downplayed the fact that the Soviets were the first to put a man-made sphere into space: "We never thought of our program as one which was in a race with the Soviets."

Then President Eisenhower, perhaps under media pressure, made the unfortunate suggestion that the Russians were first in space because they had "captured all those German scientists at Peenemünde." And soon it was circulating that the "bitterest man in the entire U.S. rocket program was Dr. Wernher von Braun, brilliant chief of the German V-2 program and now research head of the Army's Redstone Arsenal" (the center for U.S. ballistic-missile development). "As the Russian *Sputnik* went up . . . von Braun was promptly ordered not to make public comments, but it was no secret that his missile team, already repeatedly rebuffed on their ballistic missile project, was deeply distressed."[3]

U.S. officials were much more distressed about the rocket that launched *Sputnik* than about the satellite itself, which posed no direct threat to the United States. *Sputnik* required a fully developed ICBM to lift and accelerate it into space. And such an ICBM might also be able to carry a nuclear warhead into the upper atmosphere and deliver it to targets in the United States. The military implications were not lost on the U.S. Congress. Senator Lyndon Johnson, then Senate Majority Leader, reacted as follows:

The Roman Empire controlled the world because it could build roads. Later—when moved to sea—the British Empire was dominant because it had ships. In the air age, we were powerful because we had airplanes. Now the Communists have established a foothold in outer space.[4]

Johnson feared that control of the "high ground" of space would permit control of the world. Edward Teller shared this concern, claiming that if the Russians "pass us in technology, there is very little doubt who will determine the future of the world." By falling behind, he added, the United States had lost "a battle more important and greater than Pearl Harbor." Once, asked what might be found on the moon, he replied, "Russians."[5]

The media reported that "many [members of Congress] felt that investigation by the Senate would show the need for a missile czar who would have almost unlimited power, merge rival programs, control [military] service bickering and toss economy directives into the Pentagon wastebasket." Some members of Congress said that the missile czar would have to be "at least as dedicated as was General Leslie R. Groves." Senator Jackson asserted that the country needed an "Admiral Rickover of ballistic missiles." "The question," he said, "is not whether or not we are losing the race for the ICBM. We are losing it. The problem is not how to stay ahead. It is how to catch up." The alleged technological disparity between the United States and the Soviet Union became known as the "missile gap."

Soviet Premier Nikita Khrushchev exacerbated matters by boasting to a touring member of the British Parliament, "We have even more [than the ICBM] up our sleeves. . . . The age of the bomber is over. . . . The Soviet Union no longer is a peasant country."[6]

Just one month after the launch of *Sputnik I*, the Soviets announced that a second satellite was orbiting the earth. *Sputnik II* weighed 1,120 pounds (about the same as a Volkswagen "beetle") and carried a passenger, a small dog named Laika. Covered with electrodes measuring blood pressure, heartbeat and body temperature, Laika had been sent up to collect data on the effects of weightlessness on a mammal's circulatory, respiratory and digestive systems and to register the effects of cosmic rays above the earth's atmosphere. Some people called the new Soviet satellite

"Muttnik," and the American Society for the Prevention of Cruelty to Animals led groups all over the world to protest sending a dog into space. The Soviets suggested that the dog would be returned to earth unharmed, but after ten days Laika died from lack of oxygen.

On December 6, 1957, the United States tested its first Vanguard space vehicle, which carried a 3.5-pound satellite. The rocket rose several meters and stalled, then fell back onto its launch pad and exploded. This spectacular failure was televised, and coming as it did after two successful *Sputniks*, the worldwide publicity increased U.S. embarrassment. The foreign press had a field day: Vanguard was referred to as "flopnik," "kaputnik," and "stay-put-nik." More seriously, fear spread in the United States like wildfire: Did America now lie at the mercy of the Russian military, unable to protect itself and unable to maintain its prestige abroad? Wernher von Braun, feeling fully assimilated to American culture, commented on the effects of the *Sputnik* success and the Vanguard disaster:

> *The reaction to these events has been profound. They triggered a period of self-appraisal rarely equalled in modern times. Overnight it became popular to question the bulwarks of our society; our public educational system, our industrial strength, international policy, defense strategy and forces, the capability of our science and technology. Even the moral fiber of our people came under searching examination.*[7]

The London *Times* spoke of "the demon of inferiority which, since October 4, 1957 . . . has disturbed American well-being."

President Eisenhower stepped in quickly to reassure the public in this crisis of confidence. One of his first acts was to appoint a science advisor who would report to the president directly. The first Special Assistant to the President for Science and Technology was Dr. James R. Killian, President of the Massachusetts Institute of Technology, and he was granted "full access to all plans, programs, and activities involving science and technology in the government, including the Department of Defense, AEC, and CIA."[8]

Killian was a quiet, careful and deliberate man who placed little stock in any characterization of America as scientifically, industrially or militarily inferior. He was concerned about the military implications of *Sputnik*, about the Soviets' ability to keep their missile development secret, and about the near-hysteria *Sputnik* had generated in the United States, but he thought that the Russian achievement should be viewed in the context of the "lessons of the Manhattan Project." He wrote in his memoir, *Sputnik, Scientists and Eisenhower*:

The lesson of the atomic bomb, if we had the wit to learn it, was that any major industrial nation—and Russia, whatever its weaknesses, had become by mid-century a major industrial power—was capable of almost any engineering accomplishment that it considered necessary for national survival. It possessed in its manpower and in its industrial base the power to achieve almost any single goal it set, provided only that it was willing to concentrate its energies and resources on that goal.

Two years before becoming the president's science advisor, Killian had served on a special Technological Capabilities Panel of the National Security Council to evaluate the vulnerability of the United States to Soviet nuclear attack. Formed in 1954, the panel specifically addressed concerns that the U.S. bomber force had become inadequate to deter the Soviets from launching a Pearl

Harbor-type surprise attack using nuclear weapons. Pentagon studies had warned that if the Soviets felt reasonably sure that they could wipe out U.S. nuclear forces and suffer little or no retaliation, they might well consider a surprise "first strike." Military studies stressed that being able to strike back effectively would reduce any Soviet inclination to strike first.

On February 14, 1955, President Eisenhower received the panel's top-secret report, entitled "Meeting the Threat of Surprise Attack." Known as the "Killian Report," it declared that Soviet thermonuclear weapons posed a threat of terrible dimensions, and urged that the United States set for itself several objectives—among them, to increase "our capacity to get more positive intelligence about the enemy's intentions and capabilities and thus to obtain, before it was launched, adequate foreknowledge of a planned surprise attack" and to increase "still further through innovation and technology, our retaliatory power as a deterrent to surprise attack and to ensure against defeat if deterrence fails."[9]

The report specifically recommended that the Air Force develop an ICBM in "a nationally supported effort of highest priority." Also, intermediate-range (1,500-mile) ballistic missiles (IRBMs) should be developed, with consideration given to both land and ship basing. Since the IRBM's shorter range posed fewer technical problems for propulsion and guidance systems, they could be produced sooner than the ICBM. Eisenhower fully supported these recommendations, and work began on Thor and Jupiter IRBMs and on the submarine-based Polaris missile. Thors and Jupiters would be based on the territory of those NATO allies that would accept them: Britain, Italy and Turkey eventually did; France, Denmark, Greece, West Germany and Norway did not.

The report also suggested that SAC bombers be dispersed around the country or remain airborne to avoid the possibility that they could all be destroyed in a surprise attack. With regard to intelligence, "We must find ways to increase the number of hard facts upon which our intelligence estimates are based," not only to minimize the risk of surprise attack, but also "to reduce the danger of gross overestimation or gross underestimation of the threat," and to "help resolve with hard facts the contending views and fantasies that inevitably appear in our democratic process." The panel also linked reliable intelligence to arms limitation, in that intelligence could provide information about Soviet capabilities and verify whether the provisions of agreements were being honored.[10]

When *Sputniks I* and *II* went up in 1957, the public knew nothing of the Killian Report or of any actions taken in response to its recommendations; public anxiety was in part a function of public ignorance. In fact, by 1957 the SAC bomber force could have dealt a devastating blow to Soviet cities and military facilities; Soviet ICBM development was not advanced enough to prevent General Curtis LeMay's bombers from reducing the Soviet Union to a "smoking, radiating ruin."[11]

But what the public was told about U.S. capabilities during the weeks after *Sputnik* only increased the nation's anxiety. Secret reports from another defense advisory group, the Gaither panel, were leaked to *The Washington Post*, which ran a sensationalized synopsis:

The still-top-secret Gaither Report portrays a United States in the gravest danger in its history.

It pictures the Nation moving in frightening course to the status of a second-class power.

It shows an America exposed to an almost immediate threat from the missile-bristling Soviet Union. . . .

Many of those who worked on the report, prominent figures in the nation's business, financial, scientific, and educational communities were appalled, even frightened, at what they discovered to be the state of the American military posture in comparison with that of the Soviet Union.[12]

A week after the article appeared, Killian assured Eisenhower that "technically our missile development is proceeding in a satisfactory manner. Although it is probably true that we are at present behind the Soviets, we are in this position largely because we started much later and not because of inferior technology." Despite Killian's mild assurances, the most significant impact of *Sputnik*—its acceleration of the arms race in general and of a missile race in particular—was reflected in his further comments to Eisenhower:

At present the development programs of the IRBM are moving ahead very rapidly. There have been flights of both the Jupiter and the Thor which were complete technical successes. The regular production of IRBMs is soon to begin. In the immediate future a report will be prepared on Polaris, the ship-based IRBM. In the development of the ICBM the progress is also good and the recent successful flight tests of the Atlas gives confidence in the future of this missile. Another more advanced ICBM, the Titan, is reaching the stage where initial flight testing will begin in 1958.[13]

By 1959 U.S. missile-development programs were proceeding at full tilt. But *Sputnik* also stimulated other developments: The National Aeronautics and Space Administration (NASA) was established in 1958 as a civilian agency to manage the U.S. space program; National Science Foundation programs for research and science education were increased in one year from $50 million to $136 million; and Congress passed the National Defense Education Act, providing federal funds to schools and colleges for science education programs.

Public confidence was in some degree restored. President Eisenhower was able to avoid the extremely high defense-spending levels recommended by the military services and by such advisory groups as the Gaither panel. Soon, however, the nation was shaken again by an event involving the Soviet Union. This event, coincidentally, involved an aircraft the development of which had been secretly recommended five years earlier by the Killian Report.

XVI

THE U-2 AFFAIR

The State Department said today that an American plane may have drifted across the Russian border last Sunday as a result of the pilot becoming unconscious from lack of oxygen.

From the wires of *United Press International*,
May 5, 1960

Obviously we had to have accurate intelligence.

Dwight D. Eisenhower,
from his memoirs, *Waging Peace: The White House Years*,
1965

In response to the Killian Report's recommendation to improve intelligence gathering, plans were developed to design reconnaissance satellites and an airplane specially equipped for spying. The plane would be a long-range, jet-powered glider that could fly at record-breaking altitudes—too high either to be hit by antiaircraft guns on the ground or shot down by fighter aircraft. Designated the "U-2," it would carry a sophisticated camera system and equipment to intercept radio and radar transmissions. Dr. Edwin Land, Chairman of the Board of Polaroid Corporation and a member of the Killian panel, was instrumental in the development of its revolutionary photoreconnaissance system.

While Land was publicly known as the inventor of the Polaroid instant camera, he had also been working secretly on government projects aimed at developing guided missiles, infrared searchlights and a three-dimensional filter for aerial photography. As a member of the Killian panel he had emphasized that the first line of defense against surprise attack was accurate intelligence regarding an enemy's military capabilities and intentions. He knew that Soviet intelligence collectors held a clear advantage (and still do): Any Soviet agent or diplomat in the United States can buy maps showing the location of American bridges, factories, highways, ports, airbases—even atomic testing grounds. They can read accurate reports of U.S. weapons developments in the press and attend open sessions of the Senate and House Armed Services Committees.[1] But in the Soviet Union even the Moscow telephone book was restricted.

How were American military planners to know the location of vital Soviet installations? How were they to learn of new Soviet bombers, missiles, submarines and other weapons systems that could threaten the United States and its allies? And finally, how would U.S. officials know whether the Soviets were preparing for a surprise nuclear attack? Aerial reconnaissance offered the brightest possibility, but Air Force generals thought that the necessary planes and equipment could not be perfected in much less than 10 years. Land did not believe this. His proposal for a new photoreconnaissance system reached President Eisenhower via the Killian Report.[2]

Development of a high-flying aircraft to carry Land's cameras posed another set of challenging technical problems. Jet engines scarcely ran in the thin air above 70,000 feet. Also, the aircraft would have to carry an enormous amount of fuel for the long trip over the Soviet Union—and this could affect the plane's ability to fly at high altitudes. Lockheed Corporation solved these problems with a design that was less a jet airplane than a glider with a jet engine attached. To conserve fuel, the engine would turn on and off: the plane would alternately fly and glide through the stratosphere for almost 11 hours and 4,750 miles. The engineers shaved every ounce of excess weight from their design, and built the U-2 from titanium and other lightweight materials. It was a graceful-looking aircraft, with a wingspan roughly twice the length of its fuselage. The engineers at Lockheed called their creation the "Angel" but it was renamed "U-2" ("U" for Utility) by the U.S. government.[3]

The first U-2s became operational in 1956, and a regular schedule of flights over Soviet territory was initiated. The spy planes brought back valuable information concerning Soviet airfields, aircraft, missile testing, nuclear weapons production and storage and submarine production. Eisenhower considered the U-2 too sensitive to be disclosed even to the National Security Council. The project was made the responsibility of the CIA, which prepared cover stories so it could lie plausibly about the real purpose of the U-2 flights. These were tailored to suit the circumstances and geography of each flight and would be issued by Air Force public information officers at local bases in the event of an inquiry or accident.

At 6:26 A.M. on May 1, 1960, U-2 pilot Francis Gary Powers of Pound, Virginia, took off from an airbase at Peshawar, Pakistan. He was thirty years old and had logged more than 500 hours in the U-2. A .22-caliber semiautomatic pistol with a silencer rested on his hip. The red-and-blue line on his map directed him over 2,919 miles of Soviet territory en route to Bodø, Norway.[4]

On April 9, 1960, a U-2 had sighted diggings along the route Powers was to fly; U.S. photo interpreters suspected that the Soviets were building their first operational ICBM base. Powers's primary purpose was to photograph the construction before the Russians camouflaged the site or before the fog that blankets northern Russia in summer obscured it for them. Edwin Land's remarkable camera had a rotating lens that could take photographs through seven portholes in the belly of the plane. It would shoot 4,000 pictures of a strip of the Soviet Union 125 miles wide by 2,174 miles long.[5]

Before crossing the Soviet border, Powers climbed to 60,000 feet, beyond reach of Soviet fighter aircraft. He headed directly for the Soviet rocket test site at Tyuratam (the Soviet Union's Cape Canaveral), where *Sputnik* had been launched. After photographing Tyuratam, Powers set a new course toward Sverdlovsk, an industrial center near the suspected ICBM base.

The previous September, Eisenhower had spent a weekend with Soviet Premier Khrushchev at Camp David, the official presidential retreat in Maryland. During their talks, both leaders expressed their wish to devote money spent on arms and soldiers to a better standard of living for their people. Eisenhower told Khrushchev that "we really should come to some sort of agreement to stop this fruitless, really wasteful rivalry." Khrushchev nodded in agreement. As a result of the Camp David meetings, U.S.–Soviet relations had seemed to thaw, and Eisenhower was scheduled to carry the "spirit of Camp David" to a summit meeting with Soviet, British and French leaders in Paris two weeks hence. In June he was to visit the Soviet Union as Khrushchev's honored guest.

After Powers crossed into Soviet airspace, he noticed the condensation trail of a jet that was paralleling his course at a considerably lower altitude; the Soviets had detected him. A switch marked "Explosion" was located on the control panel in front of Powers, and behind him, just to the rear of the cockpit, was a three-pound charge of dynamite powerful enough to destroy the plane, its equipment—and the pilot, if he were unlucky enough to still be on board.

Powers's instructions were to destroy the plane rather than to allow it to be captured. He could do so by activating a timer, throwing the explosion switch, and ejecting from the aircraft. His seat pack held survival gear, including a collapsible life raft, clothing, water, food, a compass, signal flares, matches, chemicals for starting fires with damp wood, a first-aid kit and hunting gear. In his pocket he carried 7,500 Soviet rubles, two dozen gold Napoleon francs, and an assortment of wristwatches and gold rings to barter and bribe for assistance. If Powers was captured, he was to say as little as possible. He had been given a silver dollar with a $1\frac{1}{4}$ inch pin hidden inside. The pin held a needle tipped with a fatal dose of deadly poison: He could kill himself if he were tortured by captors or injured and without hope of rescue.[6]

Flying at 68,000 feet on the approach to the suspected Soviet ICBM base, he suddenly felt "a dull 'thump,' the aircraft jerked forward, and a tremendous orange flash lit the cockpit and sky." He lost control of the aircraft and bailed out. His plane had been hit by a new Soviet antiaircraft missile whose capabilities were unknown to the United States. Initial efforts on the part of U.S. authorities to learn the fate of Powers and his aircraft were unsuccessful.[7]

When the CIA reported that the U-2 was missing, the cover story for the May 1 flight was issued: A NASA weather plane had taken off from Turkey and—without authorization—had wandered over Pakistan. "Without authorization," because Pakistan—unlike Turkey, which is a NATO ally—was a nonaligned nation and was not supposed to provide bases from which the United States could operate. NASA had willingly allowed the CIA to use it as cover from the beginning of the U-2 project.

On May 5, 1960, in the great hall of the Kremlin, 1,300 delegates to the Supreme Soviet listened to Khrushchev speak for

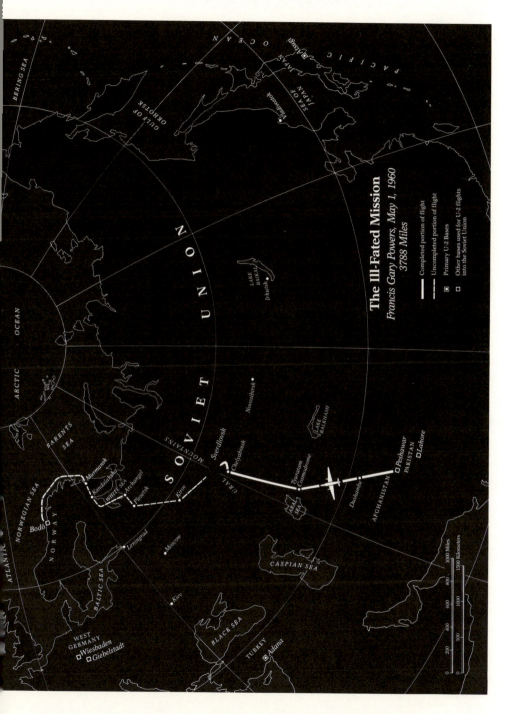

In the days before satellites, U.S. pilots flew intelligence missions over the
Soviet Union. Francis Gary Powers flew the last, unlucky flight: His U-2
aircraft was shot down by an advanced—and unanticipated—Soviet missile.

three and a half hours. Toward the end he dropped a bombshell: "Early on the morning of May Day, at 5:36 A.M. Moscow time, an American plane crossed our border and continued its flight into Soviet territory. The Minister of Defense immediately notified the government of this aggressive act. The government told him: the aggressor knows what to expect when he invades foreign territory. If he goes unpunished he will commit new provocations. The thing to do therefore is to act—shoot down the plane. These instructions were carried out, the plane was shot down."

Khrushchev asked the delegates what would have happened if a Soviet aircraft were to appear, say, over New York, Chicago or Detroit? How would the United States react? He said that U.S. officials had "repeatedly declared that they keep A-bomb and H-bomb planes on the alert and that with the approach of foreign aircraft they would take off and head for their designated bombing targets. That would mean the outbreak of war." Khrushchev reminded the delegates that he was about to meet in Paris with Eisenhower. Then he looked up toward U.S. Ambassador Llewellyn E. Thompson: "What is this, May Day greetings?" He concluded the performance by charging that the United States had deliberately tried to "torpedo" the summit talks.[8]

Eisenhower had been concerned that the worst risk run by the U-2 flights was that the Soviets would mistake the aircraft for a nuclear bomber. The U-2's size and shape did not suggest a bomber, but given imperfect radar and rumored American developments in lightweight nuclear weapons, some Soviet general might interpret the blip on his screen as the spearhead of a surprise nuclear attack and launch World War III. But Khrushchev had not complained about the flights during his talks with Eisenhower at Camp David. From this the president had deduced that the Soviets did not consider the flights a serious provocation, and that the intelligence they collected was worth the risk, even two weeks before the scheduled summit talks.[9]

Immediately following Khrushchev's speech, a small group of top U.S. officials met to decide what to do next. The group included Eisenhower, Secretary of Defense Thomas S. Gates, Jr., Deputy Secretary of State Douglas Dillon, CIA Director Allen Dulles, and others. A majority decided not to admit to espionage; there could be no turning back: They must insist on the veracity of the cover story.

Gates, however, disagreed with this strategy: If Khrushchev had evidence of espionage, Eisenhower might be associated with an "international lie" that would undermine the prestige of his presidency. Gates's objections were overruled.

State Department spokesman Lincoln White, who had not been informed that the U-2 was a spy plane, released the following statement:

The Department of State has been informed by NASA . . . [that] an unarmed plane, a U-2 weather research plane based at Adana, Turkey, piloted by a civilian, has been missing since May 1. During the flight of the plane, the pilot reported difficulty with his oxygen equipment. Mr. Khrushchev announced that a U. S. plane has been shot down over the USSR on that date. It may be that this is the missing plane. It is entirely possible that having a failure in the oxygen equipment, which could result in the pilot losing consciousness, the plane continued on automatic pilot for a considerable distance and violated Soviet air space.[10]

Capitol Hill indignantly protested shooting down an unarmed civilian weather plane while its pilot battled for life against a faulty oxygen system. Senator Styles Bridges of New Hampshire said that

Eisenhower should refuse to go to the Paris summit conference until the Soviets provided a satisfactory explanation.

On May 7, Khrushchev delivered a second speech to the Supreme Soviet:

Comrades, I must let you in on a secret. When I made my report I deliberately refrained from mentioning that the pilot was alive and healthy, and that we had the remnants of the plane. [The delegates broke into applause.]

We did this deliberately because had we given out the whole story the Americans would have thought up another version.

. . . This was a regular reconnaissance plane . . . for collecting espionage information. . . . Its assignment was to cross the entire territory of the USSR and photograph military and industrial objectives on Soviet soil.[11]

He pulled from his black briefcase two 12-inch-square enlarged photographs developed from the U-2's films. . . . Khrushchev held both pictures up, shouting repeatedly, "Here they are! Here they are!" The delegates laughed and cheered. In his speech, Khrushchev tried to divorce the U-2 operation from Eisenhower. "I am quite willing to grant that the president knew nothing about the fact that such a plane was sent into the Soviet Union . . . but this should put us even more on guard. When the military starts bossing the show, the results can be disastrous."[12]

The CIA wanted to continue denying that the U-2 was on a spy mission, but the State Department considered the cover story "blown" and wanted to admit to espionage, keeping the president out of it. Eisenhower wanted to take full responsibility, but was persuaded to follow the State Department's line. A statement was issued saying that "there was no authorization for any such flight as described by Mr. Khrushchev. Nevertheless, it appears that in endeavoring to obtain information now concealed behind the Iron Curtain, a flight over Soviet territory was probably undertaken by an unarmed civilian U-2 plane."[13]

The U-2 incident and the various official explanations now dominated front-page news. "U.S. concedes flight over Soviet, defends search for intelligence," said *The New York Times.* "Moral leadership of U.S. harmed," said the *San Francisco Chronicle.* The London *Daily Telegraph* declared, "A secret service must have some secrets from its own government. What it must never do is have more secrets from its own government than from the enemy."[14]

Then, overnight, President Eisenhower decided after all to assume full responsibility. The fourth statement in five days admitted that aerial spying, including overflights, had been conducted for years under presidential directives. It blamed the Soviet Union as ultimately responsible: "Ever since Stalin began the Cold War, the world has lived in a state of apprehension with respect to Soviet intentions"; for all the world knew, the Russians might be preparing for a nuclear sneak attack. It was "unacceptable" that the Soviet Union be allowed to make "secret" preparations for nuclear war. Despite this attempt to save face by blaming the Soviets, Eisenhower's statement marked the first time an American president had taken public responsibility for a major act of peacetime espionage.[15]

Tension between Washington and Moscow mounted during the week preceding the Paris summit. On Capitol Hill, an uneasy truce prevailed between political parties, Democrats generally rallying to support the Republican president. That week in Moscow, 500 correspondents were invited to view an exhibition of the remains of the U-2 aircraft, Powers's spy equipment, his signed confession to espionage and his personal effects. (Powers later pleaded guilty to spy charges in a Soviet court and was sentenced to ten years in prison. In 1962 he was released in exchange for Rudolf Abel, a convicted Soviet spy, and returned to the United States.)

The Paris meetings attended by Eisenhower, Khrushchev, British Prime Minister Harold Macmillan and French President Charles de Gaulle were to begin on May 16, 1960. Some scoffed at what the Paris summit might accomplish, but in fact negotiators for East and West had drawn close to reaching a limited nuclear-test-ban treaty. This would be the first major accord of the Cold War. But even before the first meeting Khrushchev delivered a memo to de Gaulle demanding that the United States halt spy flights, condemn them and punish those responsible. He also sent a copy to Macmillan—but nothing to Eisenhower. It seemed that the summit was in imminent danger of collapsing before it began.

On Monday morning, May 16, the summit began in the ornate second-floor salon of the Elysée Palace. Eisenhower did not greet Khrushchev; neither did the Russian show the American president any sign of recognition. De Gaulle, as chief of state of the host government, opened the meeting. Without waiting for permission to speak, Khrushchev put on his glasses and read a vitriolic statement that again demanded that the United States halt spy flights, condemn them and punish those responsible. "Until this is done . . . the Soviet government sees no possibility for productive negotiations. . . ." As for President Eisenhower's planned visit to Russia, the Soviet people "unfortunately" could no longer receive him "with the proper cordiality." The visit "should be postponed."

Eisenhower spoke next, in a controlled voice barely masking his anger. He announced for the first time that the United States planned no further flights over Soviet territory. He told Khrushchev, "I have come to Paris to seek agreements with the Soviet

Union which would eliminate the necessity for all forms of espionage, including overflights. I see no reason to use this incident to disrupt the conference."[16]

Then Khrushchev announced that he would publish the text of the statement he had just made at the meeting. This undiplomatic action horrified the Western leaders, and now de Gaulle made no effort to conceal his exasperation:

You have inconvenienced us. You have brought President Eisenhower from the United States and Prime Minister Macmillan from Britain. Your own ambassador came to see us two weeks ago and assured us there would be a summit. You said the same thing at Orly [airport] two days ago. You knew as much two weeks ago about the U-2 as you know now.[17]

The Paris summit conference of 1960 was clearly over. U.S. diplomat Charles Bohlen called it "the coldest gathering of human beings I believe I have ever seen." Columnist James Reston of *The New York Times* dubbed it "the conference that everyone lost."

Eisenhower returned to the United States from the most humiliating experience of his public career. The U.S. government had lied, had admitted it lied, had denied presidential responsibility and then had admitted it. The summit had been destroyed, the president had been publicly castigated by Khrushchev and his trip to Russia had been canceled.[18]

The U-2 affair occurred in the last year of Eisenhower's two-term presidency. It is a tribute to Eisenhower's long and distinguished public career (Supreme Allied Commander in Europe during World War II, first NATO commander, president of Columbia University, and president of the United States) that the U-2 incident has affected his reputation very little. Eisenhower's farewell address in January 1961 did not address the U-2 affair; instead he used his final official speech to deliver a historic warning against what he called the "military-industrial complex":

Until the latest of our world conflicts, the United States had no armaments industry. . . . [The] conjunction of an immense military establishment and a large arms industry is new in the American experience. The total influence—economic, political, even spiritual—is felt in every city, every state house, every office of the federal government. We recognize the imperative need for this development. Yet we must not fail to comprehend its grave implications. Our toil, resources, and livelihood are all involved; so is the very structure of our society.

In the councils of government we must guard against the acquisition of unwarranted influence, whether sought or unsought, by the military-industrial complex. The potential for the disastrous rise of misplaced power exists and will persist.

We must never let the weight of this combination endanger our liberties or democratic processes. We should take nothing for granted. Only an alert and knowledgeable citizenry can compel the proper meshing of the huge industrial and military machinery of defense with our peaceful methods and goals, so that security and liberty may prosper together.[19]

Eisenhower said later that this was "the most challenging message I could leave with the people of this country."

XVII

THE CUBAN MISSILE CRISIS

. . . And let every other power know that this hemisphere intends to remain the master of its own house. . . . To those nations who would make themselves our adversary, we offer not a pledge, but a request: that both sides begin anew the quest for peace, before the dark powers of destruction unleashed by science engulf all humanity in planned or accidental self-destruction.

President John F. Kennedy,
Inaugural Address,
January 20, 1961

Now war loomed large on the horizon. Weakness would only ensure it, and strength was not certain to avoid it. A single misstep on [President Kennedy's] part could extinguish the lights of civilization, but even all the right steps could turn out wrong.

Theodore C. Sorensen,
Special Counsel to the President,
1965

I recall leaving the White House that Saturday night, walking through the gardens of the White House to my car to drive back to the Pentagon and wondering if I'd ever see another Saturday night.

Robert S. McNamara,
Secretary of Defense,
1983

On January 20, 1961, Washington, D.C., prepared for the inauguration of John Fitzgerald Kennedy, the thirty-fifth president of the United States. Workmen cleared snow from the streets in 22-degree weather, but the temperature could not chill the general enthusiasm: President-elect Kennedy was youthful, articulate, determined, and he seemed to embody a new and needed idealism.

The crowd watched President Eisenhower and President-elect Kennedy take their places on the inaugural platform—the oldest man ever to have served in the office and the youngest man ever elected to it. On the platform behind Kennedy sat the men and women of his administration—"the best and the brightest," it was said, of a new generation of successful academics, businessmen, engineers, scientists and lawyers. They listened intently as Kennedy, in a clear voice, resolved to defend liberty, summoned his fellow citizens to serve their country, pledged to support U.S. allies and urged a new quest for peace in an age "where the instruments of war have far outpaced the instruments of peace."

During his presidential campaign, Kennedy had promised to take a tough stance against communism. He would build up American nuclear as well as nonnuclear forces and rectify the missile gap that he believed favored Soviet ICBM capabilities over those of the United States. In his first budget message to Congress, President Kennedy asserted that the adequacy of U.S. deterrent power should be measured by the ability of U.S. strategic forces to survive a nuclear first strike and to inflict devastating retaliatory damage on any aggressor.

The strategic-weapons programs initiated by the first Kennedy budget led to the formation of the strategic triad, the evolution of which has been described in previous chapters. Secretary of Defense Robert McNamara calculated that in addition to the Strategic Air Command's long-range bombers, 1,000 land-based missiles and forty-one submarines would guarantee a retaliatory or "second-strike" capability and thus an adequate deterrent to nuclear war.

During his first week in office Kennedy was staggered by intelligence briefings that warned of crises brewing around the world. "The only thing that surprised us when we got into office," he joked to a reporter, "was that things were just as bad as we had been saying they were." John Fischer, a journalist for *Harper's*, remarked, "While Kennedy was still trying to move in the furniture, in effect, he found the roof falling in and the doors blowing off."[1]

In Moscow, Soviet Premier Nikita S. Khrushchev spoke of a world where democracy was everywhere on the retreat and communism everywhere on the march: "There is no longer any force in the world capable of barring the road to socialism." In Washington, D.C., Kennedy's State of the Union Address presented a far gloomier picture to Congress than his inauguration speech ten days earlier might have anticipated:

Each day the crises multiply. Each day their solution grows more difficult. Each day we draw nearer to the hour of maximum danger. . . . I feel I must inform the Congress that in each of the principal areas of crisis, the tide of events has been running out and time has not been our friend.

The "areas of crisis" included Africa, where the Soviets threatened to intervene in the Congo; Southeast Asia, where Communist-led forces were close to taking over Laos; and Europe, where Khrushchev was demanding a treaty to permanently divide Germany and remove all Allied troops from Berlin. And on America's doorstep, Communists had seized political power in Cuba.

In 1959 Fidel Castro deposed Cuban dictator Fulgencio Batista, and many thought that Cuba would adopt a democratic form of government. But shortly afterward Castro declared that Cuba would be Communist, thereby bringing the Cold War to an island 90 miles off the Florida coast. Castro, Kennedy felt, had "betrayed the ideals of the Cuban revolution," transforming Cuba "into a hostile and militant satellite" of the Soviet Union. Disgruntled Cuban exiles living in Florida and Central America—some of whom had fought alongside Castro—believed so too. Eisenhower had informed Kennedy one day before the inauguration that he had secretly been supporting Cuban political exiles "to the utmost"; he recommended that "this effort be continued and accelerated." Back in March 1960 Eisenhower had approved a plan to recruit, train and arm a Cuban "army of liberation" under the direction of the CIA. 1,400 Cuban exiles had been training for nearly a year in Guatemala.[2]

After the inauguration, the CIA and military officials persuaded Kennedy to approve a military action to overthrow Fidel Castro. Cuban exiles would land at the Bay of Pigs on Cuba's southern coast, fight their way northwest to Havana and seize control of the government. Kennedy stipulated that no U.S. forces would be involved in the fighting, and on April 17, 1961, the assault was launched. But communications were botched, reconnaissance was inaccurate and supply lines were nonexistent. In three days most of the "freedom fighters" were either killed or captured by Castro's forces. In sum, the Bay of Pigs was a military fiasco and a foreign-policy disaster.

Robert F. Kennedy, attorney general in his brother's administration, said later that the president had trusted these advisors because they had been trusted by Eisenhower. Theodore Sorensen, President Kennedy's special counsel, later argued that the Bay of Pigs decision involved a no-win proposition:

[President Kennedy] was in effect asked whether he was as willing as the Republicans to permit and assist these exiles to free their own island from dictatorship, or whether he was willing to liquidate well-laid preparations, leave Cuba free to subvert the hemisphere, disband an impatient army and have them spread the word that Kennedy had betrayed their attempt to depose Castro.[3]

Nevertheless President Kennedy publicly shouldered full responsibility. He said at the time that "success has a hundred fathers and defeat is an orphan. . . . The advice of those who were brought in on the executive branch was also unanimous and the advice was wrong. And I was responsible." Robert Kennedy has said that, in private, "[the President] was more upset ·this time than he was any other. . . . He felt strongly that the Cuban operation had affected his standing as president and the standing of the United States in public opinion throughout the world. We were going to have a much harder role in providing leadership."[4]

Kennedy called Eisenhower to Camp David, where he candidly reviewed the failed operation. The two men walked slowly, heads bent, and conferred. Eisenhower asked, "Mr. President, before you approved this plan did you have everybody in front of you debating the thing so you got the pros and cons yourself and then made your decision, or did you see them one at a time?" "One at a time," Kennedy said. Eisenhower was silent.

Then Eisenhower asked, "Why didn't you provide air cover for the Cuban Brigade?" Kennedy replied, "We thought that if it was learned that we were really doing this rather than these rebels themselves, the Soviets would be very apt to cause trouble in Berlin." Eisenhower disagreed: "Mr. President, that is exactly the opposite of what would really happen. The Soviets have their own plans, and if they see us show any weakness, that is when they press us the hardest. . . . The failure of the Bay of Pigs will embolden the Soviets to do something that they would not otherwise do."[5]

Two months later, in June 1961, President Kennedy met with Nikita Khrushchev at a summit conference in Vienna, Austria. Khrushchev belligerently demanded a treaty that recognized a separate East Germany and that removed British, French and American troops from West Berlin. Secretary of State Dean Rusk described their confrontation:

Mr. Khrushchev wound up by delivering, in a very bold and intimidating way, an ultimatum on Berlin. He said to Kennedy, "Your access to Berlin will have to be worked out with the East Germans. If there is any attempt by the West to interfere with these arrangements, there will be war." And in diplomacy you almost never used the word "war." And Kennedy had to look him straight in the eye and say, "Well then, Mr. Chairman, there's going to be war."[6]

At the conclusion of the summit Khrushchev gave Kennedy just six months to agree to a treaty. Kennedy's parting words: "It will be a cold winter."

In July the president urged Americans in a television address to build bomb shelters as "national insurance":

In the event of an attack, the lives of those families which are not hit in a nuclear blast and fire can still be saved—if they can be warned to take shelter and if that shelter is available. . . . The time to start is now.

Local post offices began to carry "how-to" pamphlets, and a bomb-shelter boom was on. Shelters, however, seemed better suited to those who could afford homes with yards or basements than to people living in high-density city dwellings. Without a doubt the Civil Defense film strip "You and the Atom" offered the best advice: "The Atomic Energy Commission says the best defense against an atom bomb is to BE SOMEWHERE ELSE when it bursts."[7]

By August 1961, 3.5 million East Germans had fled to the West, many through West Berlin. As U.S.–Soviet tensions mounted and East Germans sensed that they were being imprisoned, they were escaping in numbers of up to 4,000 a day. On August 13, Khrushchev ordered that the border be sealed off. "We were losing all the best people in East Germany," Khruschev later told Kennedy's press secretary, Pierre Salinger. "I had to build a wall."[8] The Berlin Wall, a barrier of concrete and barbed wire, was erected overnight within Soviet-controlled territory and could not be defied militarily without risking war.

To emphasize their determination in Berlin, the Soviets put on a frightening display of nuclear firepower. From September to November 1961 they exploded over thirty nuclear weapons at four test sites within the Soviet Union. These had a cumulative explosive yield of 200 megatons. On October 30, the Soviets detonated a 58-megaton weapon—the largest nuclear explosion ever.[9]

By late October 1961 the Soviets had moved 300,000 Warsaw Pact troops into East Germany. American and Soviet tanks faced off at Checkpoint Charlie, the crossing point between the American and Soviet sectors of Berlin. Khrushchev sent a letter to Kennedy comparing the Berlin crisis to two stupid and stubborn goats head to head on a narrow bridge across an abyss, neither giving way and both falling to their doom. Though both Khrushchev and Kennedy threatened military confrontation, neither was prepared to precipitate a conflict that could result in nuclear war, and the Berlin crisis ended in a standoff.

According to Arkady Shevchenko, a former Soviet under secretary to the United Nations who later defected to the West:

After the Vienna summit, Khrushchev concluded that Kennedy would accept almost anything to avoid nuclear war. The lack of confidence the President displayed during both the Bay of Pigs invasion and the Berlin crisis further confirmed his view. . . . At the end of 1961, Khrushchev began to lecture us about Kennedy's "wishy-washy" behavior, ending with the remark: "I know for certain that Kennedy doesn't have a strong backbone, nor, generally speaking, does he have the courage to stand up to a serious challenge."[10]

Khrushchev did not press his deadline for a German treaty; he was contemplating something far more ambitious. If, as he believed, Kennedy would never reconcile to a Communist presence in Cuba, the United States would probably attack Cuba again. And as Khrushchev later wrote in his memoirs, "What will happen if we lose Cuba? I knew it would have been a terrible blow to Marxism-Leninism. It would gravely diminish our stature throughout the world, but especially in Latin America. If Cuba fell, other Latin American countries would reject us, claiming that for all our might the Soviet Union hadn't been able to do anything for Cuba."[11]

Castro also anticipated U.S. intervention, and therefore accepted extensive Soviet military aid. During July and August 1962 Communist-bloc and bloc-chartered vessels made over a hundred deliveries of military equipment and Soviet troops. This prompted Kennedy to increase aerial surveillance of the island. Reconnaissance photographs taken on August 31 revealed that the Soviets had installed antiaircraft missiles at Cuban airfields, stationed missile-equipped torpedo boats in Cuban ports and constructed a large shipyard and a submarine base.

The Soviet military buildup in Cuba attracted much media attention, especially as it came in a year of Congressional elections. Cuba had become, according to *Newsweek*, "an albatross around the president's neck." By the end of September, a House Republican caucus called Cuba "the biggest Republican asset" in the approaching election. Indiana Senator Homer E. Capehart "viewed with alarm" that the Executive Branch was not taking adequate steps to protect national security. On October 10, 1962, New York Senator Kenneth Keating claimed that "refugee sources" had confirmed that offensive nuclear missiles were in Cuba, and demanded military action.

On Sunday, October 14, McGeorge Bundy, the president's Advisor on National Security Affairs, appeared on a nationally televised news program. Questioned about Keating's statement, Bundy replied that there was "no present evidence" and in his judgment "no present likelihood of a major offensive capability in Cuba."

Unbeknownst to Bundy, U-2 photographs of San Cristóbal, Cuba, taken and developed that same day clearly showed a series of storage buildings and missile transporters, some carrying missiles. Identification of the missile site was aided by the fact that its configuration was identical to missile sites in the Soviet Union.[12] By Monday night the long rolls of film had been meticulously analyzed by U.S. photo interpreters. The CIA was certain that medium-range nuclear missiles were in Cuba and that they would soon be operational. Washington, D.C., Dallas, St. Louis, Cape

Canaveral and all nearby Strategic Air Command (SAC) bases lay within their 1,100-mile range; 80 million Americans could die within minutes of an attack. The evidence was delivered late Monday evening to McGeorge Bundy.

On October 16, while Kennedy was eating breakfast, Bundy told him: "Mr. President, there is now hard photographic evidence, which you will see a little later, that the Russians have offensive missiles in Cuba." Kennedy took the news calmly, although he was surprised. "I suppose," he replied, "that we will have to take them out." He asked Bundy to organize a meeting of advisors for 11:45 A.M. At 9:00 A.M., the president telephoned Robert Kennedy: "We are facing great trouble."[13]

The attorney general and other key presidential advisors assembled in the White House Cabinet Room to be briefed on an emerging crisis that, in Robert Kennedy's words, "brought the world to the abyss of nuclear destruction and the end of mankind." President Kennedy sat down at the conference table and smiled grimly: "Well, gentlemen, today we are going to earn our pay." For the next 13 days this group, known as the Executive Committee of the National Security Council ("ExCom"), would guide the United States through the Cuban Missile Crisis. The group included Secretary of Defense Robert S. McNamara, Secretary of State Dean Rusk, Director of the CIA John McCone, McGeorge Bundy, Robert Kennedy, Presidential Counsel Theodore Sorensen, Secretary of the Treasury C. Douglas Dillon, Chairman of the Joint Chiefs of Staff General Maxwell Taylor, Under Secretary of State George W. Ball, Deputy Under Secretary of State U. Alexis Johnson, Under Secretary of State for Latin America Edward Martin, Advisor on Soviet Affairs Llewellyn Thompson, Deputy Secretary of Defense Roswell Gilpatrick, and Deputy Secretary of Defense Paul Nitze. Other advisors were brought in as needed.

Mindful of Eisenhower's advice after the Bay of Pigs fiasco, the president conducted ExCom discussions openly and candidly. In contrast to the Bay of Pigs deliberations, these sessions insured that "Everybody had an equal opportunity to express himself and to be heard directly," as the attorney general said. "It was a tremendously advantageous procedure that does not frequently occur within the executive branch of government, where rank is often so important."[14]

At the first meeting, on Tuesday morning, October 16, President Kennedy pointed out that intelligence reviews had repeatedly emphasized that deploying surface-to-surface nuclear missiles outside its own territory would be "incompatible with Soviet policy."[15] Even more disconcerting than this miscalculation was the fact that the Soviets had deliberately deceived the U.S. government, the president in particular. On September 4, Robert Kennedy had been visited by Soviet Ambassador Anatoly Dobrynin, who announced that the Soviet Union was prepared to sign an atmospheric nuclear-test-ban treaty. Robert Kennedy took the opportunity to discuss the recent Soviet military buildup in Cuba:

I told Ambassador Dobrynin of President Kennedy's deep concern. . . . He told me I should not be concerned, for he was instructed by Soviet Chairman Nikita S. Khrushchev to assure President Kennedy that there would be no ground-to-ground missiles or offensive weapons placed in Cuba.

Kennedy had responded, "We will watch the buildup carefully . . . it would be of the gravest consequence if the Soviet Union placed missiles in Cuba." "That," replied Dobrynin, "would never happen." Shortly thereafter the president had announced publicly: "There is yet no proof of offensive ground-to-ground missiles or other significant offensive capability. . . . Were it to be otherwise, the gravest issues would arise."[16]

One week later, on September 11, the Soviets had issued a public statement claiming that there was no need for nuclear missiles to be transferred to any country outside the Soviet Union, including Cuba. President Kennedy had received a second message from Khrushchev reiterating that "under no circumstance would surface-to-surface missiles be sent to Cuba."

That morning of October 16, General Marshall Carter, Deputy Director of the CIA, presented enlarged U-2 photographs of Cuba to the ExCom, and photo analysts pinpointed the evidence of nuclear missiles. Those present realized that Soviet promises "had all been lies, one gigantic fabric of lies."[17] The Soviet missile base could be finished in two weeks. President Kennedy ordered daily reconnaissance flights over all of Cuba; some 2,000 missions would be flown in the next two weeks. Then he asked for opinions about possible courses of action. Since the missiles could directly threaten U.S. cities and SAC bases with almost no warning time, "Most felt, at that stage," Robert Kennedy reported, "that an air strike against the missile sites could be the only course." No final decisions were made that morning, but the president was convinced that the missiles must either be removed or destroyed; the outlook was grim.[18]

As the morning session ended, Kennedy directed that the strictest secrecy be observed. A premature leak could either precipitate a Soviet move or cause panic at home and abroad. The president warned, "You can't announce that in four days from now you're going to take them out. They may announce within three days they're going to have warheads on them; if we come and attack, they're going to fire them. Then what'll we do?"[19] Members of the

ExCom kept to their normal routines as much as possible to avoid raising suspicion.

On that Tuesday, debate focused upon the options of various air strikes. McNamara argued that an air strike could not be limited to the missile site alone; prospective nuclear-weapons storage sites, air bases and other targets would have to be attacked simultaneously. The necessity for an invasion was also deliberated. But these options would unavoidably involve killing Cuban civilians and Soviet military personnel and would certainly risk a nuclear confrontation. Instead, McNamara urged that limited pressure should be applied, to be increased as circumstances required; a naval blockade of Cuba would be a reasonable cautious preliminary move and preserve some possibility of defusing the crisis.[20]

On Wednesday, October 17, U-2 photographs brought back more ominous news. Three additional missile sites were under construction, including sites for intermediate-range ballistic missiles (IRBMs) that could travel 2,200 miles—twice as far as medium-range ballistic missiles (MRBMs). IRBMs could reach almost any target in the United States east of the Rocky Mountains. As the week wore on, six MRBM and three IRBM sites were discovered in all.

But why the sudden, secret and drastic change in Soviet policy? Arkady Shevchenko said later that "the idea to deploy nuclear missiles in Cuba was Khrushchev's own. . . . Beyond a defense for Cuba . . . the Soviet Union could get a 'cheap' nuclear rocket deterrent, and accomplish much with very little."[21] Khrushchev's memoirs explain:

We had to establish a tangible and effective deterrent to American interference in the Caribbean. The logical answer was missiles. The

U.S. had already surrounded the Soviet Union with its own bomber bases and missiles. . . . My thinking went like this: if we installed the missiles secretly and then if the U.S. discovered the missiles after they were already poised and ready to strike, the Americans would think twice before trying to liquidate our installations by military means . . . if a quarter or even a tenth of our missiles survived, we could still hit New York, and there wouldn't be much of New York left.[22]

On Thursday, October 18, President Kennedy met with Soviet Foreign Minister Andrei Gromyko; this talk had been scheduled prior to the Cuban crisis. Since the ExCom had not yet decided how to respond to the situation in Cuba, the president chose to tell Gromyko nothing of what he knew. Though anxious, Kennedy managed a smile and welcomed Gromyko to his office.

Gromyko focused not on Cuba, but on Berlin: The Soviets would proceed with an East German treaty if no U.S.–Soviet settlement was forthcoming after the American elections. Kennedy later said to Sorensen that "it all seemed to fit a pattern—everything coming to a head at once—the completion of the missile bases, Khrushchev coming to the United Nations [in November], a new drive on West Berlin."[23] Then Gromyko brought up Cuba, complaining that congressional resolutions and press reports were unduly aggressive. He read from his notes:

As to Soviet assistance to Cuba, I have been instructed to make it clear, as the Soviet government has already done, that such assistance pursued solely the purpose of contributing to the defense capabilities of Cuba and to the development of its peaceful economy.

In return, Kennedy noncommittally reread his September statement warning the Soviets against deploying offensive missiles in Cuba. Gromyko, like Dobrynin before him, assured Kennedy that this would never happen. Robert Kennedy wrote later, "The President of the United States, it can be said, was displeased with the spokesman of the Soviet Union. . . ."[24]

Back at the Executive Committee, the Joint Chiefs of Staff, and General Curtis LeMay in particular, argued heatedly for an air attack. They contended that a naval blockade would simply invite the Soviets to blockade Berlin. Arthur Schlesinger, Jr., Special Assistant to the President, has said that Kennedy was visibly upset when LeMay "boomed forth on the beauties of air attack." "These brass hats have one great advantage in their favor," Kennedy later remarked. "If we do what they want us to do, none of us will be alive later to tell them that they were wrong."[25]

Dean Acheson, former secretary of state, also addressed the ExCom in favor of an air strike. As Theodore Sorensen remembered, someone asked Acheson:

Mr. Secretary, what will the Soviets do in response to an air strike?

I think they will feel obligated to launch an attack and knock out our missiles in Turkey.

And then what do we do, Mr. Secretary?

Well, under the NATO Treaty we would be obliged to knock out Soviet missile sites in the Soviet Union.

Well, what will they then do, Mr. Secretary?

Well, we hope by that time cooler heads will prevail and everybody will talk.[26]

Dean Rusk recalled that the president "spent a good part of the day in going through a full briefing on the total effect of a nuclear war—both direct and indirect. . . . As we went through the Cabinet Room door toward the Oval Office, he looked at me with a rather strange look on his face and said, 'And we call ourselves the human race.' "[27]

Robert Kennedy argued that a sneak attack was "not in our traditions": that advocating a "surprise attack by a very large nation against a small one would call our ideals unanswerably into question." His point seemed an important one. The air strike suggested by the Joint Chiefs of Staff involved 800 separate missions and would result in hundreds or thousands of Cuban and Russian casualties. McNamara did not believe that Moscow would suffer such an attack "without resorting to a very major response," one that could quickly escalate to general nuclear war.[28]

The terms "hawk" and "dove" were later used to designate, respectively, those who favored an air strike and those who favored a blockade. The doves realized, however, that a blockade could escalate into an air strike, especially if the Soviets did not stop working to make the missile sites operational.[29] Rusk later reflected: "We never saw a warhead on a missile or a launcher prepared to fire. It's my belief that had we seen that combination— a missile ready to go—that would have produced another kind of crisis."[30] But they hadn't seen any missiles ready to go, and the majority of the Executive Committee was unwilling to put even one American city at risk by striking Cuba. It was more prudent to somehow convince the Soviets to remove their offensive missiles from Cuba.

By Thursday night only a vocal minority was holding out for an air strike. At 9:15 P.M. a group of ExCom members crammed into one car at the State Department and left for the White House.

Someone joked, "It would be some story if this car is in an accident." At the White House the alternatives were discussed with President Kennedy, who indicated that he preferred leaving Khrushchev a way out, and that he was leaning toward the milder measure.

Kennedy wanted to announce a decision soon, and called for a final recommendation on Saturday, October 20. At 2:30 P.M. on that day the ExCom met at the White House. Once more the arguments for a blockade, an air strike, and an invasion were reviewed. An awkward silence ensued. Deputy Secretary of Defense Gilpatrick broke in: "Essentially, Mr. President, this is a choice between limited action and unlimited action; and most of us here think that it's better to start with limited action." The president nodded in agreement. The group took a straw vote: eleven for a blockade, six for an air strike. Kennedy would announce the decision Monday night.[31]

During the next day—Sunday, October 21—measures were taken on domestic, diplomatic and military fronts to coincide with the president's impending message. Congressional leaders were informed. Four hundred fifty presidential messages were delivered to American embassies around the world. Letters were drafted to forty-three heads of governments. The Navy deployed 188 ships around Cuba while over 100,000 troops gathered in Florida. That night, after reviewing all the preparations, Rusk suggested that his staff get some sleep. "By this time tomorrow," he sighed, "we will be in a flaming crisis."[32]

On Monday evening, one hour before Kennedy's speech, Soviet Ambassador Dobrynin was ushered into Rusk's office. Twenty-five minutes later, visibly shaken, he left the State Department carrying a copy of the president's speech.

At 7:00 P.M., in a televised address, President Kennedy communicated what he knew about the Soviet missile sites in Cuba and told of his intention to impose a "strict naval quarantine on all offensive military equipment under shipment to Cuba." Non-military supplies, such as food or coal, could be delivered subject to American inspection. Kennedy spoke of a "quarantine" rather than of a "blockade" because under international law a blockade could be considered an act of war. A "quarantine" could yet permit a peaceful settlement of the crisis.[33] Nonetheless, he emphasized that this was only the first step in the U.S. effort to remove Soviet missiles from Cuba. "The purpose of these bases can be none other than to provide a nuclear-strike capability in the Western Hemisphere." He warned Khrushchev:

It shall be the policy of this nation to regard any nuclear missile launched from Cuba against any nation in the Western Hemisphere as an attack by the Soviet Union on the United States, requiring a full retaliatory response upon the Soviet Union.

To avoid spreading panic, Kennedy deleted from his prepared speech a comparison of the Soviet missiles' megatonnage to the bomb dropped on Hiroshima. For the same reason he did not show the enlarged U-2 photographs on television.[34] As he spoke, the Strategic Air Command and North American Air Defense Units were placed on maximum ground and air alert. B-52 bombers, fully loaded with nuclear weapons, were ordered into the air. Battle staffs were placed on 24-hour-alert duty. Kennedy continued:

The 1930s taught us a clear lesson: aggressive conduct, if allowed to go unchecked and unchallenged, ultimately leads to war. This nation is opposed to war. We are also true to our word. Our un-swerving objective, therefore, must be to prevent the use of these

missiles against this or any other country, and to secure their with-
drawal or elimination from the Western Hemisphere.[35]

Khrushchev's missiles had been uncovered. As Senator Hubert
H. Humphrey commented, "The Russians were caught with their
missiles down and the rockets exposed." Shevchenko said afterward, "Khrushchev's calculations were based upon the assumption
that he could dupe the Americans by installing the missiles rapidly
and secretly. Then he would confront the U.S. with a *fait ac-*
compli. . . . By establishing the quarantine, Kennedy has presented Khrushchev with a *fait accompli* instead of the other way
around. Once the crisis developed, Khrushchev had only two options: a nuclear war, for which the U.S. was much better prepared,
or a war limited to the area, also advantageous to the U.S."[36]

Kennedy solemnly concluded his speech: "No one can foresee
precisely what course it will take or what costs or casualties will
be incurred . . . but the greatest danger would be to do nothing."[37]
By 6:00 A.M. Wednesday, October 24, Polaris submarines had
been flushed from their ports and the Strategic Air Command was
in an intensive state of readiness. One hundred eighty-three B-47
bombers were dispersed to thirty-three civilian and military airfields. Forty-nine B-52s, with 182 nuclear weapons aboard, were
continually airborne. As one landed, another immediately took
off. Ninety Atlas and forty-six Titan ICBMs were ready to launch.[38]
And, according to Sorensen, "U.S. custodians of nuclear weapons
in Turkey and Italy were instructed to take extraordinary precautions to make certain that such weapons were fired only with
presidential authorization."[39]

Privately, President Kennedy was not particularly hopeful about
the outcome. The odds that the Soviets would go to war seemed
"somewhere between one out of three and even." Talking with

aides on the back porch of the White House just prior to delivering his speech, Kennedy had said with a grin, "I hope you realize that there's not enough room for everybody in the White House in the bomb shelter." Advisors joked darkly about who was on the list.[40]

At 10:00 A.M. on the same Wednesday, two Soviet ships were sighted just beyond the quarantine barrier extending 500 miles around Cuba. The Navy expected that at least one would have to be stopped and boarded. Then a Soviet submarine moved into position between the two ships. "I think these few minutes," Robert Kennedy recalled, "were the time of gravest concern for the President. Was the world on the brink of a nuclear holocaust? Was it our error? A mistake? . . . "[41] At 10:25 A.M., John McCone reported, "Mr. President, we have a preliminary report that some of the Russian ships have stopped dead in the water." Reaching the quarantine barrier, they stopped, turned around and sailed back toward the Soviet Union.

On Thursday, October 25, U.S. Ambassador to the United Nations Adlai Stevenson spoke to the U.N. Security Council. Soviet Ambassador to the United Nations Valerian A. Zorin charged that the CIA had manufactured evidence of missiles in Cuba. Stevenson suggested that the Soviets allow the United Nations to inspect the sites. Their dialogue went as follows:

STEVENSON: *All right sir, let me ask you one simple question: Do you, Ambassador Zorin, deny that the USSR has placed and is placing medium—and intermediate—range missiles in Cuba? Yes or no. Don't wait for the translation. Yes or no.*

ZORIN: *I am not in an American courtroom, sir.*

STEVENSON: *You are in the court of world opinion right now.*

ZORIN: *Therefore I do not wish to answer a question that is put to me in a fashion that a prosecutor does. In due course, sir, you will have your reply!*

STEVENSON: *I am prepared to wait for my answer till Hell freezes over if that's your decision! And I am also prepared to present the evidence in this room—now!*[42]

At that moment, easels supporting enlarged aerial photographs were wheeled into the Council chamber. They showed the transformation of San Cristóbal into a nuclear missile base. Zorin denied their authenticity. Stevenson persisted: "We know the facts and so do you, sir, and we are ready to talk about them. Our job here is not to score debating points. Our job, Mr. Zorin, is to save the peace. And if you are ready to try, we are."

On Friday, October 26, the Soviets continued work on the missile sites. More American troops were sent to Florida. In Washington Aleksander Fomin, a counselor for the Soviet embassy, contacted John Scali, diplomatic correspondent for ABC television. Fomin, who lunched informally with Scali from time to time, wanted to meet immediately at the Occidental restaurant. At the table, Fomin said, "War seems about to break out. Something must be done to save this situation." Scali replied, "You should have thought of that before they put the missiles in Cuba." After a silence, Fomin said, "There might be a way out. What do you think of a proposition whereby we would promise to remove our missiles under U.N. inspection, where Mr. Khrushchev would promise never to introduce such offensive weapons into Cuba again? Would the President of the U.S. be willing to promise publicly not to invade Cuba?"

Scali did not know. Fomin asked Scali to meet with people at the State Department: "This is of vital importance." Scali went immediately to the secretary of state. Rusk told Scali to convey to Fomin that the United States "saw real possibilities" for a negotiation but that time was short—the Soviets had no more than forty-eight hours. At 7:30 P.M. Scali met with Fomin, who rushed directly back to the Soviet embassy.[43]

At 9:30 P.M., the State Department received a cable for Kennedy from Khrushchev, assuring him that "the ships bound for Cuba have no armaments at all. The armaments needed for the defense of Cuba are already there." Khrushchev then expressed his wish for peace. This crisis, he said, was like a rope with a knot in the middle: the more each side pulled, the more the knot would tighten, until finally it could be severed only by a sword. If the United States promised not to invade Cuba and withdrew the quarantine, the necessity for a Soviet presence in Cuba would disappear.

On Saturday morning, October 27, Khrushchev sent a second letter of entirely different import. The Soviets would remove their missiles from Cuba and offer a nonagression pledge to Turkey if the United States would remove its missiles from Turkey.[44] Also that morning, news arrived that Major Rudolph Anderson, the U-2 pilot who had first photographed the missile sites on October 14, was shot down while flying a reconnaissance mission over Cuba. Many ExCom members felt that Soviet actions had entered a military phase. Kennedy, however, insisted that the Soviets be given time to consider their position before the United States attacked or invaded Cuba.

Advised by the attorney general, the president decided simply to ignore Khrushchev's second letter and respond to the first. Kennedy wrote that he welcomed Khrushchev's wish to seek a peaceful solution. "The first thing that must be done, however, is for work to cease on offensive missile bases in Cuba and for all weapons systems in Cuba capable of offensive use to be rendered inoperable." On Saturday evening Robert Kennedy took this message to the Soviet ambassador, adding grimly that unless assurances were received within 24 hours, the United States would take military action by Tuesday. That evening, according to Arthur Schlesinger, "was the blackest of all."[45] Driving to the Pentagon, McNamara wondered whether he would ever see another Saturday night.[46]

On Sunday morning, October 28, Khrushchev wrote that because the United States had assured the Soviets that they would not invade Cuba, the "arms which you described as offensive" would be crated and returned to the Soviet Union.

It was all over, just barely in time to prevent a war. President Kennedy reflected a few weeks later: "If we had invaded Cuba . . . I am sure the Soviets would have acted. They would have to, just as we would have to." Kennedy's advisors later concluded that U.S. nuclear superiority had not been a critical factor because a nuclear war "would have been an unexampled catastrophe for both sides."[47] Khrushchev's Sunday letter had said that the Soviets hoped to "continue the exchange of views on the prohibition of atomic and thermonuclear weapons, general disarmament, and other problems relating to the relaxation of international tension." The U.S. government heartily hoped so too.

XVIII

ARMS CONTROL AND DÉTENTE

[In the Cuban missile crisis] both sides showed that if a desire to avoid war is strong enough, even the most pressing dispute can be solved by compromise.

Nikita Khrushchev,
from his memoirs, *Khrushchev Remembers*,
1970

Perhaps now, as we step back from danger, we can together make real progress . . . I think we should give priority to questions relating to the proliferation of nuclear weapons on earth and in outer space, and to the great effort for a nuclear test ban.

John F. Kennedy,
responding to a broadcast by Khrushchev
after the Cuban Missile Crisis,
October 28, 1962

Détente becomes above all necessary because each side recognizes that the other is a potential adversary in a nuclear war. To us, détente is a process of managing relations with a potentially hostile country in order to preserve peace while maintaining our vital interests.

Henry Kissinger,
statement to Senate Committee,
April 1974

As the missiles in Cuba were dismantled, crated and shipped back to the Soviet Union, an anxious world breathed more easily. Secretary of State Dean Rusk said later, "I think both we and the Russians came out of the Cuban missile crisis somewhat more prudent because each side had a chance to look down the cannon's mouth and did not like what it saw."[1]

President Kennedy ordered that there would be "no boasting, no gloating, not even a claim of victory. We had won by enabling Khrushchev to avoid complete humiliation—we should not humiliate him now." He decided not to make a dramatic television appearance; instead, he issued a brief press release that welcomed Khrushchev's "statesmanlike decision . . . an important and constructive contribution to peace."[2]

Although 1962 was a year of confrontation, the period after the crisis was characterized by relaxed diplomatic relations. Khrushchev dropped his bluster and Kennedy tempered his anti-Communist statements. The memory of danger was fresh, and it led to efforts to improve communications in future crises. Kennedy and Khrushchev both realized that they had a common interest in avoiding long delays or scrambled communications that could lead them inadvertently into war. A direct "hot-line" communications link was set up between Washington and Moscow. Teletypes were installed instead of telephones to give each party more time to develop considered responses to events.

On June 10, 1963, President Kennedy delivered a major speech, entitled "Toward a Strategy of Peace." He decried enormous expenditures for "weapons acquired for the purpose of making sure we never need to use them." He explained that peace would not be predicated upon the absence of differences; rather peace would depend upon nations recognizing that they had a mutual interest to avoid war in a thermonuclear age—"For, in the final analysis, our most common link is that we inhabit this small planet. We all breathe the same air. We all cherish our children's future. And we are all mortal." To those who consider that war is inevitable he said, "We need not accept that view. Our problems are man-made—therefore, they can be solved by man." Nikita Khrushchev praised this as "the best speech by any President since Roosevelt."[3]

Both nations were ready to develop new initiatives to limit nuclear weapons. Attention focused first on nuclear testing. Nuclear tests loft tons of radioactive debris—smoke, soot and dust—into the atmosphere, where it is dispersed by winds before falling back to earth. The public, growing concerned about the hazards of "fallout," organized political opposition to atmospheric testing: For the first time, an informed public prepared to take political action would force its leaders to secure an arms control treaty.

By the fall of 1958 the United States, the Soviet Union and Great Britain had detonated nuclear weapons with an equivalent force of 174,000,000 tons of TNT. Radiation levels around the world had increased dramatically; one study conducted by Earlham College in Indiana found that topsoil samples analyzed in 1959 were 100 times more radioactive than samples taken from the same locations in 1950. Biologists were most concerned about strontium-90, a fallout product that remains radioactive for up to 28 years. Settling on crops, it is absorbed through the leaves and roots of plants. Humans ingest it directly by eating contaminated plants, or indirectly by eating the meat or drinking the milk of animals that have grazed on these plants. Strontium-90 is particularly dangerous because it is a "bone-seeker": Chemically similar to calcium, the basic component of bones and shells, it is attracted to and combines with calcium.[4]

Children are placed most at risk—not only because mothers

can transfer radioactivity to infants by breast-feeding, but because human skeletons grow by approximately 20 percent a year during the first five years of life. In Missouri the Greater St. Louis Citizens Committee for Nuclear Information collected 50,000 baby teeth to analyze for strontium-90. This study, and others conducted in the late 1950s, determined that strontium-90 concentrations in the bones of small children were four to seven times higher than in the bones of their parents, thus increasing the likelihood that children would develop radiation-induced diseases such as leukemia and bone cancer.

By 1963, publicity about the effects of radioactive fallout had generated enormous international political support for a nuclear-test-ban treaty. On July 15, 1963, U.S. Under Secretary of State Averell Harriman and British representative Lord Hailsham met with Nikita Khrushchev in Moscow. Getting right down to business, Khrushchev smiled and said, "Since we have decided to have a test ban let us sign now and fill in the details later." Harriman handed Khrushchev a blank sheet of paper: "Fine, you sign first." Official kidding aside, the negotiations for a Limited Test-Ban Treaty took only two weeks to conclude.[5]

The United States, the Soviet Union and Great Britain signed the Treaty Banning Nuclear Weapons Tests in the Atmosphere, Outer Space and Under Water on August 5, 1963. The Limited Test-Ban Treaty was a milestone. For the first time nations had placed some restraints on the nuclear arms race. The treaty was "limited" because underground nuclear testing was not prohibited; still, as Theodore Sorensen said with cautious optimism, "The breathing spell [brought on by the missile crisis] had become a pause, the pause was becoming a détente, and no one could foresee what further changes lay ahead."[6]

President Kennedy was assassinated in Dallas on Friday, November 22, 1963. Vice-President Lyndon Baines Johnson assumed the presidency and vowed to implement his predecessor's policies. These included an increased military commitment to the South Vietnamese, who were fighting a bitter civil war against Communist North Vietnam.

The Vietnam conflict divided the U.S. public and deflected its interest away from nuclear weapons issues. Nevertheless, throughout the war, President Johnson worked to negotiate nuclear arms control agreements under the auspices of the United Nations. The Outer Space Treaty was signed in 1967, the Treaty for the Prohibition of Nuclear Weapons in Latin America in 1967, and the Treaty on the Non-Proliferation of Nuclear Weapons (commonly known as the Non-Proliferation Treaty, or NPT) in 1968. The Outer Space Treaty required nations to "refrain from placing in orbit around the earth any objects carrying nuclear weapons or any other kinds of weapons of mass destruction, installing such weapons on celestial bodies, or stationing such weapons in outer space in any other manner." The Latin American treaty, a direct outgrowth of concerns generated during the Cuban Missile Crisis, prohibited stationing or using nuclear weapons in Latin America.[7]

As Secretary of State Dean Rusk said, the Non-Proliferation Treaty's main objective was "to make nuclear war less likely by preventing the spread of nuclear weapons to other countries."[8] As we noted in the Introduction, the nuclear materials used for peaceful and for military purposes are virtually the same. Nations without nuclear weapons can divert nuclear materials from reactors producing electricity and use them to make weapons.

The NPT, which to date has been signed by 135 nations, is the centerpiece of the world's "nonproliferation regime"—a collection of treaties, agreements, voluntary guidelines, and international institutions that collectively work to prevent the spread of nuclear weapons. Nations agree to keep accurate records of the amounts of nuclear materials they use and how they use them. Reports must be filed with the International Atomic Energy Agency (IAEA) in Vienna, Austria. IAEA inspectors may enter nuclear facilities to evaluate records and to make independent measurements of safeguarded materials. They may install cameras and other recording devices inside nuclear facilities for surveillance purposes.[9]

But by the late 1960s nuclear weapons had been tested by the United States (first test in 1945), the Soviet Union (1949), Great Britain (1952), France (1960) and the People's Republic of China (1964). These five nations continue to manufacture, maintain and deploy nuclear weapons. In 1974 India conducted a nuclear test, but it has not yet developed a nuclear arsenal as far as we know. Israel, South Africa and possibly Pakistan have an undeclared or "veiled" capability to make nuclear weapons. Argentina, Brazil, Libya and Iraq are "near-nuclear" nations who may attempt to catch up.

No one doubts that the spread of nuclear weapons will result in a more dangerous world. The risk of nuclear war precipitated by accident, miscalculation or madness would certainly increase; so too would the risk that a flare-up in a politically unstable region might escalate into a nuclear conflict involving the United States and the Soviet Union. Then why aren't nations prepared to eliminate their nuclear arsenals?

Perhaps the most significant factor is the perceived importance of nuclear deterrence. Deterrence is a centuries-old concept; it has always seemed safer to rely upon weapons for protection than to disarm, either partially or entirely. Nations have developed new nuclear weapons systems to catch up to or to keep up with, or to keep ahead of, their adversaries. Presidential advisor McGeorge Bundy has concluded:

The larger question of the historical record is that fear of the bomb has always been less powerful than fear of the adversary's bomb. . . . The weapons each side has sought have been those its government found necessary in the light of what others had done or might do.[10]

Fears of adversaries have driven technological advances in weaponry; these can both complicate ongoing arms control negotiations and render existing treaties obsolete. For example, before 1970, ICBMs and SLBMs each carried only one nuclear warhead. While the Soviets developed anti-ballistic missiles (ABMs), which could destroy enemy missiles before they reached their targets, the United States, to complicate Soviet defenses, developed MIRVs (Multiple Independently Targetable Reentry Vehicles). A single missile could now carry multiple warheads. At high altitudes, the missile's nose cone (or "bus"), carrying up to fourteen warheads, separates; at predetermined points each warhead ejects and falls on its individual target.

MIRVs did indeed complicate matters for Soviet ABM defenses; they also complicated arms control negotiations. Then the Soviets also began "MIRVing" their missiles, and the number of nuclear warheads in superpower arsenals increased drastically. MIRVs could have been outlawed. In retrospect, this was another missed opportunity to control the arms race.

Arms control is also challenged by economic and institutional resistance. The nuclear-weapons industry and associated industries that produce bombers, missiles and submarines are parts of the formidable "military-industrial complex" that Eisenhower spoke of in his farewell address. The economic well-being of many communities depends upon government defense expenditures; defense contractors employ thousands of people, who elect federal, state and local representatives to protect and perpetuate their political and economic power. Of course, entrenched nuclear constituencies are not just an American phenomenon. Every nuclear-capable nation has special-interest groups that work with varying degrees of opposition against arms control.

The U.S. nuclear arsenal peaked during President Johnson's administration.[11] Johnson became wary of the funds this arsenal drained from his efforts to create a "Great Society" to fight a "War on Poverty, to provide greater educational opportunities for all American children, to offer medical care to the elderly, to conserve on water and air and natural resources, and to tackle the country's longstanding housing shortage."[12] In June 1967, at a summit meeting in Glassboro, New Jersey, Johnson urged Soviet Premier Aleksei Kosygin (who with Leonid Brezhnev had succeeded Khrushchev) to schedule arms limitation talks. They eventually agreed to meet in Moscow the next year. But on August 21, 1968, the Soviets invaded Czechoslovakia with 400,000 troops to crush the liberal regime of Alexander Dubček. Johnson canceled his trip, and the arms talks were scuttled.

President Richard M. Nixon, in his inaugural address on January 20, 1969, spoke of conciliation: "After a period of confrontation, we are entering an era of negotiation." That same day, the Soviet Foreign Ministry expressed interest in arms negotiations. There ensued a period of "détente," an easing and relaxation of strained relations between the superpowers. In November 1969 the United States and the Soviet Union began the Strategic Arms Limitation Talks—SALT. Three principles guided U.S. negotiators: Any agreement should (1) permit the United States to maintain strategic forces at "parity"—levels at least equal to those of the Soviet Union; (2) maintain, and if possible enhance, the stability of the strategic balance, thereby reducing the threat of nuclear war; and (3) be adequately verifiable, so that violations could be detected and acted upon.

From November 1969 until May 1973, Ambassador Gerard C. Smith led a U.S. team of nearly a hundred negotiators, advisors, interpreters, administrative staff and Marine guards. During the first year, ten or so representatives from each side met twice a week in formal or "plenary" sessions. These were dry and plodding affairs; Smith and the Soviet chief negotiator, Deputy Foreign Minister Vladimir S. Semenov, read prepared statements cleared by Washington and Moscow. Semenov once said to Paul Nitze, a U.S. negotiator, "You should not be discouraged [about the slow rate of progress], for in a negotiation of this type, about one third of the business is done in the first two months, about one third of the business in the next two years, and one third during the last twenty minutes."[13]

SALT established a complex process that went beyond traditional diplomacy. John Newhouse, a historian of SALT, has described the many levels negotiations operate on:

At the outer, most obvious tier, it is a negotiation between rival powers. At another level, it is a negotiation between Washington and its chief NATO allies, whose feelings about SALT are mixed: while applauding efforts to stabilize deterrence, they are wary of the political consequences of formal parity . . . at yet another level . . . SALT is, in the United States, a negotiation between the [President] and the Congress . . . finally, and most importantly, SALT is an internal negotiation. It is within the two capitals that the critical bargaining—the struggle to grind out positions—lumbers endlessly, episodically on.[14]

In addition, unbeknownst even to the U.S. SALT delegation, President Nixon, Henry Kissinger, Soviet Premier Kosygin and Soviet Ambassador Dobrynin were conducting secret "back-channel" negotiations. U.S. Ambassador Smith and Secretary of State William P. Rogers did not learn of these efforts until May 19, 1971, one day before the final agreement was announced. Although the "back-channel" process probably hastened an agreement, many who had spent years negotiating SALT felt slighted by the secret talks.[15]

The SALT agreements placed ceilings on the numbers of ICBMs, SLBMs and missile-launching submarines that could be held by each nation. They also prohibited the deployment of anti-ballistic-missile (ABM) systems except at one site on each side. Each nation was allowed to substitute new for older weapons and to adjust the numbers of SLBMs relative to ICBMs. In May 1971 President Nixon traveled to the Soviet Union to sign the agreements. No American president had set foot on Soviet soil since World War II.

SALT II negotiations, to develop a long-term treaty limiting all nuclear weapons systems, began in November 1972. The principal U.S. objectives were to provide for equal numbers of U.S. and Soviet strategic delivery vehicles, to begin to reduce the number of these systems, and to impose restraints on new technological developments like MIRVs. But President Nixon's growing preoccupation with the Watergate scandal effectively put an end to his administration's arms control efforts. In August 1974 he resigned the presidency as a consequence of his attempts to cover up his own role, and that of his administration, in the bugging and burglary of the Democratic National Committee headquarters at the Watergate Hotel in Washington, D.C.

In November 1974, at a summit meeting in the Soviet city of Vladivostok, Leonid Brezhnev and Gerald Ford, Nixon's successor, outlined the general terms of a SALT II treaty that would set ceilings allowing each nation 2,400 "strategic delivery vehicles" (ICBMs, SLBMs and long-range bombers) and 1,320 MIRVed missiles. Was this progress? Many worried that such "ceilings" belied the very notion of arms control: Both sides would have to build up their forces even to reach them.

President Jimmy Carter's inaugural address in January 1977 expressed a hope that "nuclear weapons would be rid from the face of the earth." Two months later, Secretary of State Cyrus Vance traveled to Moscow to propose that "deep cuts"—well below the Vladivostok ceilings—be made in numbers of strategic delivery vehicles. Brezhnev took umbrage, accusing Carter of trying to change the SALT rules so painstakingly developed since 1969. One Soviet official privately admonished the chief U.S. negotiator: "You shouldn't have disregarded the fact that Brezhnev had to spill political blood to get the Vladivostok accords."[16]

After the Soviets rejected the "deep cuts" proposal, SALT II negotiators went back to work. U.S. and Soviet diplomats argued over almost every conceivable detail, including punctuation. The definition of "MIRV" for instance, went on for four pages. By 1977, the working text of the agreement was more than ten times longer than the SALT I treaty. By June 1979, after almost seven years of intense negotiations, the SALT II agreement was ready for signature.

But by 1979, Soviet–American relations were deteriorating again, and new evidence of a Soviet arms buildup was alarming the West. The U.S. Congress debated whether or not the Carter administration was responding appropriately; specifically, was SALT II contributing in some way to Soviet designs? Some members of Congress believed that SALT II gave away unwarranted, potentially dangerous concessions. On the eve of Carter's departure for Vienna, Senator Henry M. Jackson made a scathing comparison:

> . . . *Against overwhelming evidence of a continuing Soviet strategic and conventional military buildup, there has been a flow of official administration explanations, extenuations, excuses. It is ominously reminiscent of Great Britain in the 1930s, when one government pronouncement after another was issued to assure the British public that Hitler's Germany would never achieve military equality—let alone superiority. The failure to face reality today, like the failure to do so then—that is the mark of appeasement.*[17]

Old newsreels show Chamberlain carrying an umbrella when he met with Hitler in Munich in 1938. Upset by Jackson's remarks, Carter ordered that no member of the U.S. delegation carry an umbrella even though heavy rains were falling when Carter arrived in Vienna: "I'd rather drown than carry an umbrella."

The SALT II signing ceremony took place at the Hofburg Palace, amidst considerable pomp, on June 18, 1979. According to President Carter, he and Soviet Premier Brezhnev embraced warmly afterward. Carter later wrote, "There is no doubt there were strong feelings of cooperation between us at the moment."[18]

That spirit of cooperation was markedly absent in the U.S. Senate, where the treaty awaited ratification. Many members of Congress felt that arms control agreements, once sought for their own merits, should be linked to more acceptable Soviet behavior in trouble spots worldwide. After a full decade of SALT negotiations, America was beginning to reexamine arms control and détente in the light of a string of national disappointments: Vietnam, Watergate, the holding of fifty-two American hostages in Iran, and finally, in December 1979, the Soviet invasion of Afghanistan. The invasion of a nonaligned country shocked Carter: "My opinion of the Russians," he told a television interviewer, "has changed most drastically." He realized that he could not expect to get anywhere near the 67 Senate votes necessary to ratify SALT II. Early in 1980, Carter withdrew the treaty from consideration by the Senate, saving it from rejection but leaving it in limbo, where it has since remained.

Once again, an arms control initiative was shelved as a result of a jolting political event. Eisenhower's U-2 fiasco had delayed the limited test-ban treaty; Johnson's hopes for SALT were dashed when Soviet tanks rolled into Czechoslovakia; Watergate undermined Nixon's efforts to negotiate beyond SALT I; and now, the Soviet invasion of Afghanistan effectively killed Carter's Senate ratification campaign.

In 1980, presidential candidate Ronald Reagan charged that the SALT II Treaty was "fatally flawed"—it was time to rebuild the armed forces of America; they had suffered a "decade of neglect." But while it is true that the Soviet Union's strategic modernization programs more than matched U.S. programs, the United States had hardly become an inferior power. During the Carter administration alone, the United States spent nearly a trillion dollars on defense and deployed 4,000 new nuclear warheads on land- and sea-based missiles.[19] No sane leader could believe that his nation could "win" a nuclear war against the United States.

During the Carter years the Soviet Union began to deploy SS-20 intermediate-range nuclear missiles within striking range of virtually all of Western Europe. The SS-20 is an accurate, mobile missile with three independently targetable warheads. In 1977

West German Chancellor Helmut Schmidt had warned the NATO allies that in an age of strategic nuclear parity between the super-powers, the SS-20s made Western Europe vulnerable to superior Soviet tactical nuclear and conventional forces (NATO had no systems to match the SS-20). In Schmidt's view, such "disparities" had to be corrected by NATO in order to safeguard European security.

NATO responded on December 12, 1979, with a "two-track" decision: First, the United States would negotiate with the Soviets in an attempt to persuade them to withdraw the SS-20s; second, in the absence of an arms control agreement, NATO would "modern-ize" its intermediate-range nuclear forces by deploying 464 U.S. ground-launched cruise missiles and 108 Pershing II ballistic mis-siles in Western Europe. Deployment was scheduled for late 1983.

Cruise missiles are descendants of the V-1 buzz bombs devel-oped by the Germans during World War II. Like the V-1, the cruise missile is low-flying, self-guided and powered by a small jet engine. Unlike its World War II ancestors, however, it is designed to carry a nuclear warhead. Both the U.S. Pershing and the Soviet SS-20 are high-flying, nuclear-armed rockets descended from the German V-2.

In January 1981 the Reagan Administration assumed office and began an enormous expansion of U.S. strategic nuclear forces while fully supporting the modernization of NATO intermediate-range nuclear missiles. American rearmament, President Reagan be-lieved, would provide "bargaining power" in future talks with the Soviets.

The European public, however, did not favor this approach, believing that President Reagan was more interested in an arms buildup than in arms reduction. Europeans exerted intense polit-ical pressure on their leaders to seek arms control. European leaders, in turn, pressured the Reagan administration, which eventually opened Intermediate Nuclear Force (INF) talks with the Soviet Union, to deal with intermediate-range missiles and bombers able to attack Soviet territory from Western Europe and vice versa. On November 18, 1982, Reagan promised that the United States would cancel its planned deployment of 572 new Pershing II and ground-launched cruise missiles if the Soviets would dismantle their SS-20, and their older SS-4 and SS-5 (intermediate-range nuclear), missiles. If the Soviets would not agree, NATO would proceed to deploy its new missiles.

Paul Nitze had been appointed chief negotiator for the INF talks. Called the "Silver Fox"—less for his gray hair than for his ability to find ingenious solutions to snarled problems—Nitze traveled to Geneva to negotiate with his Soviet counterpart, Yuli Kvitsinsky. Vladimir Pavlichenko, a member of the Soviet delegation, said later, "We were struck by Nitze's saying almost on the first day, 'I came here to leave no stone unturned.' "[20]

By July 1982, however, nothing had been accomplished. The Soviets were not willing to destroy their SS-20s (already deployed) in exchange for NATO's scrapping its Pershing II and cruise missiles (not yet deployed). Nitze believed that European public opposition to new missile deployments could paralyze NATO and harm U.S. relations with its allies. He also knew that Brezhnev's health was failing—that the next summit meeting might be his last—and reasoned that Brezhnev might be prepared to compromise. In a private meeting, Kvitsinsky agreed that Nitze might be right. "Then shouldn't we," said Nitze, "put our heads together and explore ways to contribute to that possibility?"

Nitze suggested that discussions might be more productive if they were more private. In the weeks that followed, the two negotiators often met alone to explore compromise solutions. Their climactic meeting took place on the afternoon of July 16, 1982. They rode in Kvitsinsky's car up to a pass in the Swiss mountains near the French border where Soviet diplomats skied cross-country. Nitze wanted to walk up the mountain but Kvitsinsky preferred to walk down; he was 30 years younger but not in as good physical shape. The Soviet driver left the two diplomats near the summit.

After a short walk, they sat down on a log and Nitze began to read aloud from the outline of an agreement—a proposal for a two-thirds reduction in the number of Soviet SS-20s deployed in Eastern Europe. In exchange, the United States could keep a certain number of cruise missiles in Western Europe but not deploy any Pershing II missiles, whose quick flight time most worried the Soviets. Thus, the Soviet monopoly on intermediate-range missiles would be offset by a U.S. monopoly on cruise missiles.

Kvitsinsky listened, then suggested some changes. Nitze warned that incorporating them would make the proposal a joint paper; did Kvitsinsky understand this? "Yes," he replied. "Let's go through the rest of it." Nitze assured the Soviet, "You can blame this on me with your people." Kvitsinsky replied, "I'll tell them it's your scheme, and you tell them it's mine." "Maybe we'll both go to jail," joked Nitze. Kvitsinsky said, "No American government would send Paul Nitze to jail . . . and I have no intention of going to jail myself."[21]

The two diplomats agreed to take their "walk-in-the-woods proposal" back to their respective governments. Nitze received a mixed reaction. Some at the White House were miffed that Nitze had not "cleared" his ideas beforehand. Others worried about giving up the Pershing II missile if the Soviets would be allowed to keep some SS-20s targeted on Europe. The final decision would rest with President Reagan.

At the key cabinet meeting, proponents and opponents presented their arguments. Secretary of Defense Caspar Weinberger attacked Nitze's proposal. The president then voiced his own misgivings. He preferred his original proposal: the United States would deploy no Pershing II or cruise missiles if the Soviets would dismantle their SS-20s, SS-4s and SS-5s. "Why couldn't the Soviets live without their SS-20s if the U.S. had to live without new missiles in Europe?" "Because," replied Nitze, "there is a big difference between not deploying a weapons system still under development and removing one that is already perfected and in place." The president was not convinced. He would not agree to counter "fast-flying" SS-20s with "slow-flying" cruise missiles. "Well Paul," Reagan said, "you just tell the Soviets that you're working for one tough son-of-a-bitch."[22]

In November 1983 NATO began to deploy its new nuclear missiles. Incensed, the Soviets walked out of the INF negotiations. The INF talks were later resumed, but by 1986, NATO had deployed the majority of its cruise and Pershing II missiles and the Soviets had deployed an estimated 441 SS-20s and 270 Backfire bombers. This constituted many more missiles and bombers than the "walk-in-the-woods proposal" would have allowed.

When the Soviets walked out of the INF talks, they also quit a set of negotiations called the Strategic Arms Reduction Talks (START). These latter talks had focused on limiting nuclear warheads (rather than delivery vehicles) and had made negligible progress. Initiating START, President Reagan had hoped to divorce himself entirely from the SALT process. However, the major provisions of both the SALT I treaty and the unratified SALT II agreement continue to be observed. In general, the Reagan administration's policy was to avoid actions that would undercut SALT II, provided the Soviets exercise equal restraint. Both nations have thus far acknowledged that the world is better off observing limitations than not.

In 1983 the Reagan administration turned its attention to a new idea that continues to generate enormous controversy and that complicates future arms control negotiations. Edward Teller and others, seeking ways to exploit the significant U.S. lead in space-age technology, convinced President Reagan to begin a Strategic Defense Initiative (SDI), popularly known as "Star Wars." SDI advocates assert that a mix of land- and space-based weapons can be built to destroy Soviet nuclear missiles in case of an attack against the United States. It is far better, they assert, to save lives with defensive systems than to threaten lives with offensive nuclear weapons; deterrence based on defense is morally more acceptable than deterrence based on the threat of nuclear retaliation.

In a televised address on March 23, 1983, President Reagan urged that the nation commit itself to a long-term multibillion-dollar strategic defense research effort, a program that would rival, in cost, the Manhattan Project and the Apollo moon program. "Star Wars" has received mixed reviews. Defense consultant Simon Ramo said he thought "it was a great idea [for President Reagan] to make this announcement," but he cautioned that "we don't know how to do this yet, and there will be pitfalls and problems all the way." SALT I negotiator Gerard Smith expressed disapproval: "Instead of one nuclear arms race, we would have two." Zbigniew Brzezinski, former national security advisor to President Carter, wondered, "How will the Soviets respond?"

Soviet Premier Yuri Andropov (Brezhnev's successor) responded quickly and vehemently. Four days after Reagan's announcement, Andropov claimed that the U.S. strategic nuclear buildup, coupled with an anti-ballistic-missile program, represented a "bid to disarm the Soviet Union in the face of the U.S. nuclear threat." Andropov warned that if Reagan's "Star Wars" became a reality, it would "open the floodgates to a runaway race of all types of strategic arms, both offensive and defensive."

Soviet objections to "Star Wars" run deep. A great benefit of détente, from the Soviet point of view, is that it permits them to maintain military equality with the United States. Since the Nixon administration, the United States had accepted strategic parity as an inevitable aspect of nuclear deterrence. "Star Wars" appeared to the Soviets, however, to be a U.S. effort to regain strategic superiority. If a leak-proof U.S. system of defense could be built, the great Soviet achievement of strategic nuclear parity would be nullified.

In November 1984 Ronald Reagan was reelected in a landslide vote. In March 1985, Mikhail Gorbachev took over as the new Soviet premier. A new agenda was set for wide-ranging arms control negotiations covering strategic nuclear arms, INF, and defensive and space weapons. The two leaders arranged a summit meeting in November 1985 at Geneva, Switzerland. Reagan sought to demonstrate to the American public that in spite of his having only harsh things to say about the Soviet Union during his first term in office, he could yet meet and negotiate with the Soviet leader. Gorbachev, newly installed in office, wished to show that he could hold his own against the telegenic and experienced U.S. leader. At one point during their meeting, Reagan and Gorbachev sat before a roaring fire. Reagan remarked, "Between us, we could come up with things that could bring peace for years to come."

At the Geneva summit, little of consequence was accomplished. Reagan and Gorbachev did, however, agree to hold another meeting—one that turned out to be an extraordinary encounter.

At the two-day meeting in Reykjavik, Iceland, on October

11–12, 1986, U.S.–Soviet negotiating protocol was all but abandoned. The United States had anticipated that this meeting would
be a preliminary summit for planning purposes; instead, Reagan
and Gorbachev appeared to pull out all the stops as they improvised
ways to restructure and reduce their huge stockpiles of nuclear
weapons. Working groups of experts toiled through the night to
achieve compromises on issues that years of negotiation had failed
to resolve.

At Reykjavik the two leaders agreed, in Reagan's words, "to a
figure of 100 intermediate-range missile warheads for each side
worldwide. . . . And for the first time we began to hammer out
the details of a 50% cut in strategic forces over 5 years. And we
were a sentence or two away from agreeing to new talks on nuclear
testing. And maybe most important, we were in sight of an historic
agreement on completely eliminating the threat of offensive ballistic missiles by 1996."[23]

Reagan and Gorbachev failed to overcome the principal obsta-
cle: They could not resolve how to constrain SDI. Gorbachev
insisted that the program would give the United States military
superiority and a first-strike capability against the Soviet Union.
Reagan insisted that SDI would produce a purely defensive shield
against offensive nuclear forces and was therefore the moral alternative to traditional deterrence based on mutual assured destruction. Neither leader would accept the other's reasoning. The
Reykjavik meeting collapsed.

Although no accords were signed, the deliberations apparently
came closer than had ever been thought possible to producing an
agreement that would effect sweeping changes in U.S.–Soviet nuclear arsenals. Many people were startled to learn that after years
of tough talk about the Soviets and the need for an arms buildup,
Reagan would even discuss such far-reaching disarmament pro-

posals. People were also surprised, after the slow, painstaking processes of SALT I and II, that the two leaders could have moved so fast toward an agreement. After Reykjavik Reagan said, "I'm still optimistic that a way will be found, the door is open and the opportunity to begin eliminating the nuclear threat is within reach. . . ."

Throughout 1987, amid controversy over the Iran-contra Affair and concerns about the tumbling stock market and the growing federal budget deficit, U.S. arms control negotiators worked diligently. The Soviets faced their own difficulties, including international opposition to their eight-year war in Afghanistan, heavy criticism on human rights issues, and a stagnant economy. Notwithstanding, the two nations forged an Intermediate-Range Nuclear Forces Treaty that would eliminate from Europe 859 U.S. and 1752 Soviet missiles with a range of 300 to 3,000 miles, among them the U.S. Pershings and cruise missiles and the Soviet SS-20s that had been the subject of the "walk in the woods" proposal. Although the agreement would eliminate only approximately 4 percent of the superpowers' total weaponry, it was widely hailed as a major step toward negotiating deeper cuts in nuclear arsenals.

On December 8, 1987, at the signing ceremony in Washington, D.C., President Reagan said:

We can only hope that this history-making agreement will not be an end in itself, but the beginning of a working relationship that will enable us to tackle the other . . . urgent issues before us. . . .

Soviet General Secretary Gorbachev responded:

We can be proud of planting this sapling, which may one day grow into a mighty tree of peace. . . . May December 8, 1987, become a date that will be inscribed in the history books—a date that will mark the watershed separating the era of a mounting risk of nuclear war from the era of a demilitarization of human life.

A few U.S. senators expressed misgivings that removal of U.S. missiles from Europe will leave our NATO allies vulnerable to superior Soviet conventional forces, but the Senate ratified the INF Treaty by an overwhelming vote of 93 to 5 on May 27, 1988. Ratification by the Soviets followed the next day.

The INF Treaty represents three "firsts" that warrant considerable optimism for future progress in arms control: For the first time, an entire class of nuclear weapons would have to be destroyed as the result of an arms control agreement. Also, and again for the first time, both sides appear to recognize that we have many more nuclear weapons than is required for mutual deterrance. And, finally, for the first time in the nuclear age, the Soviets have accepted the principle of on-site inspection. As Jonathan Schell, author of *The Fate of the Earth*, has noted, this principle is so important that the treaty might well be renamed "The On-Site Inspection Agreement." The treaty calls for "Nuclear Risk Reduction Centers" to be used by each side to request inspections, to notify the other of the movement of missiles or of the elimination of weapons, and to provide a means for other exchanges of information. A new United States–Soviet "Special Verification Commission" will resolve disputes about compliance with the agreement. These breakthroughs are important precedents that can pave the way for sweeping verifiable nuclear and conventional arms treaties in the future.

Before, during, and after the INF signing ceremony, "summit fever" gripped Washington, and other parts of the country. President Reagan hosted a lavish state dinner at the White House, and General Secretary Gorbachev and his wife Raisa entertained influential Americans at the Soviet Embassy. Following his final meeting with Reagan, Gorbachev ordered his motorcade to stop at a street corner in downtown Washington where a crowd had gathered in the rain. The Soviet General Secretary climbed out of his armored Zil limousine to wave and shake hands with the cheering crowd. Gorbachev's security guards were aghast, but both Gorbachev and the American crowd were delighted by the informal contact. Attracted by the racket, Washington restaurateur Duke Zeibert stepped outside. He said later, "Gorbachev caught my eye and waved to me. I'm 76 years old and it takes a lot to get me excited, but I was excited. I'm still excited."

The Washington summit of 1987 raised hopes for 1988, 1989, and beyond; after years of arms buildups and harsh rhetoric, many saw the occasion as ushering in a new era of U.S.–Soviet détente. Another summit conference convened in June of 1988, in Moscow: The superpowers sought a 50-percent cut in long-range-nuclear-weapons systems, but verification problems and other differences forestalled an agreement. The authors hope that a verifiable agreement is achieved soon. However, even if 50-percent reductions are accomplished, we still cannot assume that the world is safe from the threat of nuclear war.

Realistically, we are likely to confront many obstacles in our quest for a safer future. We should anticipate that periods of détente will continue to alternate with other times in which fear and distrust prevail. Episodes of espionage such as those involving Klaus Fuchs, the Rosenbergs, and the U-2 may temporarily derail arms control efforts. Technical breakthroughs and their military applications by one side may threaten the other, causing reactions that are not compatible with long-term efforts in the interests of peace. We should also expect to face some institutional opposition to arms control from the military-industrial complex and other special-interest groups in the United States, the Soviet Union, and elsewhere. Whatever the future brings, we need to avoid drastic swings in the national mood and maintain a consistent commitment to reducing and eventually eliminating the nuclear threat.

XIX

NUCLEAR DEMOCRACY

The very fact that knowledge is itself the basis of civilization points directly to openness as the way to overcome the present crisis.

Niels Bohr

Neither the President nor the Congress can ignore the new constituency for arms control that has forced the President to the negotiating table and the Congress into a crash course on the intricacies of national security policy. Like it or not, nuclear policy-making is fast becoming democratized.

Representative Edward F. Feighan (Ohio),
1983

The threat posed by nuclear weapons concerns everyone, but citizens of the United States and other democratic nations bear a special responsibility to actively confront the dramatic and often divisive issues that are raised by weapons of mass destruction. Indeed, many are doing so: Religious leaders and lay persons are wrestling with the moral acceptability of threatening nuclear retaliation as a means to deter nuclear war. Psychologists are examining the effects on individuals of living under the threat of nuclear annihilation and are studying factors that promote aggression and inhibit cooperation. Involved citizens are debating the social and economic trade-offs that result from large military budgets—how much deterrence can we afford in light of competing needs to relieve poverty and support education, health care and medical research?

By way of our elected representatives and our free press, citizens have the last word on a broad range of national security alternatives. We can urge—or forbid—our leaders to build, limit or eliminate nuclear weapons either unilaterally, or through agreements with other nations. It may be startling to some that we wield such power, but that is the nature of democracy.

Nuclear debates are particularly vigorous in the Western European democracies. Europeans, who have hosted two World Wars in this century, are horrified at the prospect of a third conflagration—one that probably would involve nuclear weapons. And many object to a controversial NATO strategy which anticipates the possible first use of nuclear weapons if NATO conventional forces are unable to stop a conventional attack by the Warsaw Pact. That is, NATO's deterrence strategy is based on the ability to respond to any Warsaw Pact aggression at an equal or even higher level of conflict. As a consequence of this policy, approximately 6,000 U.S. nuclear weapons are based in West Germany alone, a country about the size of Oregon. Even if the INF Treaty of 1987 is ratified and implemented, about 4,000 nuclear weapons are slated to remain.

Not surprisingly, public reaction to nuclear issues is especially strong in West Germany. In the early 1980s a new German political party, the "Greens," amassed a large coalition made up primarily of young people. They organized demonstrations and gathered some 1.5 million signatures to protest Pershing and cruise missile deployments. They intended, they said, to prevent a "Euroshima." Members of the Greens ran for election on an antinuclear platform and gained twenty-seven seats in the West German parliament. To mobilize more support, they conducted a "Nuremberg Tribunal

Against First-Strike Weapons and Other Instruments of Mass Destruction in East and West." The tribunal published an appeal that reads, in part:

We call upon people everywhere to never accustom themselves, to never allow themselves to be accustomed, to the idea of war and the preparation for war. . . . Through this commitment to peace, even fear itself may perform a useful service by being transformed into a creative force.

We call upon people everywhere to work for peace, to forget the quiet comfort of their homes, to leave behind their fears and feeling of powerlessness, their privileges and possessions, and join us as active participants and co-workers for peace.[1]

Some Americans have wondered whether these Germans are ungrateful for U.S. contributions to the defense of Europe. But West Germany has more nuclear weapons per square mile than any other nation in the world; and as former West German Chancellor Helmut Schmidt said to visiting American newspaper editors, "if the state of New York had some 6,000 nuclear weapons on its territory, then I suggest you Americans would have a highly vocal peace movement as well."

The wave of West European protest spilled over into the United States, building momentum for a "nuclear freeze." The movement was the brainchild of Randall Forsberg, a woman who sensed that Americans were worried enough about the arms race to do something about it. In August 1980, she published a memorandum entitled "A Call to Halt the Nuclear Arms Race." It reads, in part:

To improve national and international security, the United States and the Soviet Union should stop the nuclear arms race. Specifically, they should adopt a mutual freeze on the testing, production and deployment of nuclear weapons and of missiles and new aircraft designed primarily to deliver nuclear weapons. This is an essential, verifiable first step toward lessening the risk of nuclear war and reducing the nuclear arsenals.[2]

Forsberg's "Call to Halt" generated resolutions across the United States, and by 1981 freeze organizations were active in all fifty states and in a majority of congressional districts.

Nuclear freeze activities concentrated on four fundamental democratic processes: education, outreach, political action and fundraising. Volunteers organized meetings in homes and "teach-ins" in schools, churches and synagogues. They wrote letters to local newspapers. They urged local libraries to order up-to-date books dealing with nuclear weapons issues; many libraries set up special sections and display cases. To build a broad base of political support, activists solicited endorsements from businesses, labor unions, minority groups and religious communities. They wrote to and visited their congressional representatives in their local and Washington offices. They organized "telephone trees" to contact congressional offices before key votes and publicized congressional voting records on national security issues. They marched, rallied and held candlelight vigils; they raised funds by sponsoring concerts, walkathons and bikeathons.

The nuclear freeze was a major issue in the 1982 congressional elections. Democratic Congressman Edward Feighan has recalled: "On every talk show, and in every forum in which candidates sought to get their message across, they had to have a position on the nuclear-weapons freeze." Congressional hearings were held, and resolutions appeared in the Senate and House of Representatives. On August 6, 1982, members of Congress who favored a freeze argued that it served both sides because the United States and the Soviet Union had achieved strategic parity—that is, both had roughly comparable strategic nuclear forces. Opponents, supported by President Reagan, argued that the Soviet Union possessed a margin of strategic superiority. The United States, therefore, must build up its arsenals before a freeze could be considered; a freeze at current levels would place the nation at a military disadvantage.

In November 1982 freeze resolutions appeared on twenty-eight state and local ballots and were approved on twenty-five of these. However, in the House of Representatives opponents of the freeze won a narrow victory by a vote of 204–202. But the debate was not over: in the November 1982 elections, freeze supporters won twenty-eight seats; and opponents won sixteen. On May 4, 1983, the freeze resolution passed in the House with a bipartisan majority of 278–149. The vote was not binding—that is, it could not force the president to freeze weapons levels; nevertheless, it officially registered the public's deep concern about the arms race.

Nonetheless, President Reagan was able to generate public and Congressional support for a U.S. arms buildup. Encouraged by the president, new organizations advocating a buildup worked with energy and conviction to convert citizens to their cause. They used many of the same techniques as the freeze movement and pursued their views just as adamantly as those advocating arms control and disarmament. The Committee on the Present Danger and the Coalition for Peace Through Strength stressed the dangers of the Soviet military threat. The Committee on the Present Danger declared that "the Soviet Union has not altered its long-held goal of a world dominated by a single center—Moscow" and that American military policies were leaving the United States "adrift in a hostile world, facing the unremitting pressures of Soviet policy backed by an overwhelming preponderance of [military] power."[3] The Coalition for Peace Through Strength promoted a policy advocating "overall military/technological superiority over the Soviet Union."[4] In the early 1980s these arguments largely prevailed, and a massive U.S. arms buildup was the consequence.

The authors believe that the nuclear debate of the early 1980s has a deeper significance than which side "won" or "lost": For the first time, conservative and liberal citizens alike realized that "grass-roots" political activity could influence the development of nuclear weapons policy. As a result, citizens are becoming better informed and more determined than ever to question their political candidates' knowledge and views on a wide range of nuclear issues, and to vote accordingly. There are also signs that the press is determined not to allow uninformed candidates to slide by on their charm or good looks alone. "Nuclear democracy" promises to figure significantly in the 1988 and future elections.

By the late 1980s, after years of a U.S. arms buildup, there are few who can plausibly argue that the United States is inferior in strength to the Soviet Union. The United States can now certainly negotiate from a position of strength, and arms control has resurfaced as a priority on the national agenda. With the accession of Mikhail Gorbachev to the Soviet leadership, prospects for arms control continue to improve. His policy of *glasnost* (openness) makes him appear more approachable and more reasonable than any Soviet leader of recent memory.

The early 1980s were years of unstable leadership in the Soviet Union. Leonid Brezhnev governed as a semi-invalid before his death in 1982. His successor, Yuri Andropov, died in 1984 after serving less than two years in office. Andropov's successor, the frail and elderly Constantine Chernenko, lived only one year. By this time Soviet society was suffering: Divorce rates climbed, along with increasing numbers of abortions and illegitimate births, and alcoholism was on the rise. Life expectancy actually declined, especially among Russian males—an unprecedented development in a modern industrial society not at war.

A deeply troubled economy contributed significantly to the Soviet malaise. While the Soviets matched the United States in military might, they were hardly equal in economic performance, lagging far behind the West in most technologies. The gap between the Soviet Union and the capitalist countries in microelectronics and computers, keys to economic progress in the last years of the twentieth century, was wide and growing wider.[5]

Mikhail Gorbachev has inherited the huge task of revitalizing his country. He is vigorous, articulate and (in his fifties) relatively young for a Soviet leader. He has gambled his political career on a new policy called *perestroika* (restructuring), which is designed to overhaul Soviet society. According to Gorbachev, perestroika is a "policy of accelerating the country's social and economic progress and renewing all spheres of life. . . . Many problems have accumulated and it won't be easy to solve them. But the change has begun and society cannot now turn back."[6] Perestroika involves grafting certain economic, social, and even political elements borrowed from the West onto the Soviets' centralized authoritarian system. Economic decentralization and even "democratization" are the new order of the day: The plan involves introducing profit sharing and other incentives, improving the quality of products, firing inefficient workers, and closing unproductive factories and shops. Certainly it is an ambitious and difficult undertaking, even under the best of circumstances.[7]

If perestroika is to succeed, Gorbachev must prevent military spending from continuing to drain the Soviet economy, thus crippling progress in other sectors. To do this, he will need to promote a new era of détente—a less militarized, less confrontational, less dangerous relationship than the United States and the Soviet Union have had in the past. Consequently, the possibility that deep cuts in nuclear arsenals can be made over the next few years is a very real one. The Reykjavik summit of 1986 illustrated how far and how fast we and the Soviets can go if both sides have the will to make progress; for reasons described in the preceding chapter, the INF Treaty of 1987 also warrants optimism—as do the imperatives of perestroika.

Many well-meaning and dedicated individuals have put forward their visions and hopes for solving the problem of nuclear weapons. President Reagan and others believe that "Star Wars" might be the answer. Others believe that only a big scare—such as a localized nuclear conflict in smaller countries or a limited nonnuclear conflict involving U.S. and Soviet forces—will bring the superpowers to their senses. Some people would like to see the very concept of nations abolished or at least have them subordinated to a world government. Still others hope that technological advances will increase economic prosperity worldwide, which will in turn alleviate tensions between the United States and the Soviet Union; or that new techniques of nonviolence will simply render military force useless.[8]

The authors believe that the arms control process—a nonviolent approach to the arms race—is the key to a safe path to the future. It brings Americans and Soviets together to face off across the negotiating table. It presents opportunities to alleviate tensions by limiting the size and content of nuclear and conventional arsenals. Although both Soviet and American arms-control critics argue that rival negotiators merely seek unilateral advantage and military superiority, in fact, all arms control agreements may be abandoned (or abrogated) if they prove not to serve national interests.

Although we believe that the arms control process holds our best prospect for the future, it is important to remember that, as Paul Nitze has said, "arms control is not an end in itself but a means":

The object of arms-control negotiations is to support foreign policy and security policy by negotiating agreements that will contribute to reducing the risk of war, primarily nuclear war. Other purposes— stopping the arms race, saving money, increasing stability, assuring predictability, providing the foundation for a better East–West relationship—may well be desirable, but only if they contribute to the more important goal of reducing the risk of war and strengthening the prospects of peace.[9]

Reducing the risk of war is our primary objective, but it is not our only goal. Otherwise, we could simply unilaterally dismantle our armed forces and hope for the best; but, as hardly needs to be said, preserving democracy and individual freedom are fundamental national goals. Our dual objective—of preventing war and defending what we have fought for—means that diplomacy in the nuclear era is a difficult, and at times a precarious, balancing act. To maintain our values, we must avoid being coerced by the armed forces of other nations while refraining from the use of our own devastating military power.

Negotiations with the Soviets will benefit if we learn from the mistakes that have derailed arms control opportunities in the past. While we have little control over Soviet political or negotiating behavior, we must at least ensure that our own political representatives (and the negotiators they select) understand in some depth just how and why the nuclear threat has evolved. As we have seen, this involves much more than just a simple grasp of the numbers and kinds of weapons in our arsenals.

We also need to understand our potential adversaries better than we do. It is notable that while 30 million Soviet citizens study the English language, only 15,000 Americans study Russian. According to Senator Paul Simon of Illinois, "there are more teachers of English in the U.S.S.R. than there are students of Russian in the United States."[10] We must recognize that basic societal differences, coupled with a long-standing experience of hostile political relations, continue to create misunderstanding and tension between our two countries—with the result that each side often misconstrues the intentions and actions of the other. The Russians, whose history has been punctuated by foreign invasions, are understandably suspicious of the outside world. The Nazi invasion and occupation of Russia in World War II remains to this day a rallying point for Soviets who wish to maintain a powerful military establishment.

Citizens of the Soviet Union and the Communist countries of Eastern Europe remain isolated and uninformed by comparison to the citizens of the West. Only a small number of people from the East are allowed to travel to, or even have contact with, the world outside their own nation. In stark contrast to the western democracies, very little, if any, public debate of nuclear issues is permitted in the Soviet Union or in the Warsaw Pact nations; more information about Soviet nuclear capabilities appears in the western press than is available to the Soviet people themselves. It is to be hoped that Mikhail Gorbachev's policy of openness will be a moderating influence that reduces Soviet isolation and promotes better understanding between us.

As we have seen, mutual fear has led us to a quest for more and more nuclear weapons. We have constructed the very "doomsday machine" portrayed in the 1964 movie *Dr. Strangelove*, subtitled *How I Stopped Worrying and Learned to Love the Bomb*. The movie was meant as a spoof of the arms race; somehow its most fantastic notions have come true. Some government officials will acknowledge only privately that a conflict between the superpowers would very likely escalate into an all-out nuclear war. It is imperative that we dismantle this doomsday machine by reducing the levels of nuclear weaponry so that no conflict could possibly lead to total annihilation.

We believe that unilateral disarmament is no safe or practical solution to the dangers we face. We also believe that the concept of nuclear deterrence should not be shelved until we arrive at a better alternative. U.S. presidents since Eisenhower have relied on nuclear weapons for deterrence to avoid the high economic and social costs of maintaining huge conventional forces to match those of the Soviets. Unlike the United States, the Soviet Union is a militarized society, with a large standing army, compulsory military service and a citizenry accustomed to making deep economic sacrifices for arms.[11] In our view, U.S. society would not accept such measures in peacetime. Accordingly, we believe that deep reductions in U.S. and Soviet nuclear arsenals (for example, from the current level of 25,000 weapons each down to 5,000 each) should be accompanied by reductions in the Soviets' superior conventional military strength.

As we reduce arms levels, the ability of both sides to execute a surprise first strike must be eliminated. This will require giving high priority to the reduction of very fast, accurate, multiwarhead missiles that could be launched with the goal of winning a war by destroying an enemy's retaliatory forces. Whether or not such a war can be "won" is highly questionable, but these types of weapons are especially dangerous because they raise suspicions about a nation's stated intentions to use nuclear weapons <u>only</u> in retaliation. If these suspicions harden into convictions, the "threatened" nation could decide to beat the other to the punch and launch a preemptive attack. If we are to have nuclear weapons to deter war, they should be better suited for retaliation than for a first strike; deterrence is best served by weapons that could survive a surprise nuclear attack and still be capable of retaliation. If both sides limit their arsenals to such weapons, a war is much less likely to begin.

Crisis communications systems need to be continually improved. As an extension of the "Nuclear Risk Reduction Centers" to be established pursuant to the INF treaty, we favor an idea advanced by William L. Ury and Richard Smoke in *Beyond the Hotline*. They propose that the United States and the Soviet Union establish a nuclear crisis control center with joint facilities in Washington and Moscow. These facilities would be connected by instant teleconferencing. U.S. and Soviet diplomats and military officers would continuously monitor potential crisis situations that could inadvertently lead to war.[12]

Finally, we must agree upon adequate verification measures to ensure that each side is fully aware of the military capabilities of the other and to ensure that each is making the weapons reductions required by any given treaty. With so many lives at stake, we need not rely on one another's word as our only proof. As a corollary to this issue, we must avoid building weapons systems whose size, mode of deployment and other characteristics make verification difficult or impossible.

The superpowers need to achieve significant progress in bilateral negotiations before they attempt to persuade the other nuclear powers—Great Britain, France and China—to reduce their nuclear arms. U.S.–Soviet bilateral agreements that accomplished, for example, the 50-percent cuts in superpower arsenals hoped for in 1988 and 1989 could convince the other members of the "nuclear club" that a serious opportunity was at hand to <u>enhance</u> their national security by participating in mutual, balanced reductions in world arsenals. Negotiators set aside issues surrounding "Star Wars" in order to achieve the INF Treaty, but SDI is likely to reemerge as an issue—as it did at Reykjavik—when deep reductions in long-range strategic weapons are considered. The issue of limiting conventional military forces also needs to be addressed: After all, by reducing or eliminating nuclear weapons, we do not want to make the world "safe" for another "conventional war."

Once the United States and the Soviet Union enlist the cooperation of the other nuclear-armed nations, we must collectively convince the "near-nuclear" or "undeclared" nuclear nations to freeze their growing capabilities and end nuclear proliferation. Innovative regional and local security arrangements, backed by both the United States <u>and</u> the Soviet Union, may be necessary before certain nations are willing to abandon their nuclear ambitions.

We can eliminate nuclear weapons from the earth only if all nations agree not to build them. No country is likely to give up its nuclear weapons (or nuclear ambitions) while potential enemies continue to build, maintain, or seek to build nuclear arsenals. The superpowers must take the lead in a process that will require supreme effort and great patience. We believe that momentum for progress is building—and that each one of us can play an important role.

Edward Teller (left) and Enrico Fermi at a meeting in Chicago, 1951.

General Curtis E. LeMay, head of the U.S. Strategic Air Command, 1954.

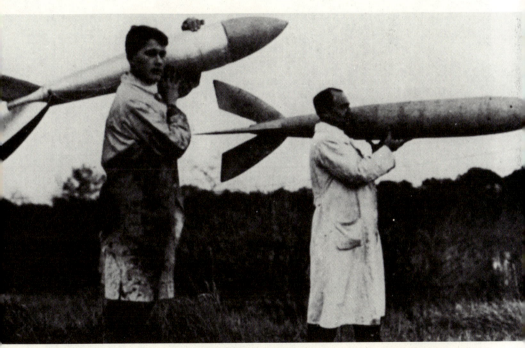

Wernher von Braun (left) and colleague carrying early rockets to the launch pad, 1932.

Admiral Hyman G. Rickover on board the U.S.S. *Nautilus*.

An unarmed Minuteman ICBM being launched from Vandenberg Air Force Base, California.

Nikita S. Khrushchev berating the United States over the U-2 affair.

MEDIUM RANGE BALLISTIC MISSILE BASE IN CUBA

ERECTOR ON LAUNCH PAD

MISSILE READY BLDGS

OXIDIZER VEHICLES

PROB HYDROGEN PEROXIDE TANKS

MISSILE READY BLDGS

FUELING VEHICLES

TENTS

ERECTOR ON LAUNCH PAD

MISSILE ON TRAILER

U.S. Air Force reconnaissance photo of an IRBM base under construction in Cuba, October 1962.

President John F. Kennedy (right) and his brother, Attorney General Robert F. Kennedy, share a pensive moment on the back porch of the White House during the Cuban Missile Crisis.

A U.S. Minuteman missile in its silo.

Demonstration in New York City calling for a nuclear freeze and reduction of nuclear arsenals, June 12, 1982.

XX

LOOKING THE TIGER
IN THE EYE

I know of no safe depository for the ultimate powers of society but the people themselves, and if we think them not enlightened enough to exercise their control with a wholesome discretion, the remedy is not to take it from them but to inform their discretion.

Thomas Jefferson

Oh say does that star-spangled banner yet wave
O'er the land of the free
And the home of the brave?

Francis Scott Key,
1814

I believe that until we have looked this tiger in the eye, we shall be in the worst of all possible dangers, which is that we may back into him.

J. Robert Oppenheimer,
1953

Thomas Jefferson did not have to confront the threat of nuclear war. When Francis Scott Key wrote the "Star-Spangled Banner," "the rockets' red glare" did not refer to intercontinental ballistic missiles, and "the bombs bursting in air" were not thermonuclear. J. Robert Oppenheimer, on the other hand, was in a unique po-

275

sition to understand the threat of nuclear annihilation, and this book is an effort to heed his warning—to look this tiger in the eye. Over the last forty years we have lived with the existence of nuclear weapons and the threat of nuclear war. Up to now, it has been asserted, nuclear weapons may have saved lives by deterring nations from a major war. But the long-term prognosis for this strategy may not be favorable, particularly if nuclear stockpiles remain enormous and the number of nuclear nations continues to grow.

What would Jefferson have said and done about the nuclear threat had he been born in this century? We can only speculate; what we do know is that his principles of democratic participation have persisted, have in fact grown stronger over the last 200 years. As Derek Bok, President of Harvard University, has said,

We should not forget that it was an informed public opinion that pressed for an end to slavery; that sought an end to child labor; that helped persuade politicians to protect the environment; to integrate schools, and even to place a limited ban on the testing of nuclear weapons.[1]

Public influence on national security issues has increased dramatically since World War II; we should remember that the force of public opinion compelled leaders to end American involvement in Vietnam. At one time even Vice-President Truman was kept from knowing about the Manhattan Project; these days congressional debates about nuclear issues are often televised. Our responsibility as citizens of a free country (voters as well as those approaching voting age) is to learn as much as we can about national security issues and insist that our candidates for public office know about them too. When we choose our leaders, we have an opportunity to choose policies for preventing nuclear war. That opportunity can be lost if we thoughtlessly empower others to make crucial decisions for us.

The fact that the Soviet system often appears impervious to public opinion should provide more, not less, incentive to become involved. Jonathan Schell, in *The Fate of the Earth*, writes:

We do not know what the peoples of the totalitarian states, including the people of the Soviet Union, may want. They are locked in silence by their government. In these circumstances, public opinion in the free countries would have to represent public opinion in all countries, and would have to bring its pressure to bear, as best it could, on all governments.[2]

Our book depicts three different but related nuclear races. The first, involving the United States, Great Britain and Nazi Germany, began during World War II and ended at Hiroshima and Nagasaki. The second race, between the United States and the Soviet Union, began before the end of World War II and continues today. As we have seen, it has resulted in the building of enormous nuclear arsenals by the superpowers and smaller stockpiles by a growing number of other nations. The third race involves all of us: it is the human race to prevent nuclear war, our ultimate enemy. Anyone who thinks that he or she is irrelevant to this struggle needs to reconsider; we need fresh ideas, commitment and informed judgment.

The authors have tried to give our best sense of the motivations of the individuals who made the discoveries and decisions that brought us into our present nuclear predicament. We have stressed, and McGeorge Bundy, former national security advisor to Presidents Kennedy and Johnson, has said that <u>fear</u> is primarily responsible for the development and proliferation of nuclear weapons:

When we review the record, looking at the motives for the decisions of major governments, we find that while motive is . . . frequently somewhat mixed, the dominant theme, beginning with Franklin Roosevelt in 1941, is fear—if we don't get it first, he [Hitler] may. . . . [Roosevelt] got it so we must—Stalin in 1945; they are doing it, so must we—Britain and France; they have done it, and we will—Mao. . . . Less fearful motives do operate: we will win; we will catch up; we will be great; we will even, perhaps, be safe. But fear dominates.[3]

But if we are numbed or paralyzed by fear of nuclear war, we risk falling prey to the hopelessness that shirks responsibility, to the apathy that may invite what we fear. It is neither necessary nor inevitable that fear dominate our behavior. Ultimately, it is more satisfying and life affirming—indeed thrilling—to confront reality rather than spend time seeking distraction.

Once we learn to look this tiger in the eye, we can begin to face him down. The task will require courage, dedication and patience; we should not expect nuclear weapons to suddenly disappear, as with the wave of a wand. But there will be frequent opportunities for informed individuals to correct a misapprehension, to make an influential point, to raise the level of discussion and debate. "Great acts are made up of small deeds," said the Chinese philosopher Lao-tzu. And every effort can yield an immediate reward: It will combat the helplessness so many feel in the face of these complicated problems. The example we set can encourage others to participate in this quest.

French philosopher Jean-Paul Sartre wrote that, in war, "we are all embued with the feeling of participating in a world event. In fact, we have always participated in world events and not an instant has gone by when we were not historic. . . ." Sartre emphasizes that "it's during peacetime that we should have had that dedication and that seriousness—we'd perhaps have avoided the war."[4]

Nuclear-weapons issues have been ignored by too many of us for too long. We should remember that other species have become extinct because they could not adapt to their circumstances. Most people would agree that a nuclear war, no matter how "limited," would be an unprecedented, almost unimaginable catastrophe. Aside from the immediate effects of blast, fire and radiation there would be prolonged suffering and probable genetic damage to future generations of all living things. In the aftermath of a nuclear war, some have said, the living would envy the dead. Such a catastrophe can be avoided. Humans have choices—and possess a more conscious understanding of their situation than any species before them. Whether we take advantage of this consciousness, and act to end the threat of nuclear war, remains to be seen.

William Faulkner, who won the Nobel Prize for Literature in 1949 for his novels about the rural American South, chose the occasion of his Nobel Prize acceptance speech to address the threat of nuclear war:

I decline to accept the end of man. It is easy enough to say that man is immortal simply because he will endure: that when the last dingdong of doom has clanged and faded from the last worthless rock hanging tideless in the last dead and dying evening, that even then there will be one more sound: that of his puny inexhaustible voice, still talking.

I refuse to accept this. I believe that man will not merely endure: he will prevail. He is immortal, not because he alone among creatures has an inexhaustible voice, but because he has a soul, a spirit capable of compassion and sacrifice and endurance. . . .[5]

We must prove Faulkner right.

Chronology

(Events related to the development of nuclear weapons are set in Italic type.)

1895—Wilhelm Roentgen discovers the "X ray."

1895—Henri Becquerel discovers that the element uranium has radioactive properties.

1896—Marie and Pierre Curie discover radium.

1905—Albert Einstein publishes his Theory of Relativity.

1914–1918—World War I.

1917–1918—The Russian Revolution.

1919—The Treaty of Versailles is signed, dictating the terms of victory over Germany and Austria-Hungary.

1919—German National Socialist Party and Italian Fascist Party are founded.

September 18, 1931—Japan invades the Chinese province of Manchuria.

1932—James Chadwick discovers the neutron.

January 30, 1933—Adolf Hitler becomes Chancellor of Germany.

1934—Enrico Fermi bombards uranium with neutrons, producing several radioactive elements.

October 1935—Italy invades Abyssinia (Ethiopia).

March 7, 1936—Germany occupies the Rhineland, in defiance of the Treaty of Versailles.

October 21, 1936—Hitler and Mussolini sign a secret protocol forming the Rome–Berlin "Axis."

March 1938—Hitler invades and annexes Austria.

September 1938—At Munich, France and Britain cede the Czechoslovakian Sudetenland to Germany.

December 22, 1938—Otto Hahn and Fritz Strassmann bombard uranium with neutrons and, unknowingly, split the atom. Lise Meitner and Otto Frisch, in exile, explain the results.

March 3, 1939—Leo Szilard's experiments confirm the possibility of an atomic chain reaction.

March 15, 1939—Hitler invades and occupies Czechoslovakia, where the richest known European sources of uranium are located.

March 18, 1939—A French research team led by Joliot-Curie publishes an article confirming the possibility of a self-sustaining chain reaction.

August 2, 1939—Albert Einstein signs a letter drafted by Leo Szilard and Eugene Wigner warning President Franklin Roosevelt of German atomic research.

September 1, 1939—The German army invades Poland. World War II begins.

September 26, 1939—German scientists form the "Uranium Society," which concludes that power from the fission of Uranium-238 could create a tremendous explosion.

October 21, 1939—Roosevelt appoints a U.S. "Uranium Committee," which investigates the feasibility of building and exploding an atomic device.

May 10, 1940—Hitler invades France through neutral Belgium. France surrenders six weeks later.

July 1940—Germany launches massive bombing raids against England, concentrating heavily on London. The "Battle of Britain" begins.

June 22, 1941—Hitler invades the Soviet Union.

October 1941—The British begin atomic-bomb research under the code name "Tube Alloys."

1941—Glenn T. Seaborg at the University of California produces the first measurable quantities of an element he names "plutonium."

December 7, 1941—Japan launches a surprise attack against the U.S. Pacific Fleet moored at Pearl Harbor, Hawaii; the next day the United States declares war on Japan; four days later, Germany declares war on the United States.

June 17, 1942—The U.S. atomic-bomb project is organized under the code name "Manhattan Project."

December 2, 1942—At the University of Chicago, Enrico Fermi and his scientific team sustain the first controlled atomic chain reaction.

December 7, 1942—The Los Alamos Ranch School is appropriated by the U.S. Government as headquarters of the Manhattan Project.

June 6, 1944—"D-Day": the allies launch "Operation Overlord" against Germany; *the "Alsos Mission" follows the invasion forces into Germany to discover the extent of German atomic research.*

June 13, 1944—The first V-1 rockets hit London.

September 8, 1944—The first V-2 rockets hit London and Antwerp, Belgium.

April 12, 1945—President Franklin D. Roosevelt dies. Harry S Truman becomes President of the U.S.

May 5–8, 1945—Germany surrenders. The Allies declare victory in Europe (V-E) Day.

June 11, 1945—The "Franck Report," written by seven Manhattan Project scientists, warns that an unannounced atomic attack on Japan will lead to an arms race.

June 26, 1945—The charter of the United Nations is signed in San Francisco.

July 16, 1945—The first atomic bomb is detonated at a test site in Alamogordo, New Mexico.

July 24, 1945—President Truman, still at the Potsdam conference, mentions the successful testing of a "powerful explosive" to Josef Stalin, who congratulates the president and expresses hope that it will be used against Japan.

July 26, 1945—The U.S. and its allies issue the "Potsdam Declaration," calling for the immediate and unconditional surrender of the Japanese forces. The Japanese refuse to surrender.

August 2, 1945—President Truman, on board the cruiser U.S.S. Augusta, *gives the order to drop atomic bombs on Japan.*

August 6, 1945—The B-29 Enola Gay *drops an atomic bomb on the city of Hiroshima, Japan.*

August 9, 1945—The B-29 Bock's Car *drops the second atomic bomb on the city of Nagasaki, Japan.*

August 10, 1945—President Truman suspends further atomic bombing of Japan.

August 14, 1945—U.S. aircraft armed with conventional bombs make their heaviest raid of the war on Japanese targets. Japan surrenders, and "V-J Day" is celebrated.

February 26, 1946—Stalin makes his "Cold War" speech.

March 5, 1946—Winston Churchill delivers his "Iron Curtain" speech in Fulton, Missouri.

1946—The U.S. begins regular testing of atomic bombs.

June 16, 1946—Bernard M. Baruch presents the United Nations with a U.S. proposal for the international control of atomic energy.

August 1, 1946—A civilian Atomic Energy Commission (AEC) is established as sole controller of the research and development of atomic energy in the U.S.

June 5, 1947—U.S. Secretary of State George C. Marshall announces the European Recovery Program (better known as the Marshall Plan).

June 24, 1948—Stalin blocks all land routes to West Berlin. In response, Truman institutes the "Berlin Airlift" with the help of Great Britain and France.

1948—Communist coup in Czechoslovakia.

April 4, 1949—The North Atlantic Treaty Organization (NATO) is formed.

September 23, 1949—President Truman announces that the Soviet Union has exploded its own atomic bomb.

1949—China falls under Communist control.

January 31, 1950—President Truman authorizes the development of the hydrogen bomb.

February 9, 1950—The Red Scare is intensified when U.S. Senator Joseph McCarthy accuses State Department employees of membership in the Communist party.

June 25, 1950—North Korean troops invade the Republic of South Korea. The Korean conflict begins.

November 2, 1952—The first U.S. hydrogen bomb is tested at Bikini Atoll in the Pacific.

November 1952—Dwight D. Eisenhower is elected president of the United States.

1952—The United Kingdom tests its first nuclear weapon.

March 5, 1953—Stalin dies; Malenkov assumes power.

January 17, 1955—The first nuclear-powered submarine, the Nautilus, *is launched.*

1955—The Warsaw Pact Treaty Organization is established.

August 27, 1957—The Soviets test the first ICBM.

October 4, 1957—*Sputnik I* is launched by the USSR.

March 27, 1958—After a five-year power struggle following Stalin's death, Nikita S. Khrushchev assumes power in the Soviet Union.

May 1, 1960—A U.S. U-2 spy plane is shot down over the Soviet Union.

May 16, 1960—The Paris summit meeting collapses.

1960—France tests its first nuclear weapon.

November 1960—John F. Kennedy is elected president of the U.S.

October 1962—Kennedy orders a naval blockade of Cuba, forcing the Soviets to remove offensive missiles from the island and ending the Cuban Missile Crisis.

August 5, 1963—The Limited Test-Ban Treaty goes into effect.

November 22, 1963—President Kennedy is assassinated; Lyndon B. Johnson takes office.

1964—Nikita Khrushchev is deposed as Soviet Leader; Leonid Brezhnev takes over.

1964—The People's Republic of China tests its first nuclear weapon.

1967—Treaties banning nuclear weapons in Latin America and in outer space go into effect.

August 21, 1968—The Soviets invade Czechoslovakia.

November 1968—Richard M. Nixon is elected president of the United States.

1968—The Nuclear Non-Proliferation Treaty is signed.

1970—The U.S. develops multiple independently targetable reentry vehicles (MIRVs).

May 5, 1971—The SALT I agreement is signed.

May 26, 1972—The Anti-Ballistic Missile (ABM) Treaty is signed.

August 9, 1974—President Nixon resigns; Gerald Ford assumes office.

1974—India tests a nuclear device.

November 1974—Ford and Brezhnev meet in Vladivostok and agree to an outline for SALT II.

November 1976—Jimmy Carter is elected president of the United States.

1977—Soviets begin deploying new SS–20 missiles; West German Chancellor Helmut Schmidt warns of the threat they pose to NATO.

June 18, 1979—The SALT II Treaty is signed, but the U.S. Senate refuses to ratify.

December 1979—Soviet forces invade Afghanistan.

August 1980—Randall Forsberg issues "Call to Halt"; the Nuclear Freeze movement begins.

November 1980—Ronald Reagan is elected president of the United States.

July 1982—Nitze and Kvitsinsky develop their arms-control proposal; President Reagan refuses its terms.

1982—Leonid Brezhnev dies; Yuri Andropov assumes power in the USSR.

March 1983—President Reagan announces the U.S. Strategic Defense Initiative.

1983—NATO deploys Pershing II and ground-launched cruise missiles in response to Soviet missiles.

November 1983—Soviets walk out of the INF and START talks.

1984—Andropov dies; Constantine Chernenko takes over in USSR.

March 1985—Chernenko dies; Mikhail Gorbachev assumes power in USSR.

October 11–12, 1986—Reykjavik summit between Reagan annd Gorbachev.

December 8, 1987—Reagan and Gorbachev sign INF Treaty in Washington, D.C.

Notes

Complete bibliographical information on these references will be found in "Sources and Suggested Reading," beginning on page 297.

CHAPTER I: Zero Hour

1. Groves, *Now It Can Be Told.*
2. Jette, *Inside Box 1663.*
3. Clark, *The Greatest Power on Earth.*
4. Lamont, *Day of Trinity.*
5. Groves, *Now It Can Be Told.*
6. *ibid.*
7. Goodchild, *J. Robert Oppenheimer.*
8. Groves, *Now It Can Be Told.*
9. Feis, "The Secret that Traveled to Potsdam."
10. Mee, *Meeting at Potsdam.*

CHAPTER II: Hiroshima and Nagasaki

1. Manchester, *The Glory and the Dream.*
2. Groves, *Now It Can Be Told.*
3. Manchester, *The Glory and the Dream.*
4. Truman, *Year of Decisions.*
5. Stimson and Bundy, *On Active Service.*
6. Lyon and Evans, *Los Alamos.*
7. Bernstein and Matusow, *The Truman Administration.*
8. Stimson, "The Decision to Use the Atomic Bomb."
9. Churchill, *Triumph and Tragedy.*
10. Lilienthal, *The Journals of David E. Lilienthal.*
11. Donovan, *Conflict and Crisis.*
12. Groves, *Now It Can Be Told.*
13. Chinnock, *Nagasaki.*
14. Laurence, *Men and Atoms.*
15. *ibid.*

16. Groves, *Now It Can Be Told.*
17. Herken, *The Winning Weapon.*
18. Craig, *The Fall of Japan.*
19. Teller with Brown, *The Legacy of Hiroshima.*

CHAPTER III: The March to World War II

1. Shirer, *The Rise and Fall of the Third Reich.*
2. Hardy, *Hitler's Secret Weapon.*
3. Fussell, *The Great War and Modern Memory.*
4. Washington, Farewell Address.
5. Churchill, *The Gathering Storm.*
6. Federal Republic of Germany, *Questions on German History.*
7. Churchill, *The Gathering Storm.*
8. Leeds, *Italy Under Mussolini.*
9. Churchill, *The Gathering Storm.*
10. *ibid.*
11. Toland, *The Rising Sun.*
12. U.S. Department of State, *Peace and War.*

CHAPTER IV: A Walk in the Woods

1. Meitner, "Looking Back."
2. Crawford, *Lise Meitner.*
3. Moore, *Niels Bohr.*
4. MacPherson, *Time Bomb.*
5. Irving, *The German Atomic Bomb.*
6. Segrè, *From X-rays to Quarks.*
7. *ibid.*
8. Curie, *Madame Curie.*
9. Fermi, Laura, *Atoms in the Family.*
10. Hahn, "The Discovery of Fission."
11. Massachusetts Institute of Technology, *The Nuclear Almanac.*
12. Frisch, *What Little I Remember.*
13. Weart and Szilard, *Leo Szilard.*

CHAPTER V: Early Warning

1. Weart and Szilard, *Leo Szilard.*
2. Joliot et al., "Liberation of Neutrons."
3. Weart, *Scientists in Power.*
4. Einstein, Letter to Franklin Roosevelt.
5. Jungk, *Brighter Than a Thousand Suns.*
6. Rhodes, *The Making of the Atomic Bomb.*
7. U.S. Department of State, *Peace and War.*

CHAPTER VI: The Manhattan Project

1. Jette, *Inside Box 1663*.
2. Burroughs, "Comments on Los Alamos Boys' Ranch School."
3. Goodchild, *J. Robert Oppenheimer*.
4. Los Alamos Historical Society, *When Los Alamos Was a Boys' School*.
5. *ibid.*
6. Hewlett and Anderson, *The New World*.
7. Clark, *The Greatest Power on Earth*.
8. MacPherson, *Time Bomb*.
9. Blow, *The History of the Atomic Bomb*.
10. Hewlett and Anderson, *The New World*.
11. Hawkins, *Manhattan District History*.
12. Jette, *Inside Box 1663*.
13. *ibid.*
14. U.S. Atomic Energy Commission, *Transcript of Hearing*.

CHAPTER VII: The Uranium Society

1. Irving, *The German Atomic Bomb*.
2. *ibid.*
3. Heisenberg, Werner, "Research in Germany."
4. Irving, *The German Atomic Bomb*.
5. Szasz, *The Day the Sun Rose Twice*.
6. Gallagher, *Assault in Norway*.
7. Irving, *The German Atomic Bomb*.
8. Goodchild, *J. Robert Oppenheimer*.
9. Heisenberg, Werner, *Physics and Beyond*.
10. Goudsmit, *Alsos*.
11. Heisenberg, Werner, *Physics and Beyond*.
12. *ibid.*
13. *ibid.*
14. Heisenberg, Elizabeth, *Inner Exile*.
15. Moore, *Niels Bohr*.
16. Irving, *The German Atomic Bomb*.
17. Speer, *Inside the Third Reich*.
18. Jones, *The Most Secret War*.
19. Brown and MacDonald, *The Secret History of the Atomic Bomb*.
20. Goudsmit, *Alsos*.
21. Pash, *The Alsos Mission*.
22. Heisenberg, Werner, *Physics and Beyond*.
23. Goudsmit, *Alsos*.
24. Dower, "Science, Society and the Japanese Atomic Bomb."

CHAPTER VIII: Dejection, Grief, Jubilation

1. Hahn, *My Life.*
2. *ibid.*
3. Irving, *The German Atomic Bomb.*
4. Groves, *Now It Can Be Told.*
5. Irving, *The German Atomic Bomb.*
6. Heisenberg, Werner, *Physics and Beyond.*
7. Groves, *Now It Can Be Told.*
8. Goudsmit, *Alsos.*
9. Groves, *Now It Can Be Told.*
10. Irving, *The German Atomic Bomb.*
11. U.S. Army Manhattan Engineering District, *The Atomic Bombings of Hiroshima and Nagasaki.*
12. *ibid.*
13. Satterfield, *The Home Front.*
14. Craig, *The Fall of Japan.*
15. Blow, *The History of the Atomic Bomb.*
16. *Time* magazine, "Atomic Age."

CHAPTER IX: Joe I

1. Hewlett and Anderson, *The New World.*
2. Baruch, *Baruch.*
3. Congressional Record, "The Naval A-Bomb Experiment," "Debate on Bikini Tests" and "Cancellation of the Bikini A-Bomb Test."
4. Shurcliff, *Bombs at Bikini.*
5. Herken, *The Winning Weapon.*
6. Lippman, *The Cold War.*
7. Congressional Quarterly, *The Soviet Union.*
8. Kennan, *Russia and the West.*
9. Acheson, *Present at the Creation.*
10. Kennan, "X, The Sources of Soviet Conduct."
11. Mee, *The Marshall Plan.*
12. Herken, *The Winning Weapon.*
13. *ibid.*
14. Cochran, Arkin and Hoenig, *U.S. Nuclear Forces and Capabilities.*
15. Millis, *The Forrestal Diaries.*
16. Lilienthal, *The Journals of David E. Lilienthal.*
17. Brown and MacDonald, *The Secret History of the Atomic Bomb.*
18. Holloway, *The Soviet Union.*
19. Brown and MacDonald, *The Secret History of the Atomic Bomb.*
20. *Bulletin of the Atomic Scientists*, "The Soviet Bombs."
21. Hewlett and Anderson, *The Atomic Shield.*
22. Lilienthal, *The Journals of David E. Lilienthal.*

23. Chafe, *The Unfinished Journey*.
24. Griffith, *Politics of Fear*.

CHAPTER X: Atom Bomb Spies

1. Hyde, *The Atom Bomb Spies*.
2. Radosh and Milton, *The Rosenberg File*.
3. Hyde, *The Atom Bomb Spies*.
4. *ibid*.
5. *ibid*.
6. *ibid*.
7. *ibid*.
8. Radosh and Milton, *The Rosenberg File*.
9. *ibid*.
10. *ibid*.
11. *ibid*.
12. Meeropol, *We Are Your Sons*.

CHAPTER XI: The Super

1. Dyson, *Weapons and Hope*.
2. Clark, *The Greatest Power on Earth*.
3. *ibid*.
4. Lilienthal, *The Journals of David E. Lilienthal*.
5. Truman, *Years of Trial and Hope*.
6. *The New York Times*, "Text of Senator McMahon's Address."
7. MacArthur, *Reminiscences*.
8. York, *The Advisors*.
9. Eisenhower, *Mandate for Change*.
10. Ambrose, *Eisenhower*.
11. *Foreign Relations of the United States*.
12. *ibid*.
13. *ibid*.
14. Ambrose, *Eisenhower*.
15. Schwartz, *NATO's Nuclear Dilemmas*.
16. Wolfe, *Soviet Power and Europe*.
17. Brodie, "The Development of Nuclear Strategy."
18. Wolfe, *Soviet Power and Europe*.

CHAPTER XII: From Kitty Hawk to Strategic Bombers

1. Christy, *American Air Power*.
2. Kennett, *A History of Strategic Bombing*.
3. Sallagar, *The Road to Total War*.
4. *ibid*.
5. *ibid*.

6. Coffey, *Iron Eagle*.
7. LeMay with Kantor, *Mission with LeMay*.
8. *ibid.*
9. *ibid.*
10. Rosenberg, "The Origins of Overkill."
11. LeMay with Kantor, *Mission with LeMay*.
12. Sallagar, *The Road to Total War*.

CHAPTER XIII: From V-Rockets to ICBMs

1. Winter, *Prelude to the Space Age*.
2. Dornberger, *V-2*.
3. *ibid.*
4. *ibid.*
5. Speer, *Inside the Third Reich*.
6. Bar-Zohar, *The Hunt for German Scientists*.
7. *ibid.*
8. Lasby, *Project Paper Clip*.
9. Bar-Zohar, *The Hunt for German Scientists*.
10. Ordway and Sharpe, *The Rocket Team*.
11. Khrushchev, *Khrushchev Remembers*.

CHAPTER XIV: From U-Boats to Nuclear Submarines

1. Franck, *The Sea Wolves*.
2. Hewlett and Duncan, *The Nuclear Navy*.
3. Polmar and Allen, *Rickover*.
4. Hewlett and Duncan, *The Nuclear Navy*.
5. *ibid.*
6. Polmar and Allen, *Rickover*.
7. *ibid.*
8. Hewlett and Duncan, *The Nuclear Navy*.
9. Polmar and Allen, *Rickover*.
10. *ibid.*

CHAPTER XV: Sputnik

1. *Time* magazine, "Red Moon Over the U.S."
2. *Newsweek*, "Man's Awesome Adventure."
3. *ibid.*
4. Killian, *Sputnik, Scientists, and Eisenhower*.
5. *ibid.*
6. *Newsweek*, "Man's Awesome Adventure."
7. Shelton, *Soviet Space Exploration*.
8. Killian, *Sputnik, Scientists, and Eisenhower*.
9. *ibid.*

10. *ibid.*
11. Rosenberg, "A Smoking Radiating Ruin."
12. Killian, *Sputnik, Scientists, and Eisenhower.*
13. *ibid.*

CHAPTER XVI: The U-2 Affair

1. Beschloss, *MayDay.*
2. *ibid.*
3. *ibid.*
4. *ibid.*
5. Wise and Ross, *The U-2 Affair.*
6. Beschloss, *MayDay.*
7. Powers with Gentry, *Operation Overflight.*
8. Beschloss, *MayDay.*
9. *ibid.*
10. *ibid.*
11. *ibid.*
12. *ibid.*
13. *ibid.*
14. *ibid.*
15. *ibid.*
16. *ibid.*
17. *ibid.*
18. Wise and Ross, *The U-2 Affair.*
19. Eisenhower, "Liberty Is at Stake."

CHAPTER XVII: The Cuban Missile Crisis

1. Sorensen, *Kennedy.*
2. Schlesinger, *A Thousand Days.*
3. Sorensen, *Kennedy.*
4. Schlesinger, *Robert Kennedy.*
5. Ambrose, *Eisenhower.*
6. American Broadcasting Company, ABC News, No. 45-85.
7. Carey, "The Schools and Civil Defense."
8. American Broadcasting Company, ABC News, No. 45-85.
9. Sands, Norris and Cochran, *Known Soviet Nuclear Explosions.*
10. Shevchenko, *Breaking with Moscow.*
11. Khrushchev, *Khrushchev Remembers.*
12. Hilsman, "The Cuban Crisis."
13. Kennedy, Robert, *Thirteen Days.*
14. *ibid.*
15. Central Intelligence Agency, "The Military Build-up in Cuba."
16. Kennedy, Robert, *Thirteen Days.*
17. *ibid.*

18. *ibid.*
19. Trachtenberg, "The Influence of Nuclear Weapons."
20. Sloan Foundation, Transcript, June 28, 1983.
21. Shevchenko, *Breaking With Moscow.*
22. Khrushchev, *Khrushchev Remembers.*
23. Sorensen, *Kennedy.*
24. Kennedy, Robert, *Thirteen Days.*
25. Schlesinger, *Robert Kennedy.*
26. American Broadcasting Company, ABC News, No. 45-85.
27. Sloan Foundation, Transcript, June 28, 1983.
28. Schlesinger, *Robert Kennedy.*
29. *ibid.*
30. Sloan Foundation, Transcript, June 28, 1983.
31. Sorensen, *Kennedy.*
32. Hilsman, *To Move a Nation.*
33. Sorensen, *Kennedy.*
34. *ibid.*
35. Kennedy, John, "Arms Quarantine of Cuba."
36. Shevchenko, *Breaking With Moscow.*
37. Kennedy, John, "Arms Quarantine of Cuba."
38. Sagan, "Nuclear Alerts."
39. Sorensen, *Kennedy.*
40. *ibid.*
41. Kennedy, Robert, *Thirteen Days.*
42. Sorensen, *Kennedy.*
43. Hilsman, "The Cuban Crisis."
44. Bernstein, "The Cuban Missile Crisis."
45. Schlesinger, *A Thousand Days.*
46. Sloan Foundation, Transcript, June 28, 1983.
47. Rusk, "The Lessons of the Cuban Missile Crisis."

CHAPTER XVIII: Arms Control and Détente

1. American Broadcasting Company, ABC News, No. 45-85.
2. Sorensen, *Kennedy.*
3. *ibid.*
4. Fowler, *Fallout.*
5. Whelan, *Soviet Diplomacy and Negotiating Behavior.*
6. Sorensen, *Kennedy.*
7. U.S. Arms Control and Disarmament Agency, *Arms Control and Disarmament Agreements.*
8. U.S. House of Representatives, *Fundamentals of Nuclear Arms Control.*
9. International Atomic Energy Agency, *IAEA Safeguards: Arms, Limitations, Achievements.*
10. Bundy, "Existential Deterrence."

11. Cochran, Arkin and Hoenig, *U.S. Nuclear Forces and Capabilities*.
12. Johnson, *The Vantage Point*.
13. Sloss and David, *A Game for High Stakes*.
14. Newhouse, *Cold Dawn*.
15. Whelan, *Soviet Diplomacy and Negotiating Behavior*.
16. Talbott, *Endgame*.
17. *ibid.*
18. Carter, *Keeping Faith*.
19. Krepon, "The SALT Decade."
20. Talbott, *Deadly Gambits*.
21. *ibid.*
22. *ibid.*
23. Reagan, "The Significance of Reykjavik."

CHAPTER XIX: Nuclear Democracy

1. Kelly and Verbeeck, "Appeal at the Nuremberg Tribunal."
2. Forsberg, "A Call to Halt."
3. Wells, "The United States and the Present Danger."
4. Fisher, "Coalition for Peace Through Strength."
5. Mandelbaum and Talbott, *Reagan and Gorbachev*.
6. Gorbachev, *Perestroika*.
7. *Princeton Alumni Weekly*, "Perestroika," December 9, 1987.
8. Wagner, Richard L., Jr.
9. Nitze, *Ethics and Nuclear Arms*.
10. Simon, *The Tongue-Tied American*.
11. Mandelbaum and Talbott, *Reagan and Gorbachev*.
12. Ury and Smoke, *Beyond the Hotline*.

CHAPTER XX: Looking the Tiger in the Eye

1. The Harvard Nuclear Study Group, *Living With Nuclear Weapons*.
2. Schell, *The Fate of the Earth*.
3. Bundy, "Existential Deterrence."
4. Sartre, *War Diaries*.
5. Faulkner, Nobel Prize acceptance speech.

Sources and Suggested Reading

What follows is an alphabetical listing of the major sources used for this book. We have chosen not to list every documentary source and interview conducted in the course of our research, but have cited sources based on our assessment of their historical accuracy and interest to our readers. Our suggestions for further reading are marked by asterisks.

Acheson, Dean. *Present at the Creation: My Years in the State Department.* New York, Norton, 1969.

Ambrose, Steven E. *Eisenhower: The President*, Vol. 2. New York: Simon & Schuster, 1984.

American Broadcasting Company. ABC News, No. 45-85, transcript of television program broadcast on September 18, 1985.

Angell, Joseph W. "Guided Missiles Could Have Won." In *Atlantic Monthly*, Vol. 121, No. 12 (January 1952), pp. 57–63.

Baruch, Bernard M. *Baruch: The Public Years.* New York: Holt, 1960.

Bar-Zohar, Michel. *The Hunt for German Scientists.* New York: Hawthorn Books, 1967.

Beech, Edward L. *Around the World Submerged.* New York: Holt, 1962.

Bernstein, Barton J. "The Cuban Missile Crisis: Trading the Jupiters in Turkey." In *Political Science Quarterly*, Spring 1980, pp. 97–125.

*———, and Allen J. Matusow, editors. *The Truman Administration: A Documentary History*. New York: Harper Colophon Books, 1966.

*Beschloss, Michael R. *MayDay: Eisenhower, Khrushchev and the U-2 Affair.* New York: Harper & Row, 1986.

*Bethe, Hans. "Comments on the History of the H-Bomb." In *Los Alamos Science*, Fall 1982, pp. 43–53.

Blair, Clay, Jr. *The Atomic Submarine and Admiral Rickover.* New York: Henry Holt and Co., 1954.

Blow, Michael. *The History of the Atomic Bomb.* New York: American Heritage, 1968.

Broad, William J. *Star Warriors.* New York: Simon & Schuster, 1985.

Brodie, Bernard. "The Development of Nuclear Strategy." In Steven E. Miller, editor, *Strategy and Nuclear Deterrence*. Princeton, N.J.: Princeton University Press, 1984.

Brown, Anthony Cave, and Charles B. MacDonald, editors. *The Secret History of the Atomic Bomb*. New York: Delta Publishers, 1977.

Bulletin of the Atomic Scientists. "The Soviet Bombs: Mr. Truman's Doubts," March 1953, pp. 43ff.

*Bundy, McGeorge. "Existential Deterrence." In McGeorge Bundy, editor, *The Security Gamble: Deterrence Dilemmas in the Nuclear Age*. Totowa, N.J.: Rowan and Allanheld, 1984.

———. "The Missed Chance to Stop the H-Bomb." In *New York Review of Books*, May 13, 1982, pp. 13–14.

Carey, Michael. "The Schools and Civil Defense: The Fifties Revisited." In *Teachers College Record*, Vol. 84, No. 1 (Fall 1982), pp. 115–127.

Carter, Jimmy. *Keeping Faith: Memoirs of a President*. New York: Bantam, 1982.

———. *Why Not the Best?* New York: Bantam, 1976.

Center for Defense Information. "Quotes: Nuclear War" (pamphlet, no date).

Central Intelligence Agency. "The Military Build-up in Cuba." Special National Intelligence Estimate, No. 85-3-62.

Chafe, William H. *The Unfinished Journey: America Since World War II*. New York: Oxford University Press, 1986.

Chinnock, Frank W. *Nagasaki: The Forgotten Bomb*. New York: World, 1969.

Christy, Joe. *American Air Power: The First 75 Years*. Blue Ridge Summit, Pa.: Tab Books, 1982.

*Churchill, Winston S. *The Gathering Storm. The Second World War*, Vol. I. Boston: Houghton Mifflin, 1948.

*———. *Triumph and Tragedy. The Second World War*, Vol. VI. Boston: Houghton Mifflin, 1953.

*Clark, Ronald W. *The Greatest Power on Earth*. New York: Harper & Row, 1980.

Cochran, Thomas B., William M. Arkin and Milton M. Hoenig. *U.S. Nuclear Forces and Capabilities. Nuclear Weapons Databook*, Vol. I. Natural Resources Defense Council, Cambridge, Mass.: Ballinger, 1984.

Coffey, Thomas M. *Iron Eagle*. New York: Crown, 1986.

Cole, Paul M., and William J. Taylor, Jr., editors. *The Nuclear Freeze Debate: Arms Control Issues for the 1980s*. Boulder, Colo.: Westview Press, 1983.

Collier, Basil. *The Battle of the V-Weapons, 1944–1945*. London: Hodder & Stoughton, 1964.

Compton, Arthur H. *Atomic Quest*. New York: Oxford University Press, 1956.

Congressional Quarterly. *The Soviet Union*. Washington, D.C.: Congressional Quarterly, Inc., 1982.

Congressional Record. 79th Congress, 2nd Session:
"Cancellation of the Bikini A-Bomb Test," March 29, 1946, pp. 2790–2795;

"Debate on Bikini Tests, Use of Naval Vessels as Targets," March 11, 1946, pp. 2117–2131;

"The Naval A-Bomb Experiment," January 31, 1946, p. 624.

————. 97th Congress, 2nd Session: "Providing for Consideration of House Joint Resolution 521, Calling for a Mutual and Verifiable Freeze on and Reduction of Nuclear Weapons for Approval of the SALT II Agreement," August 5, 1982, pp. H 5220–H 5264.

Cooper, Bryan. *The Story of the Bomber 1914–1945*. London: Octopus Books, 1974.

Craig, William. *The Fall of Japan*. New York: Dial, 1967.

Crawford, Deborah. *Lise Meitner: Atomic Pioneer*. New York: Crown, 1969.

Curie, Eve. *Madame Curie: A Biography*, translated by Vincent Sheean. Garden City, N.Y.: Doubleday, 1943.

Donovan, Robert J. *Conflict and Crisis: The Presidency of Harry S Truman 1945–1948*. New York: Norton, 1977.

*Dornberger, Walter. *V-2: The Nazi Rocket Weapon*. New York: Viking, 1954.

Dower, John W. "Science, Society and the Japanese Atomic Bomb Project During World War II." In *Bulletin of Concerned Asian Scholars*, April–June 1978, pp. 41–54.

*Dyson, Freeman. *Weapons and Hope*. New York: Harper & Row, 1984.

Einstein, Albert. Letter to Franklin Roosevelt, August 2, 1939. In Maurice Goldsmith, Alan Mackay, and James Woudhuysen, editors, *Einstein: the first hundred years*. Oxford: Pergamon Press, Ltd., 1980.

Eisenhower, Dwight D. "Liberty Is at Stake." In *Vital Speeches*, Vol. XXVII, No. 8 (February 1, 1961), pp. 228–231.

————. *Mandate for Change 1953–1956*. New York: Doubleday, 1963.

Faulkner, William. Acceptance speech for the 1949 Nobel Prize for Literature, December 10, 1950. In Houston Peterson, editor, *A Treasury of the World's Great Speeches*. New York: Simon & Schuster, 1954, pp. 814–816.

Federal Republic of Germany. *Questions on German History*. Bundestag, Bonn, 1984.

Feis, Herbert. *The Atomic Bomb and the End of World War II*. Princeton, N.J.: Princeton University Press, 1966.

————. "The Secret that Traveled to Potsdam." In *Foreign Affairs*, Vol. 38, No. 2 (January 1960), pp. 300–317.

Fermi, Enrico. "The Development of the First Chain-Reacting Pile." In *Proceedings of the American Philosophical Society*, Vol. 20 (January 1946), pp. 20–24.

Fermi, Laura. *Atoms in the Family*. Chicago: University of Chicago Press, 1954.

Fisher, John M. "Coalition for Peace Through Strength." In American Security Council, *Washington Report*, October 1978.

Foreign Relations of the United States 1952–1954. Volume XV, *Korea*, Part I, pp. 817–818.

Forsberg, Randall. "A Call to Halt the Nuclear Arms Race." Washington, D.C.: Nuclear Freeze Campaign, 1982.

Fowler, John M., editor. *Fallout: A Study of Superbombs, Strontium 90 and Survival.* New York: Basic Books, 1960.

Franck, Wolfgang. *The Sea Wolves: The Story of German U-Boats at War.* New York: Ballantine, 1955.

*Frisch, Otto. *What Little I Remember.* Cambridge: Cambridge University Press, 1979.

———, and John A. Wheeler. "The Discovery of Fission." In *Physics Today,* Vol. 20 (November 1967). Part I: "How It All Began," by Otto Frisch, pp. 43–48. Part II: "The Mechanism of Fission," by John A. Wheeler, pp. 49–52.

Fujino, Toshie. "The Stars Are Looking On." In *Give Me Water: Testimonies of Hiroshima and Nagasaki,* Center for Defense Information, March 1972.

*Fussell, Paul. *The Great War and Modern Memory.* New York: Oxford University Press, 1975.

Gallagher, Thomas. *Assault in Norway: Sabotaging the Nazi Nuclear Bomb.* New York: Bantam, 1981.

Golovin, Igor. "Father of the Soviet Bomb." In *Bulletin of the Atomic Scientists,* December 1967, pp. 13–18.

———. *I. V. Kurchatov: A Socialist-Realist Biography of the Soviet Nuclear Scientist.* Bloomington, Ind.: Selbstverlag Press, 1968.

*Goodchild, Peter. *J. Robert Oppenheimer, Shatterer of Worlds.* London: British Broadcasting Corporation, 1980.

*Gorbachev, Mikhail. *Perestroika.* New York: Harper & Row, 1987.

*Goudsmit, Samuel A. *Alsos.* New York: Henry Schuman, 1947.

Griffith, Robert. *Politics of Fear: Joe McCarthy and the Senate.* Lexington, Ky.: University of Kentucky Press, 1970.

*Groves, Leslie R. *Now It Can Be Told: The Story of the Manhattan Project.* New York: Harper & Row, 1962.

Hahn, Otto. "The Discovery of Fission." In *Scientific American,* Vol. 198, No. 2 (February 1958), pp. 76–84.

*———. *My Life: A Scientific Autobiography.* New York: Herder and Herder, 1970.

Hardy, Alexander G. *Hitler's Secret Weapon: The "Managed" Press and Propaganda Machine of Nazi Germany.* New York: Vantage, 1967.

Harvard Nuclear Study Group. *Living With Nuclear Weapons.* New York: Bantam, 1983.

Hawkins, David. *Manhattan District History: Project Y, the Los Alamos Project.* Los Angeles: Tomash, 1983.

Heisenberg, Elizabeth. *Inner Exile.* Boston: Burkhauser, 1984.

*Heisenberg, Werner. *Physics and Beyond.* New York: Harper & Row, 1971.

———. "Research in Germany on the Technical Application of Atomic Energy." In *Nature,* August 16, 1947, pp. 211–215.

————. "The Third Reich and the Atomic Bomb." In *Bulletin of the Atomic Scientists*, June 1968, pp. 34–35.

Herken, Gregg. *The Winning Weapon: The Atomic Bomb in the Cold War 1945–1950*. New York: Knopf, 1980.

Hermann, Armin. *Heisenberg*. Hamburg: Rowohlt, 1984.

*Hersey, John. *Hiroshima*. New York: Knopf, 1946.

*Hewlett, Richard G., and Oscar E. Anderson, Jr. *The Atomic Shield 1947–1952. A History of the U.S. Atomic Energy Commission*, Vol. II. Philadelphia: University of Pennsylvania Press, 1969.

————. *The New World 1939–1946: A History of the U.S. Atomic Energy Commission*, Vol. I. University Park, Pa.: Pennsylvania State University Press, 1962.

*Hewlett, Richard G., and Francis Duncan. *The Nuclear Navy, 1946–1962*. Chicago: University of Chicago Press, 1974.

Hilsman, Roger. "The Cuban Crisis: How Close We Were to War." In *Look*, Vol. 28, No. 17 (August 25, 1964), pp. 17–21.

————. *To Move a Nation*. Garden City, N.Y.: Doubleday, 1967.

Hitler, Adolf. *Mein Kampf*. New York: Reynal, 1940.

*Holloway, David. *The Soviet Union and the Arms Race*. New Haven: Yale University Press, 1983.

Hyde, H. Montgomery. *The Atom Bomb Spies*. New York: Atheneum, 1980.

International Atomic Energy Agency. *IAEA Safeguards: Arms, Limitations, Achievements*. No. IAEA/SG/INF/4. Vienna, 1983.

————. *IAEA Safeguards: An Introduction*. No. IAEA/SG/INF/3. Vienna, 1981.

*Irving, David. *The German Atomic Bomb: The History of Nuclear Research in Nazi Germany*. New York: Simon & Schuster, 1967.

*Jette, Eleanor. *Inside Box 1663*. Los Alamos, N.M.: Los Alamos Historical Society, 1977.

Johnson, Lyndon Baines. *The Vantage Point: Perspectives of the Presidency 1963–1969*. New York: Holt, 1971.

Joliot, Frédéric, et al. "Liberation of Neutrons in the Nuclear Explosion of Uranium." In *Nature*, March 18, 1939, pp. 470–471.

Jones, Robert V. *The Most Secret War*. London: Hamish Hamilton, 1978.

Jungk, Robert. *Brighter than a Thousand Suns: A Personal History of the Atomic Scientists*. New York: Harcourt, 1958.

Kaku, Michio, and Jennifer Trainer. *Nuclear Power, Both Sides*. New York: Norton, 1982.

Kaplan, Fred. *The Wizards of Armageddon*. New York: Simon & Schuster, 1983.

Keaney, Thomas A. *Strategic Bombers and Conventional Weapons*. Washington, D.C.: National Defense University Press, 1984.

Kelly, Petra Karin, and Hermann Verbeeck. "Appeal at the Nuremberg Tribunal Against First-Strike Weapons and Other Instruments of Mass Destruction in East and West." Die Grünen, Bundesgesellschaftsstelle, Bonn, February 20, 1982.

Kennan, George F. *Memoirs 1925–1950*. Boston: Little, Brown, 1967.

———. *Russia and the West Under Lenin and Stalin*. Boston: Little, Brown, 1961.

*———. "X, The Sources of Soviet Conduct." In *Foreign Affairs*, Vol. 25, No. 4 (July 1947), pp. 566–582.

Kennedy, John. F. "Arms Quarantine of Cuba." In *Vital Speeches*, Vol. XXIX, No. 3 (November 15, 1962), pp. 66–68.

*Kennedy, Robert F. *Thirteen Days: A Memoir of the Cuban Missile Crisis*. New York: Norton, 1969.

*Kennett, Lee. *A History of Strategic Bombing*. New York: Scribner's, 1982.

Khrushchev, Nikita S. *Khrushchev Remembers*. Boston: Little, Brown, 1971.

———. *The Last Testament*. Boston: Little, Brown, 1971.

*Killian, James R., Jr. *Sputnik, Scientists, and Eisenhower*. Cambridge, Mass.: MIT Press, 1977.

Kissinger, Henry. *The White House Years*. Boston: Little, Brown, 1979.

Krepon, Michael. "The SALT Decade: A Post Mortem." Paper given at the University of Vermont, 1985.

*Kunetka, James W. *City of Fire: Los Alamos and the Atomic Age 1943–1945*. Albuquerque: University of New Mexico Press, 1979.

———. *Oppenheimer: The Years of Risk*. Englewood Cliffs, N.J.: Prentice-Hall, 1982.

Kurzman, Dan. *Day of the Bomb: Countdown to Hiroshima*. New York: McGraw-Hill, 1986.

Lamont, Lansing. *Day of Trinity*. New York: Atheneum, 1965.

Lapp, Ralph E. "The Einstein Letter That Started It All." In *New York Times Magazine*, August 2, 1964, pp. 13ff.

Lasby, Clarence G. *Project Paper Clip: German Scientists and the Cold War*. New York: Atheneum, 1971.

*Laurence, William L. *Men and Atoms*. New York: Simon & Schuster, 1959.

Lawrence, Ernest O. "Atomic Engineering." Address delivered to the American Society of Mechanical Engineers on July 26, 1946. Lawrence Papers, University of California Bancroft Library, Berkeley, California, Carton 40, Folder 29.

Leeds, Christopher. *Italy Under Mussolini*. The Documentary History Series. London: Wayland Publishers, 1972.

*LeMay, General Curtis E., with MacKinlay Kantor. *Mission with LeMay: My Story*. New York: Doubleday, 1965.

Ley, Willy. *Rockets, Missiles and Men in Space*. New York: Viking, 1968.

*Lifton, Robert Jay. *Death in Life. Survivors of Hiroshima*. New York: Random House, 1967.

Lilienthal, David E.. *The Journals of David E. Lilienthal: The A. E. C. Years 1945–1950*, Vol. II. New York: Harper & Row, 1964.

*Lippmann, Walter. *The Cold War: A Study in U.S. Foreign Policy*. New York: Harper & Row, 1958.

Los Alamos Ranch School alumni recollections, responses to requests from the authors.

Los Alamos Historical Society. *When Los Alamos Was a Boys' School* (pamphlet, no date).

Los Alamos National Laboratory. *Los Alamos 1943–1945: The Beginning of an Era*, No. LASL-79-78. Reprint: May 1984.

Lyon, Fern, and Jacob Evans, editors. *Los Alamos: The First Forty Years*. Los Alamos, N.M.: Los Alamos Historical Society, 1984.

MacArthur, Douglas. *Reminiscences*. New York: McGraw-Hill, 1964.

MacPherson, Malcolm C. *Time Bomb: Fermi, Heisenberg and the Race for the Atomic Bomb*. New York: Dutton, 1986.

Manchester, William. *The Glory and the Dream: A Narrative History of America 1932–1972*. Boston: Little, Brown, 1973.

Mandelbaum, Michael, and Strobe Talbott. *Reagan and Gorbachev*. New York: Random House, 1987.

Massachusetts Institute of Technology. *The Nuclear Almanac: Confronting the Atom in War and Peace*. Reading, Mass.: Addison-Wesley, 1984.

McDougall, Walter A. . . . *The Heavens and the Earth: A Political History of the Space Age*. New York: Basic Books, 1985.

McGovern, James. *Crossbow and Overcast*. New York: Morrow, 1964.

Mee, Charles L., Jr. *The Marshall Plan*. New York: Simon & Schuster, 1984.

———. *Meeting at Potsdam*. New York: M. Evans and Company, 1975.

Meeropol, Robert and Michael. *We Are Your Sons*. Boston: Houghton Mifflin, 1975.

Meitner, Lise. "Looking Back." In *Bulletin of the Atomic Scientists*, November 1964, pp. 2–7.

———, and Otto R. Frisch. "Disintegration of Uranium by Neutrons: A New Type of Nuclear Reaction." In *Nature*, February 11, 1939, pp. 239–240.

Miller, Samuel Duncan. *An Aerospace Bibliography*. Washington, D.C.: Office of Air Force History, 1978.

Millis, Walter, editor. *The Forrestal Diaries*. New York: Viking, 1951.

Mondey, David. *An International Encyclopedia of Aviation*. New York: Crown, 1977.

Moore, Ruth. *Niels Bohr*. Cambridge, Mass.: MIT Press, 1985.

Moorehead, Alan. *The Traitors*. London: White Lion, 1974.

The New York Times. "Text of Senator McMahon's Address on the Hydrogen Bomb," February 3, 1950, p. 2.

*Newhouse, John. *Cold Dawn: The Story of SALT*. New York: Holt, 1973.

Newsweek. "After Four Years of Castro. Cuba Today." October 22, 1962, pp. 35ff.

———. "Man's Awesome Adventure." October 14, 1957, pp. 37–41.

———. "The Simmering Summer." May 23, 1960, pp. 31–38.

Nitze, Paul H. Foreword to *Ethics and Nuclear Arms: European and American Perspectives*. Washington, D.C.: Ethics and Public Policy Center, 1985.

————. *Is SALT II a Fair Deal for the United States?* Washington, D.C.: Committee on the Present Danger, May 16, 1979.

Nuclear Weapons Freeze Campaign manual. "Organization for a Nuclear Weapons Freeze." St. Louis, Mo.: Freeze National Clearing House, 1984.

*Oppenheimer, J. Robert. "Atomic Weapons and American Policy." In *Foreign Affairs*, Vol. 31, No. 4 (July 1953), pp. 525–535.

*Ordway, Frederick I., and Mitchell R. Sharpe. *The Rocket Team*. New York: Crowell, 1979.

Pash, Colonel Boris T. *The Alsos Mission*. New York: Award House, 1969.

Phillips, T. R. "The U-2 Incident." In *Bulletin of the Atomic Scientists*, June 1960, p. 222.

Pilat, Oliver. *The Atom Spies*. New York: Putnam, 1952.

Pimlott, John. *B-29 Superfortress*. Englewood Cliffs, N.J.: Prentice-Hall, 1983.

*Polmar, Norman, and Thomas B. Allen. *Rickover*. New York: Simon & Schuster, 1982.

*Powers, Gary, with Curt Gentry. *Operation Overflight*. New York: Holt, 1970.

Princeton Alumni Weekly. "Perestroika," December 7, 1987, pp. 21–27.

Pynchon, Thomas. *Gravity's Rainbow*. New York: Viking, 1973.

*Radosh, Ronald, and Joyce Milton. *The Rosenberg File*. New York: Holt, 1973.

Reagan, Ronald. "The Significance of Reykjavik," address given on October 14, 1986. In U.S. Department of State, *Current Policy*, No. 880.

*Rhodes, Richard. *The Making of the Atomic Bomb*. New York: Simon & Schuster, 1986.

*Rosenberg, David Alan. "The Origins of Overkill: Nuclear Weapons and American Strategy 1945–1960." In *International Security*, Vol. 7, No. 4 (Spring 1987), pp. 3–71.

————. "A Smoking Radiating Ruin at the End of Two Hours: Documents on American Plans for Nuclear War with the Soviet Union, 1954–1955." In *International Security*, Vol. 6, No. 3 (Winter 1981–82), pp. 3–38.

Rusk, Dean, et al. "The Lessons of the Cuban Missile Crisis." In *Time*, September 27, 1983, pp. 85–86.

Sagan, Scott D. "Nuclear Alerts and Crisis Management." In *International Security*, Vol. 9, No. 4 (Spring 1985), pp. 99–140.

*Sallagar, Frederick M. *The Road to Total War*. New York: Van Nostrand Reinhold, 1969.

Sands, Jeffrey I., Robert S. Norris, and Thomas B. Cochran. *Known Soviet Nuclear Explosions 1949–1985*. In *Nuclear Weapons Databook* Working Paper. Washington, D.C.: Natural Resources Defense Council, February 1986.

Sartre, Jean-Paul. *War Diaries November 1939–March 1940*, translated by Quentin Hoare. New York: Pantheon, 1985.

Satterfield, Archie. *The Home Front*. New York: Playboy Press, 1981.

*Schell, Jonathan. *The Fate of the Earth*. New York: Knopf, 1982.

Schlesinger, Arthur M., Jr. *Robert Kennedy and His Times*, 2 vols. Boston: Houghton Mifflin, 1978.

*————. *A Thousand Days: John F. Kennedy in the White House*. Boston: Houghton Mifflin, 1978.

Schneir, Walter and Miriam. *Invitation to an Inquest*. New York: Doubleday, 1965.

*Schwartz, David N. *NATO's Nuclear Dilemmas*. Washington, D.C.: Brookings Institution, 1983.

Seaborg, Glenn T. *Kennedy, Khrushchev and the Test Ban*. Berkeley: University of California Press, 1981.

*Segrè, Emilio. *From X-Rays to Quarks: Modern Physicists and Their Discoveries*. New York: W. H. Freeman, 1980.

Shapley, Deborah. "Nuclear Weapons History: Japan's Wartime Bomb Projects Revealed." In *Science*, Vol. 199 (January 13, 1978), pp. 152–157.

Shelton, William. *Soviet Space Exploration: The First Decade*. London: Barker, 1969.

Sherwin, Martin. *A World Destroyed: The Atomic Bomb and the Grand Alliance*. New York: Random House, 1975.

Shevchenko, Arkady. *Breaking with Moscow*. New York: Knopf, 1985.

Shirer, William L. *The Nightmare Years: 1930–1940*. Boston: Little, Brown, 1984.

*————. *The Rise and Fall of the Third Reich*. New York: Simon & Schuster, 1960.

Shurcliff, W. A. *Bombs at Bikini: The Official Report of Operation Crossroads*. New York: Wise, 1947.

Simon, Paul. *The Tongue-Tied American: Confronting the Foreign Language Crisis*. New York: Continuum, 1980.

Alfred Sloan Foundation. Transcript of a discussion about the Cuban Missile Crisis, June 28, 1983.

Sloss, Leon, and M. Scott David. *A Game for High Stakes: Lessons Learned in Negotiating with the Soviet Union*. Cambridge, Mass: Ballinger, 1986.

Smoke, Richard. *National Security and the Nuclear Dilemma: An Introduction to the American Experience*. Reading, Mass.: Addison-Wesley, 1984.

Smyth, Henry DeWolf. *Atomic Energy for Military Purposes: The Official Report of the Atomic Bomb under the Auspices of the United States Government 1940–1945*. Princeton: Princeton University Press, 1945. (Also known as "The Smyth Report.")

*Sorensen, Theodore C. *Kennedy*. New York: Harper & Row, 1965.

Speer, Albert. *Inside the Third Reich*. New York: Macmillan, 1970.

Stalin, J. V. Text of a speech delivered at an election rally in Moscow, February 9, 1946. Washington, D.C.: Embassy of the U.S.S.R., March 1946.

*Stimson, Henry L. "The Decision to Use the Atomic Bomb." In *Harper's Magazine*, Vol. 194, No. 1161 (February 1947), pp. 97–107.

————, and McGeorge Bundy. *On Active Service in Peace and War*. New York: Harper & Row, 1948.

Stoiko, Michael. *Soviet Rocketry*. New York: Holt, 1970.

Strauss, Lewis L. *Men and Decisions*. Garden City, N.Y.: Doubleday, 1962.

*Szasz, Ferenc Morton. *The Day the Sun Rose Twice: The Story of the Trinity Site Nuclear Explosion July 16, 1954*. Albuquerque: University of New Mexico Press, 1984.

*Talbott, Strobe. *Deadly Gambits*. New York: Knopf, 1984.

*————. *Endgame: The Inside Story of SALT II*. New York: Harper Colophon, 1979.

Taylor, T. "Long-Range Lessons of the U-2 Affair." In *The New York Times Magazine*, July 24, 1960, pp. 20ff.

Teller, Edward, with Allen Brown. *The Legacy of Hiroshima*. Garden City, N.Y.: Doubleday, 1962.

Tibbetts, Paul W., with Clair Stebbins and Harry Franken. *The Tibbetts Story*. New York: Stein and Day, 1985.

Time. "Atomic Age," August 20, 1945, pp. 29–36.

————. "Confrontation in Paris," May 23, 1960, pp. 18–20.

————. "Red Moon Over the U.S.," October 14, 1957, p. 27–28.

Time-Life Books editors. *The U-Boats*. Time-Life Books Seafarers series. New York: Time-Life Books, 1979.

*Toland, John. *The Rising Sun*. New York: Random, 1970.

Trachtenberg, Marc. "The Influence of Nuclear Weapons in the Cuban Missile Crisis." In *International Security*, Vol. 10, No. 1 (Summer 1985), pp. 137–203.

Truman, Harry S. *Year of Decisions*. Garden City, N.Y.: Garden City Historical Society, 1955.

————. *Years of Trial and Hope*. Garden City, N.Y.: Garden City Historical Society, 1956.

Ulam, Adam B. *Expansion and Coexistence: Soviet Foreign Policy, 1917–1973*. New York: Praeger, 1974.

United States Air Force Historical Division. *Army Air Forces in World War II*, Vol. V. Chicago: University of Chicago Press, 1948–1958.

U.S. Arms Control and Disarmament Agency. *Arms Control and Disarmament Agreements: Texts and Histories of Negotiations*, 1982.

U.S. Army Manhattan Engineering District. *The Atomic Bombings of Hiroshima and Nagasaki*, 1945.

U.S. Atomic Energy Commission. In the matter of J. Robert Oppenheimer. Transcript of Hearing before Personnel Security Board and Text of Principal Documents and Letters. Cambridge, Mass.: MIT Press, April 1971, p. 81.

U.S. Department of Defense. *Soviet Military Power*, 1986.

U.S. Department of State. *Peace and War: U.S. Foreign Policy 1931–1941*. Washington, D.C.: Government Printing Office, 1942.

————. *The United States and the United Nations*. Report Series No. 7 (Washington, 1947), pp. 169–178.

U.S. House of Representatives. "Report on Soviet Espionage Activities in Connection with the A-Bomb." U.S. House Un-American Activities Committee Report, September 28, 1948.

————. *Fundamentals of Nuclear Arms Control: Historical Overview*, Part I. Subcommittee on Arms Control, International Security and Science. Washington, D.C.: Congressional Research Service, 1985.

Urey, Harold C. "The Atomic Explosion in Russia." In *Bulletin of the Atomic Scientists*, October 1949, p. 265.

*Ury, William L., and Richard Smoke. *Beyond the Hotline: Controlling a Nuclear Crisis*. Cambridge, Mass.: Harvard Nuclear Negotiation Project, 1984.

*von Braun, Wernher, and Frederick I. Ordway. *History of Rocketry and Space Travel*. New York: Crowell, 1975.

Wagner, Dr. Richard L., Jr., former assistant to the Secretary of Defense for Atomic Energy. Conversations with the authors.

Washington, George. Farewell Address, September 17, 1796. In Saxe Commins, editor, *Basic Writings of George Washington*. New York: Random House, 1948.

Weart, Spencer R. *Scientists in Power*. Cambridge, Mass.: Harvard University Press, 1979.

*————, and Gertrude Weiss Szilard, editors. *Leo Szilard: His Version of the Facts*. Cambridge, Mass.: MIT Press, 1978.

Weisgall, Jonathan M. "Micronesia and the Nuclear Pacific Since Hiroshima." In *SAIS Review*, Vol. V, No. 2 (Summer–Fall 1985), pp. 41–55.

Wells, Samuel F., Jr. "The United States and the Present Danger." In *Journal of Strategic Studies*, Vol. 4, No. 1 (March 1981), pp. 60–70.

Whelan, Joseph G. *Soviet Diplomacy and Negotiating Behavior: Emerging Context for U.S. Diplomacy*. Special Studies Series on Foreign Affairs Issues, Vol. I. Congressional Research Service, House Committee on Foreign Affairs, Document No. 96-238, July 11, 1979.

*Winter, Frank H. *Prelude to the Space Age: The Rocket Societies 1924–1940*. Washington, D.C.: Smithsonian Institution Press, 1983.

*Wise, David, and Thomas B. Ross. *The U-2 Affair*. New York: Random, 1962.

Wolfe, Thomas W. *Soviet Power and Europe, 1945–1970*. Baltimore: Johns Hopkins University Press, 1970.

York, Herbert F. "The Debate over the Hydrogen Bomb." In *Scientific American*, Vol. 233, No. 4 (October 1975), pp. 106–113.

————. "Multiple-Warhead Missiles." In *Scientific American*, Vol. 229, No. 5 (November 1973), pp. 18–27.

————. *The Advisors: Oppenheimer, Teller and the Superbomb*. San Francisco: W. H. Freeman, 1976

Zumwalt, Elmo R., Jr.. *On Watch*. New York: Quadrangle, 1976.

Index

We are grateful for permission to use illustrative material from the following sources:

Page 53: Courtesy Princeton University Press

Page 66: Painting by Gary Sheahan. Courtesy American Institute of Physics, Niels Bohr Library

Page 68: © American Heritage Publishing Co., Inc.

Pages 95, 96, 97, 98, and 101 (bottom): Los Alamos National Laboratory

Page 99: Otto Hahn. *A Scientific Autobiography*. New York: Charles Scribner's Sons, 1966. Courtesy American Institute of Physics, Niels Bohr Library

Pages 100 and 265: Courtesy American Institute of Physics, Niels Bohr Library

Page 101 (top): International Communication Agency. Courtesy American Institute of Physics, Niels Bohr Library

Page 102 (top): Margaret Rice Jette and Los Alamos Historical Museum Archives

Page 102 (bottom): Photo by P. Ehrenfest, Jr. Courtesy American Institute of Physics, Niels Bohr Library, Weisskopf Collection

Page 103: National Archives photo number 80-G-473733

Page 176: Courtesy of Department of Energy for Hewlett and Duncan, authors of *Nuclear Navy 1946–1962*, and University of Chicago Press

Page 197: Endpaper map by George Colbert in *MayDay: Eisenhower, Krushchev and the U-2 Affair* by Michael R. Beschloss. Copyright © 1986 by Michael R. Beschloss. Reprinted by permission of Harper & Row, Publishers, Inc., and by permission of Russell and Volkening, Inc., as agents for the author

Pages 266, 269, 271, and 273: U.S. Air Force Photo

Page 267: National Air and Space Museum, Smithsonian Institution

Page 268: Official U.S. Navy Photograph

Page 270: UPI/Bettmann

Page 272: Photo. No. ST 423-2-62, in the John F. Kennedy Library

Page 274: Committee for a Sane Nuclear Policy